# BETWEEN THE LINES

By the same author

*Emergency Retold, 1977*
*India—The Critical Years, 1971*
*Distant Neighbour—A Tale of the Subcontinent, 1972*
*Supersession of Judges (ed.), 1973*
*India After Nehru, 1975*

# BETWEEN THE LINES

KULDIP NAYAR

Konark Publishers Pvt Ltd
New Delhi • Seattle

**Konark Publishers Pvt. Ltd**
206, First Floor,
Peacock Lane, Shahpur Jat,
New Delhi- 110 049
Phone: +91-11-41055065
e-mail: india@konarkpublishers.com, us@konarkpublishers.com
website: www.konarkpublishers.com



First published 1969
Paperback Edition 2014
Sixth Impression 2022



**Cataloging in Publication Data--DK**
Courtesy: D.K. Agencies (P) Ltd. <docinfo@dkagencies.com>

**Nayar, Kuldip, 1923-**
Between the lines / Kuldip Nayar. – Pbk. ed.
p. cm.
Reprint.
ISBN 9789322008284

1. India--History--1947---Sources. I. Title.

DDC 954.04 23

Typeset by Saanvi Graphics, Noida

Printed and bound at Saurabh Printers Pvt. Ltd

*Dedicated*

*to a Gurgaon teashop*wala *who struck me as having a more realistic and down-to-earth approach to Indian problems than leaders in Delhi.*

# Contents

# Preface to the Paperback Edition

Politics in India has not changed much. In fact, it is old wine in new bottle. As I look back, since I wrote *Between The Lines* some 45 years ago, politics has not changed in intrigue or secrecy. But it has become dirtier and defamatory. Back then, power was the end. Now, power is the motivating force.

One good thing about that time was that politicians confided in you, and you, as a media person, seldom betrayed their trust.

This is my first book, a wish come true. I was visiting Tirupati Temple as part of the Home Minister, Govind Ballabh Pant's entourage. On an early morning of December, he had a bath in cold water before visiting the temple. As we sat on the floor, I asked a police officer sitting next to me, to explain the importance of the temple. I had never seen Pant*ji* doing all this, I said. He asked me whether it was my first visit. When I said yes, he told me that when you faced the deity, whatever you wished would come true. When it was my turn, I prayed that I would one day write a book.

When the book was published, I told my wife about my visit to Tirupati and my wish coming true. Soon after, when I received my first royalty cheque, she took me to Tirupati and made me put the cheque in the *handi*. Since then, I have written 14 more books and have gone back to the temple many times. Was I destined to write books or was I determined enough to write them? Whatever the reason, I am now an author of sorts.

*Between The Lines* reconstructs four important events of India's history. The readers will have inside information of developments as they unfolded. In addition, there is my diary, in which I would jot down day-to-day happenings within the government. As Shastri's Press Officer, I was privy to correspondence and notes. This has made the diary something of a source material.

I propose to publish all my books, because nearly all of them are out of print. Much will depend on the response to *Between The Lines*.

# Argument

Should a newspaperman tell? This is always a difficult decision to make, because in the process of doing so, he always runs the risk of annoying someone. In the case of the government, the tendency to hide and to feel horrified once the truth is uncovered is greater than in an individual. This is reportedly so because, to use official jargon, "repercussions" are wider. What are these repercussions? Who assesses these repercussions? How real are these? These questions are never answered.

Somehow those who occupy high positions in the government labour under the belief that they—and they alone—know what the nation should be told and when. And it troubles them to see news, which they do not like, appear in print. Their first attempt is to contradict it and dub it mischievous. Later, when it is realized that a mere denial will not convince even the most gullible, a lame explanation is offered that things have not been put "in proper perspective". Probably, at that time, the government gets away with its version of the story.

But what they do not realize is that such methods only decrease the credibility of official assertions. Even honest claims of the government begin to be questioned. In a democracy, where faith stirs the people's response, the government cannot afford to have even an iota of doubt raised about what it says or does. Somehow, New Delhi is not conscious of this fact.

During my time with the *United News of India* and *The Statesman,* many of my stories—such as the "Reorganization of Assam" and the "Kutch Tribunal Award"—were contradicted. But later, they were proved right. One recent example was the denial of the Prime Minister's note on the government servants' token strike. It was a belated effort. It was not the content but the divulgence which made the government unhappy. To disprove the story, the "secret" note was taken out of the files and destroyed. The publication of the note might have caused some embarrassment to certain quarters, but they cannot extricate themselves from political difficulties by sacrificing what they need most: credibility.

In a free society, the media has a duty to inform the public without fear or favour. At times it is an unpleasant job, but it has to be performed because a free society is founded on free information. If the media were to publish only government handouts or official statements, there would be nothing to pinpoint lapses, deficiencies or mistakes. In fact, the truth is that the media is already too niminy-piminy, too nice, altogether too refined, too ready to leave out. The government should not ask for more.

Most of the information given in the book is based on the notes which I was keeping when I was the Government of India's Information Officer, first attached to Mr Gobind Ballabh Pant when he was Home Minister, and then to Mr Lal Bahadur Shastri until he became Prime Minister. I have met many ministers and others again to reconstruct events of those days.

The deliberations of the Parliamentary Committee on the official Language Commission's report have hitherto remained unpublished, and the catalogue of events of the Chinese invasion on India is from the diary which I maintained when Mr Shastri was Home Minister, and I was his PRO.

# Hat Trick

In the hush of a summer night in 1963, five men groped their way to a sequestered bungalow overlooking an expansive valley in the temple town of Tirupati down south. One was ungainly and heavy, another portly, the third brisk and breezy, the fourth, slight in stature, and the fifth looked like a muscular wrestler. All of them came from different directions to avoid detection, and they succeeded in doing so. There was hardly anybody in the streets. Most people had gone to bed so they could be up early for the pre-dawn call of the temple.

By the time the five settled themselves at a large wooden table, the late moon appeared in the sky. Their profiles were now recognizable: dark-glassed Atulya Ghosh, chubby, double-chinned S. Nijalingappa, thin-faced Sanjiva Reddy, Cassius-like Sirinavas Mallayya from South Kanara, and high-cheekboned K. Kamaraj. They looked like a family of contending sons on the eve of their father's death.

It was a business-like meeting, shorn of generalities; enough thinking seemed to have been done already.

They came straight to the point. The Congress Party had been losing popularity since the Chinese had licked India in October 1962. All three parliamentary by-elections—in the constituencies of Farrukhabad, Amroha and Rajkot—had been lost to the Opposition. People had an increasing feeling of being let down by the government. Something had to be done to reverse the trend. The gold control and compulsory deposit schemes which Morarji Desai, the then Finance Minister, had sponsored to check smuggling as well as inflation, had made the Congress still more unpopular.

On the other hand, after the humiliation at the hands of China, Jawaharlal Nehru was like a god that had failed. They did not think he would last very long, not even physically. Who should step into his shoes? Or, still more pertinent, who could step in? Their own stakes were equally high. Three among them were Chief Ministers of States—Kamaraj from Madras, Nijalingappa from Mysore and Sanjiva Reddy from Andhra Pradesh. Atulya Ghosh wanted West Bengal to remain his preserve. Mallayya was not a heavyweight in politics but did not want to lose his eminence as a senior Congress parliamentarian.

How could they turn public opinion again in favour of the Congress? Or, as Kamaraj put it, how to stop the rot? They resolved to act in unison, as a syndicate, a name which has stuck to them ever since. Having decided to sink or swim together, they planned to control the party itself. The organizational platform was considered a convenient springboard for jumping to the top governmental position. But they would not make it obvious; they could not. To begin with, they would have their "own man" as Congress president.

Their choice fell on diminutive Lal Bahadur Shastri, "the third man", who was absent from the meeting, but was otherwise close to them. As an election organizer, he had helped them get their men nominated in the 1962 poll. They had also seen him functioning, both in the Congress Party and in the government. He made very few enemies, and appeared most acceptable to the public. People liked him for his modesty and unobtrusive manners, and he had come to be regarded as a key that fitted many locks. The Syndicate also needed a man who would be beholden to them. Shastri fit the bill.

Morarji Desai's name cropped up at the meeting, but the discussion was confined to thinking up ways to keep him out. In him, they found an uncompromising and intractable man. He was too rigid in his views. Were he to become Congress president, he would be too strong to be pulled down later, when the question of succession to Nehru arose. He must be weeded out now.

Once the five agreed to nominate Shastri for the party's presidentship, Kamaraj took it upon himself to talk to Nehru. "But suppose Shastri were to refuse, whom else do we have then?" asked Nijalingappa. "No, no, we must make him agree," said Sanjiva Reddy. "We must force him to accept the office." All of them, however, knew that Shastri would never say "yes" without consulting Nehru, who might have other plans. They had heard that Nehru wanted to punish certain Congress leaders for holding him responsible for the defeat in NEFA. Some, to his anger, were parties to the move to oust Krishna Menon from the cabinet. The rumour was that Nehru might combine the offices of prime minister and Congress president and have a go at his critics. If Nehru was in the field, the Syndicate realized it could do very little. But if he was not and had nobody else in view, then Shastri was the man he would accept and they would have to agree.

Nijalingappa's question—"who if Shastri was not available?" —had remained unanswered so far. All eyes automatically turned towards Kamaraj, who went on saying "illai, illai" ("no" in Tamil). Ghosh, who had been unusually quiet that evening, clinched the issue by saying, "Kamaraj will have to agree". Kamaraj gave in, confident that Shastri's name would go through without difficulty. Saying "yes" to a hypothetical proposition was not so bad. And even if the office was thrust upon him, it would be a good change from Madras politics which was getting stickier day by day due to his ambitious Finance Minister, C. Subramaniam. Kamaraj said "yes", and now his eyes were fixed on the pole star—Delhi.

Shastri, if possible, or Kamaraj, if necessary. With this alternative, the Syndicate members rose to disperse. They felt confident that their nominee would be the Congress president. And they were quite conscious that in the process they had also selected Nehru's successor. The moon was now at its zenith. The entire area was visible to the tiniest detail—huge boulders, the winding road, spacious houses and the temple steeple. The "suprabhatam", the pre-dawn invocations at the shrine, was approaching. The worshippers of the deity considered this the most auspicious time of day. These five devout Hindus knew this only too well.

Morarji Desai was furious when he learnt about the Tirupati meeting. Sanjiva Reddy and Atulya Ghosh rushed to assure him that Shastri's selection was not meant to jeopardize his chances but to block certain other elements from coming to power after Nehru's death. One of them was more precise: "We thought that this was the best way to keep Indira Gandhi out." Desai remained unconvinced. He could see that the Congress presidentship was a stepping stone to the prime ministership. "They have left me out because they know Shastri will be easy to manage," he told his associates. And he made it known that he would contest against Shastri for the presidentship. This upset the Syndicate's calculations.

Nehru was opposed to a contest. He was afraid that the party's differences might be further accentuated. His mind was working on how to cleanse the Congress, or still more specifically, on how he could cut down to size the party leaders he did not like. A contest under the circumstances would only cloud the real issue.

Some Syndicate members began doubting Shastri's pull with Nehru. But Shastri assured them that Nehru was not against him but wanted a unanimous choice. "I don't know why Morarji *bhai* is so keen to become the Congress president. Panditji does not want him," Shastri said openly. He and the Syndicate spread this word around; but this did not deter Desai, who continued to be in the field.

When Kamaraj mentioned Shastri's name to Nehru, he did not reject it, but the burden of his arguments was that the Congress needed a jolt to shed its complacency and sluggishness. Certain persons who had occupied governmental positions for too long should quit and work in the organization at the grassroots.

"Why don't you take up this job yourself?" Nehru asked Kamaraj. He was not prepared for that kind of question. Nehru added: "You had yourself once suggested that top leaders should leave their present positions and work in the organization to strengthen the Congress." Kamaraj had discussed this kind of plan in a letter to Nehru but little did he realize at that time that he would be asked to wield the axe. He could not say no now. Only the plan made at Tirupati would go awry, but probably temporarily. Shastri could always be brought in when the time came.

Now the Syndicate's second name—Kamaraj's—held the field. Desai was opposed to Shastri on the grounds that as Congress President, Shastri would strengthen his claim to succeed Nehru. Kamaraj was a different kettle of fish. Desai therefore did not oppose him. On the other hand, Shastri envisaged no danger from Kamaraj because he knew that when it came to choosing a prime minister, Kamaraj stood no chance. By giving him unflinching support now, Shastri thought he would completely win over Kamaraj—and the Syndicate. This was precisely what happened. When the time came, Kamaraj stood him in good stead.

Nehru punished all those who had raised their voices against him when he was busy installing Kamaraj as Congress President or when he was teetering from the blow in NEFA. Desai, Jagjivan Ram, S.K. Patil and many other central and chief ministers were thrown out of office on the plea of activising the Congress. This "cleansing" operation came to be known as the Kamaraj Plan because he was the author. Desai's comment was that through the Kamaraj Plan, Nehru had removed all possible successors from the path of his daughter, Indira Gandhi. Many others echoed the same thought, but never in public because of the fear of Nehru. Desai and Jagjivan Ram made no secret that Nehru's real purpose was to drop them from the Cabinet. There is some weight in the charge because they were never assigned organizational work, even when they pressed for it. In fact, they were reduced in importance and consigned to a life of inactivity.

It is often said that Shastri was dropped from the Cabinet at the insistence of Mrs Gandhi, who saw in him a potential danger. This is not correct, although Mrs Gandhi's dislike for Shastri was an open secret by that time. Certain indiscreet remarks the Shastri family had made about her, vis-á-vis her supporters, had reached her. She had reason to feel annoyed. However, Nehru was keen to retain Shastri. But Shastri himself asked Nehru to relieve him, and his argument was: "You must drop some of your own men to take the wind out of Morarji's sails." It is, however, surprising how Nehru came to retain Pratap Singh Kairon at the last minute. Shastri had communicated to his supporters in Punjab that Kairon was being dropped. He had, however, warned them: "Let us keep our fingers crossed. Kairon is Panditji's blind spot, and he might change his mind at the last minute." Things turned out as he had feared. Kairon was retained.

The Kamaraj Plan only accentuated the group rivalries in the Congress. It was the haves against the have-nots. Those who went out of the government felt dispossessed of the authority they thought was rightly theirs. Nehru was too tall for them and they could not pull him down. But they could talk behind his back. And they did so unabashedly; the criticism of Nehru's rule was never whispered so loudly and so widely as then.

Shastri kept himself away from this tittle-tattle. Even when people mentioned the futility of the Kamaraj Plan, he would either defend it or keep quiet. He was opposed to the Plan on other grounds. His feeling was that the Congress would not gain by a few top leaders leaving the government because they would not put their heart into organizational work. He himself was far from happy, but was too careful to get mixed up with intrigue or petty talk. However, his contact with the Syndicate—which had come to include S.K. Patil from Bombay and Biju Patnaik from Orissa by that time—was open and intimate, but he did not become a part of it. This gave him a halo of neutrality, which stood him in good stead at the time of succession.

His refusal to get involved and the impression that he was Nehru's favourite made him the cynosure of those who were looking beyond Nehru. Shastri continued to have an image of wide acceptability, and even without the trappings of office, he was closely followed and respected. In him, people saw Nehru's successor.

Nehru's sudden illness at Bhubaneshwar on June 9, 1963, provided the Syndicate with an opportunity to have their candidate, Shastri, back in the government. First Kamaraj and then Ghosh spoke to Nehru about recalling Shastri. The State Chief Ministers also asked the Prime Minister to shed a part of his burden, and some of them specifically suggested that Shastri should take over some responsibilities. Nehru called him at Bhubaneshwar itself and said: "You will have to help me now." But it was only in Delhi, many days later, that Shastri was sworn in as a minister without portfolio.

What delayed the appointment was the pressure which Nehru faced once Shastri's name went out. Gulzari Lal Nanda, the then Home Minister, tried to dissuade Nehru from taking back anybody from among the "Kamaraj-ed" ministers. This would be "discriminatory" and "misunderstood", he said. Later, he and T.T. Krishnamachari, the then Finance Minister, saw to it that Shastri was ranked fourth in the Cabinet. Shastri had the impression that Nehru would make him No. 2. The downgrading of the rank did disappoint him. Morarji Desai expressed his negative indifference to Shastri's entry; Jagjivan Ram made it publicly known that he opposed Shastri being taken back. Recalling the Kamaraj Plan, he said quite indignantly, that on the carrom board of politics, Nehru had used Shastri as the "striker" to drive out "unwanted men". And now he wanted him back. It came to be believed that the real purpose of the Kamaraj Plan was to oust Morarji Desai and Jagjivan Ram. Shastri's stock, therefore, increased in the eyes of the public.

That Nehru had picked only Shastri was bound to boost his prestige. But this action incensed Nehru's opponents, not so much because they had been left out but because he was openly nominating his successor. When he therefore tried to make Shastri Leader of the

House there was opposition, particularly from Desai. The proposal had to be dropped. Nehru did not want a contest lest the party should split in his lifetime. He devalued the post and a relatively unknown person was appointed Leader of the House. Shastri was unhappy, but from that day, he realized that he would have to brave Desai's stern opposition if he wanted to become prime minister. Shastri had a knack for keeping his own counsel. He therefore never showed any disrespect to Desai, nor did he project himself as a candidate. But he tilted still more on the side of the Syndicate, while at the same time giving an impression of being a non-party, non-controversial person.

If Shastri nurtured the belief that his ministership was a stepping stone to prime ministership, he was mistaken. As soon as Nehru recovered from his illness, all important files and papers went directly to him and Shastri would come to know about them many days later through the Deputy Secretary or Joint Secretary. "I am only a glorified clerk," he often said.

One day he received a request from an African country to nominate a delegate to an international labour conference. He suggested the name of Abid Ali, known for his interest in labour problems. A senior official of the External Affairs Ministry, who later became its Secretary, did not accept the recommendation and went to the extent of having it changed by Nehru. Shastri came to know about the rejection of his recommendation only through the routine papers, which the lower echelons of bureaucracy, after scoring a point against a minister, share with them to spite them. Shastri felt humiliated.

As the days went by, such instances piled up. In fact, he had to wait even to get an appointment with Nehru. He thought he would quit the ministry. Once he told me that he would go back to Allahabad. "There is nothing for me here now," he said. He then added woefully: "If I continue to stay in Delhi I am bound to clash with Panditji. I would rather retire from politics than join issue with him." But two considerations made him stay. One, the Syndicate did not want him to give up the position of vantage he occupied as cabinet minister, even though No. 4 in rank. Two, by quitting, Shastri feared that the impression that Nehru had nominated him successor when he brought him back into the government, would weaken. He decided to wait.

Many people at that time said—and told him so—that Nehru's behaviour was influenced by Indira Gandhi's "hostility" towards him. First, he would never encourage such talk but later he used to go out of the way to find out if that was true. And in due course, he became convinced that he was not uppermost in Nehru's mind as his successor. There was somebody else.

I ventured to ask Shastri at that time: "Who do you think Nehru has in mind as his successor?"

"His daughter,"* Shastri said, without even a second's delay, as if he had already pondered the problem.

---

* In 1962, Nehru reportedly asked U.N. Dhebar, the outgoing Congress President, to propose the name of Mrs Gandhi as his successor. Dhebar convened a special meeting of the Working Committee. When he put up her name, the Congress Working Committee members were not prepared for it. They had decided to nominate

"But it wouldn't be easy," he added.

"People think you are such a staunch devotee of Nehru that you would yourself propose Indira Gandhi's name after his death," I said.

"I am not that much of a sadhu as you imagine me to be," was Shastri's reply.

Later, events showed that he did try to work for a consensus in Mrs Gandhi's favour.

Nehru's death was sudden. In fact, the news came when the general impression was that he was recovering. Everybody was caught unprepared, the contenders as well as the king-makers. Kamaraj hurried back to Delhi in a chartered plane, Atulya Ghosh from Calcutta and Desai from a place near Delhi. Nehru's body was still at Teen Murti House when the discussion on the succession began. Some leaders went into a huddle, not very far from where the body lay. One of them told Shastri there itself that he was the obvious choice. Shastri merely said: "Yes, I know but now it is for Nandaji to take over." By that time, Nanda had been sworn in as Prime Minister. This was on the suggestion of President Radhakrishnan who had advised that the

---

Nijalingappa. Pant opposed Mrs Gandhi's name on the grounds of her fragile health. Other members repeated the same view. But when Nehru intervened to say that she was quite healthy and, in fact, "healthier than some of the members present", everybody accepted her as Congress President.

seniormost minister in the cabinet should take over until the Congress Party elected a new leader.

By the following evening, when Nehru was only a handful of ashes, all those who counted were talking more about possible successors than his loss. The Syndicate was sitting pretty; its only anxiety was to stay united, and it did. Somebody in the Central Bureau of Intelligence read too much into the succession issue, and sent a message to all state governments that there was great tension in Delhi. This was quickly followed by a decision that the security forces should take all precautions against subversive activities. Military officials and men were recalled from leave and ordered back to their posts. But there was never even a thought of a coup d'état.*

In fact, the Chief of the Army Staff, General Chaudhuri, was down with a heart attack on Nehru's funeral day. It is true that he had summoned 6,000 troops from the Western Command to Delhi, but they were for ceremonial purposes, to line the route and control the mammoth crowd at Shantivan where Nehru was cremated. Moreover, Chaudhuri had informed the President about the movement of these 6,000 men.

Nehru might not have designated his successor but he had left behind a durable political structure which could smoothly elect a leader. And this happened in a normal manner.

---

* Desai, later commenting to me on the possibility of the military taking over in India, said: "They are no different from us."

The real place of activity on Nehru's cremation day was Desai's house at Thyagaraja Marg. The lawn and the verandah were full of people, and at least two of his supporters, Mrs Tarakeshwari Sinha and Suresh Desai, were armed with a list of Congress MPs, with ticks against their names to indicate whether they were favourable to Desai or doubtful. Shastri's supporters were unmarked.

As a newsman, I went to Desai's house to find out whether he was a candidate. He was not available. But his supporters gave me this reply: "Come what may, Morarji will contest and win hands down." One person took pains to explain how strong men like Kairon from Punjab, Biju Patnaik from Orissa, Balwant Rai Mehta from Gujarat, C.B. Gupta from UP and P.C. Sen from West Bengal and many MPs had already pledged their loyalty to him.

I reached Shastri's house late in the evening but a member of the Syndicate was still closeted with him. When I asked him who would be the next prime minister, Shastri first directed me to that person, who said nothing and left. Later, Shastri said: "I shall prefer a unanimous election, and I, for one, favour Indiraji if Morarji accepts her." After a pause, he added: "Were a contest to become inevitable, I would like to stand against Morarji because I can defeat him, not Indiraji." And then, as if he was talking of an ideal arrangement, he said: "We need a person like Jayaprakash Narayan to head the Government at this juncture."

After assessing the climate in the two camps, I wrote this story for *United News of India,* a news agency which I headed then. The story said:

"Mr Morarji Desai, former Finance Minister, is the first one to throw his hat in the ring. He is believed to have told his associates that he is a candidate.

"Mr Desai is understood to have said that there must be an election, and he, for one, will not withdraw."

"The Minister without portfolio, Mr Lal Bahadur Shastri, is considered another candidate, though he himself is reticent. According to circles close to him, he would like to avoid a contest as far as possible..."

I never realized that the news item would do as much harm to Desai as it did. His supporters said that it cost them at least 100 votes. Word went round that he was so ambitious that he hadn't even waited for Nehru's ashes to go cold before he made a bid for the leadership. I realized how much it had helped Shastri, when, the day the story appeared in the Delhi papers, he called me to his house to say: "Thank you. Now no more writing. The contest for leadership is practically over." I vainly explained to him that the story was never meant to harm or to help anybody. He concluded the interview by placing a finger on his lips. Later, when he was elected leader of the party, he embraced me before everybody on the outer steps of Parliament House and took me aside to say: "Thank you."

I realized how much I had unwittingly helped him when he asked me to be his press officer, and said: "Now Morarji *bhai* will be convinced that I am repaying you for that news story." I did not join his staff. But Desai remains convinced to this day that I wrote the story to help Shastri. Whenever I have broached this topic to him, he has said: "Shastri had his own way of using people, even without their realising it." Desai should in fact blame his own supporters, who were confiding in everybody on the day of Nehru's cremation that the prime ministership was in their pocket.

Mrs Gandhi's name as a successor was in circulation only for a while. Shastri told me that he had sent word to Desai to accept Mrs Gandhi as the unanimous choice. Desai never heard from Shastri directly. It was D.P. Mishra, a veteran Congress leader from Madhya Pradesh, who met Desai to suggest her name. Mishra reportedly told him this move was meant to block Shastri and ultimately get Desai elected. Whatever the truth, Desai's reaction was hostile. He said he would prefer Shastri any day to Mrs Gandhi. A contest looked inevitable. The Congress Parliamentary Party's executives met to plead for a unanimous choice. After Nehru, the need was to get together, not to fall apart. But their wish appeared to remain unanswered. The Left-wingers tried to have the election postponed for two months. When this did not succeed, Krishna Menon and K.D. Malviya threw their support behind Desai. They thought that by electing Desai, they would be accelerating the process of polarization, between the Left and the Right. This, they thought, would help the country in the long run because the choice before the nation would be clear and categorical; even if the Right were to come into power, the pendulum would ultimately swing towards the Left.

With this naive thinking, the Left-wingers stayed with Desai until the end. But others, whom he had counted on, withdrew their support. Ghosh made it clear that he would not abandon the Syndicate. Chavan, who was sitting on the fence, arrayed himself behind Shastri. So did the stop-gap Prime Minister, Nanda, for whatever he counted.

Morarji still did not withdraw and began ringing up MPs personally to seek their support. However, the plea for a unanimous choice was gaining ground. His determination to contest, come what may, wilted under pressure. He finally agreed, with great reluctance, to accept an informal consensus which Kamaraj was asked to determine. Desai never forgave himself for having agreed to it. Desai's two supporters, Hare Krushna Mahatab of Orissa and Ravindra Varma of Kerala, tried to retrieve the situation by challenging the Congress High Command's right to advise the Parliamentary Party on how to choose the new leader. But what could they do when Desai himself had offered up his neck?

Kamaraj, being a Syndicate member, was suspect in Desai's eyes. Some MPs on his side confirmed his misgivings, by telling him that Kamaraj never took down their name or preference when ascertaining their wishes. Hence, when Kamaraj called his home to announce that the consensus was in favour of Shastri, Desai said: "You are telling a lie. You had made up your mind beforehand." Kamaraj never forgave him for those remarks. But the real damage was done by U.N. Dhebar, the former Congress President. He was leaving for Rajkot on the day the consensus result was to be available. Before going, he asked Kamaraj about the trend. Kamaraj's reply was that it looked like going in Shastri's favour but he could not say for certain. Dhebar told Desai that Kamaraj had said that Shastri had won. Naturally, when Kamaraj met Desai during the day, the latter charged him with making up his mind even before the process of ascertaining opinion was complete.

After Kamaraj's announcement that the majority of the Congress members favoured Shastri, his election was a formality. Desai himself seconded his name, which Nanda had proposed. Shastri was elected leader unanimously. It was considered a foregone conclusion that he would offer the No. 2 position to Desai. But he did not. When he talked to Desai about joining his cabinet, Shastri said Nanda would have to be No. 2 because he had officiated as prime minister. Desai ended the interview by saying that he would feel humiliated if he were to accept an inferior position. That day was one of the very few occasions when Shastri did not wait till his visitor's car had left. Somehow Desai's car did not start immediately. Shastri waited for a while, and then went in.

After Desai's "refusal", Shastri did not approach Jagjivan Ram. He wanted to take a somewhat plausible stand in public: no one who had been sent out under the Kamaraj Plan had been taken back. Instead, Shastri offered ministerships to Dr H.J. Bhabha and Dr D.S. Kothari, both scientists. Both declined the invitation.

Mrs Gandhi's inclusion in the cabinet was taken for granted. All were surprised—and her friends disappointed—when she got only the Ministry of Information and Broadcasting. This was, as Shastri told me, on her own insistence. She wanted a comparatively light burden so as to be able to look after arrangements connected with the perpetuation of her father's memory.

But later, when she was available for a portfolio of more importance, Shastri was reluctant to give her one.

After his heart attack, soon after taking office—for some reason the government continued to clumsily deny the attack and described it as fatigue—Shastri wanted to part with the Foreign Affairs portfolio. Mrs Gandhi was the obvious choice, but he feared that the External Affairs portfolio might make her "too important". Chagla, Education Minister, was in his mind, but he thought that a Muslim would be unnecessarily rigid towards Pakistan to appease communal opinion in India. The choice fell on unflashy but steady Swaran Singh.

Just as Shastri was unhappy as a minister without portfolio and wanted to quit the Nehru Cabinet, so was Mrs Gandhi as Minister of Information and Broadcasting. Her friends kept telling her that her presence in the cabinet gave her a vantage position. The king-maker, Kamaraj, who was pulling away from Shastri for having been ignored, had become very close to her. It looked like history was repeating itself.

I interviewed Mrs Gandhi on November 11, 1965, so as to synchronize the release of a story with Nehru's birthday three days later. Her contempt for the Government was apparent. "Where is non-alignment? Are our policies socialistic?" She spoke on these questions at length and gave instance after instance of how "India had swerved from the right path" since Nehru's death. It was obvious that Mrs Gandhi was drifting away from Shastri. And when he dropped T.T. Krishnamachari, Finance Minister, from the Cabinet, her annoyance knew no bounds. T.T.K. was very close to her because he had kept her father's company in his last days.

Shastri's death at Tashkent was even more sudden than Nehru's. Nobody had the slightest warning. In the case of Nehru, his illness at Bhubaneshwar had somewhat prepared the Congress top brass. But Shastri's departure was most unexpected, and it caught the aspirants to the prime ministership, and their supporters, unprepared, once again. Morarji Desai was in Koraput, Orissa, Kamaraj in Madras, Atulya Ghosh in Calcutta and S.K. Patil in Bombay. All rushed to Delhi by the earliest flight.

It was a familiar pattern. Just as the talk of succession to Nehru began even before the cortege left Teen Murti, so did the exercise of "who would be next?" before Shastri's body reached Delhi. At the airport itself, the name of Mrs Gandhi started gaining currency as the next prime minister. A busybody astrologer was at Palam airport. Biju Patnaik asked him: "What do the stars foretell?" "It will be a hat trick," the man replied, meaning that Nehru and Shastri were from Allahabad and the new leader would also be from there. The Congress Working Committee met, as it did after Nehru's death, to pass a resolution paying glowing tributes to Shastri on the first day, and to look for a successor on the second day. By that time, word had gone around that there would be more than two candidates. Indira Gandhi and Morarji Desai were there, but the names of Nanda, Chavan and Jagjivan Ram were also mentioned. It was suggested at the Working

Committee's meeting that the winning candidate must secure more than half the votes cast. If this was not possible on the first count, two or more ballots would be taken till one of the candidates had an absolute majority. Patil proposed that each member of the party be asked to write the name of the candidate of his choice on the ballot paper. This would bring to the fore all candidates and thus facilitate the process of elimination.

The Working Committee hoped the election would be unanimous. A suggestion was made to repeat the consensus formula of 1964. Morarji's reaction was violent. He insisted on a contest. An informal committee was constituted to effect unity with Kamaraj, Desai and Jagjivan Ram as members. But the move was stillborn. Desai distrusted Kamaraj; he still harboured the suspicion that Kamaraj had "manoeuvred the consensus" which gave Shastri the prime ministership in 1964.

Nanda, who had been again sworn in as a stop-gap prime minister, made the first move. "Why should I step down this time?" he asked Kamaraj. He thought he would woo Mrs Gandhi, a possible candidate. He took her to the airport in his car to meet the plane bringing Shastri's body from Tashkent. The following morning he asked her directly whether she was in the field. She did not reply to that query but said: "Why don't you try?" This was enough for Nanda to throw his hat in the ring. He had, however, misunderstood her. She was a candidate; it was part of her strategy not to say so. Kamaraj had asked her to remain quiet. Later, when pressed to divulge her plans, she said she would contest if the Congress President asked her to stand.

Kamaraj himself was under great pressure. The Syndicate did not want Mrs Gandhi, Desai or Nanda. Ghosh started a campaign to "draft" Kamaraj in. Behind this move were the party bosses of eastern India, particularly Biju Patnaik. Twice, the Syndicate met at Sanjiva Reddy's house to discuss the draft Kamaraj Plan. But they always got stuck because of Kamaraj's "No". Ultimately, he put a stop to the move by saying that he neither knew English nor Hindi, and that India's Prime Minister should be able to speak at least one of these languages. In the absence of Kamaraj, the Syndicate had no firm name in view. As Atulya Ghosh told Nanda: "Everything is in the hands of Kamaraj, who will select from a panel of given names—Nanda, Mrs Gandhi, Chavan, Patil and Reddy—or someone else." Patil proposed a 10-person "Cabinet of composite talents", led by Nanda. Patil backed him continuously and he really believed that Nanda could be a compromise candidate. He brought round Patnaik; Reddy also preferred Nanda to Mrs Gandhi.

Nanda hoped against hope, up to the last moment, that he would be selected, because he thought Mrs Gandhi would support him. He checked with her again. If she was a candidate, he would withdraw, he told her. Mrs Gandhi said she would support him if others did. But Nanda read in newspapers certain "inspired" stories that the Congress Party would prefer a younger person. Chavan met Nanda and argued in the same vein. Nanda said he, for one, would not object to a younger person, but Chavan should better note that the choice of Indira Gandhi would block his own chances at some later date. Nanda knew he had lost the game. He almost lost the Home Ministership as well. Before the cabinet was sworn in, Mrs Gandhi, accompanied by Satya Narayan Sinha, Minister for Parliamentary Affairs, called on Nanda. Sinha did most of the talking. He said that there was no question of taking away Nanda's seniority. He would remain No. 2, but some chief ministers did not want him to hold Home. He should, therefore, accept some other portfolio. Nanda said he would rather quit. Mrs Gandhi tried again on the eve of the announcement of the cabinet to persuade Nanda to yield, but he stuck to his guns.

Coming back to the succession, Kamaraj, the Syndicate's leader, was all for Mrs Gandhi and he was dead set to have her elected. He had not forgiven Desai for having called him a liar at the time of Shastri's selection. He was willing to compromise on Nanda but he proved with facts and figures that Nanda was too weak to defeat Desai. Kamaraj, therefore, went on arguing night after night to break down the Syndicate's opposition to Mrs Gandhi till he succeeded. Sanjiva Reddy, who had once taunted her by observing that the Congress president was her *chaprasi*, was the last one to give in. Others fell like nine pins.

For Kamaraj to get Mrs Gandhi elected was also the realization of a promise he had made to himself. After getting Shastri into the cabinet, Kamaraj was anxious that Mrs Gandhi should also join. His impression was that she too was keen to do so. When he mentioned her name to Nehru at the time of proposing Shastri, Nehru kept quiet for a while as if he was thinking. Then he said:

"No, not yet. Indu, probably later," was all that Nehru said. That day, Kamaraj promised to himself that he would first make Shastri the Prime Minister, and then Indira Gandhi, the order in which Nehru mentioned their names. And Kamaraj did so. But did Nehru have a successor in mind? Kamaraj never asked that question. In a democracy, the prime ministership was not a plug of tobacco which could be passed on as one liked, Nehru would often say (incidentally, this was the observation which Bernard Shaw had made when Mahatma Gandhi was pressed to give the reins of leadership to Nehru).

Desai, reported as being dogmatic and ruthless, also created a fear in the minds of the Syndicate members who sincerely believed that she would be more pliable and tractable than he was. A last-minute effort was made to persuade Desai to withdraw in favour of Mrs Gandhi, but he remained adamant. He said he would contest even if his was the only vote in his favour. But he was hopeful that a secret ballot might result in his victory. It was a vain hope.

D.P. Mishra, the Madhya Pradesh Chief Minister, whom she had helped to rehabilitate in the Congress, was the first to jump onto Mrs Gandhi's bandwagon. He brought together several other chief ministers at Madhya Pradesh Bhawan in New Delhi's Chanakyapuri. Among them were Naik from Maharashtra, Bhaktavatsalam from Madras, Brahmananda Reddy from Andhra Pradesh, Sadasiva Tripathi from Orissa, Nijalingappa from Mysore and Sadiq from Kashmir. All of them came out publicly on Mrs Gandhi's side. The Bihar Chief Minister, Sahay, was present but did not commit himself. He said he wanted to consult his Cabinet colleagues. Ram Kishen of Punjab, issued from Chandigarh, a statement in favour of Mrs Gandhi.

Desai was peeved at the Chief Ministers' statement. These were pressure tactics, he said, and added: "I hope members of Parliament are mature enough to exercise their votes in national interest." Atulya Ghosh issued a strong rejoinder. He said Desai's statement was "an insult to every single Congress MP and to the Congress organization as a whole". Ghosh went to the extent of saying that Morarji Desai's own decision to be a candidate without consulting the Congress High Command was "highly undemocratic".

Ghosh's rejoinder did not stop Desai from issuing a three-page personal letter to all Congress MPs. This was more in the nature of an election manifesto. He wrote that many MPs had told him of the "pressures" being put upon them to prove their loyalty to chief ministers. "This would foil the secrecy of the ballot," he said. "If we surrender this right or allow it to be eroded by the use of extraneous pressures, we will be bringing into disrespect the sacred institution of Parliament."

He added: "I never shirked the responsibility to take measures of economic reform or other action which were in the interest of the country and democratic socialism, even if such measures sometimes brought odium to one who initiated them." He was referring to the gold control and compulsory deposit schemes which his opponents were criticising to seek votes for Mrs Gandhi. A staunch prohibitionist and Hindi*wala* as he was, many members considered him obstinate, as well as obdurate. In his letter, Desai explained: "I have no personal fads or obsessions of my own as alleged. All that I have done is to stand firmly for whatever the organization has accepted as its goal and policy." Desai followed up the letter with a telephone call to every member.

The response from MPs of at least six states to Desai's appeal was an open declaration in favour of Mrs Gandhi. The Chief Ministers' pressure on them was quite apparent. The General Election was only a year away, and the MPs would once again want tickets as well as other assistance in terms of funds and influence. They could not afford to annoy the Chief Ministers. At the same time, many of them genuinely preferred Mrs Gandhi, the daughter of their hero, Nehru, to Morarji Desai. The members had also to reckon with the Congress President, Kamaraj, who was on her side and who had a major say in nominating the party's candidates.

Desai was angry, helpless and exasperated. He told pressmen that the election was between him, "the MPs' candidate", and Mrs Gandhi, "the Congress President's candidate". This had no effect. The pro-Gandhi trend was too strong to be reversed or deflected. Her election was a foregone conclusion. But it did not "look" like a unanimous choice. Chavan's candidature was in the field for only a brief time. Nijalingappa scotched any possibility by saying that he would not accept a man who only thought of Maharashtra all the time. Nijalingappa was referring to Mysore's dispute with Maharashtra. Patil from Bombay was also opposed to Chavan due to rivalries at the State level. Chavan himself preferred Mrs Gandhi to Desai. "There is a generation gap, and I, for one, want a young person to come to power," he told me.

Jagjivan Ram was never a serious candidate. He supported Morarji Desai till he found out that Desai would not win. He switched over to Mrs Gandhi's side only after telling Desai that he was doing so. Jagjivan Ram's explanation for changing his loyalty was that while Desai's supporters were moneyed people, his associates were ordinary men; the two could not go together.

Kamaraj thought of making one last effort on the eve of election to avoid a contest. His brief from the Congress Working Committee was to work for a unanimous choice. The party was also literally praying for that. The members' main concern was that the contest would divide the party. Most of them were also diffident about taking a public stand and being counted for or against. Some had promised support to both.

The meeting between Desai and Kamaraj was short. Neither had forgotten the brief encounter they had had at the time of Shastri's election. But now, Morarji had mellowed, and his was a voice of anguish and helplessness. When Kamaraj began talking in terms of unity in the party, Desai said: "What crime have I committed? Does unity mean that I should withdraw?"

"But the majority is not in your favour," Kamaraj said. "Who knows, if there had been no pressure on the MPs, they might have come out in my favour. They may still," said Desai. Kamaraj replied: "The other candidate will get a larger number of votes." "Tomorrow, the ballot box will show," Desai retorted.

He proved to be wrong. The voting was 355 for Mrs Gandhi and 169 for Desai. The Intelligence Bureau, more royalist than the King, had informed officiating Prime Minister Nanda beforehand that it would be 357 to 167. Probably for the first time in its existence, the IB came close to guessing correctly.

Desai took his defeat stoically, as he always did. But he rationalized it by telling his supporters: "I can prove pressure was exerted on the MPs. I personally feel that the interest the Congress President has taken is unfair to me." This time he was respectful to Kamaraj. He had learnt the hard way that Kamaraj was too tall a person to be annoyed or alienated. He must win back his goodwill. Desai started doing that, but it was too late. By the time he had him on his side, Kamaraj was a spent force. Desai realized this when he was pitted against Mrs Gandhi for the second time.

As time went by, Kamaraj's own stock went down. When he installed Shastri in the Prime Minister's chair, he was at the top of his form. He could tilt the scales much the way he liked. Shastri did not like this, even though he was beholden to Kamaraj. Shastri's chagrin with Kamaraj came through in the irritated comment he once made: "He is not only the party boss but also the king-maker."

No sooner did he get Shastri elected as the leader, Kamaraj's own decline began. Shastri began asserting himself. In fact, he went beyond that; he tried to erase the general impression that Kamaraj always had his way. Some distance between the two was perceptible even when Shastri was finalising the list of cabinet members. Kamaraj was kept waiting in an adjoining room. Shastri did not show him the list until he had decided on each and every name. To Kamaraj's humiliation, Shastri consulted a couple of civil servants and his son-in-law, his unofficial adviser, who were in his room at the time.

The relationship between the two was to become increasingly cold and formal; they would not meet for weeks together. Once they rode in a special train to a place in Rajasthan for the inauguration of a canal but never exchanged a word throughout the journey. When Shastri dropped T.T.K. from the Cabinet, he never consulted Kamaraj. Not that it was necessary, but T.T.K. was Kamaraj's man. The gulf between Shastri and Kamaraj widened still further. The Syndicate could sense the estrangement, because the two would often avoid each other, even at an accidental meeting. Some Syndicate members, especially Reddy, tried to bring the two together but this did not happen. In fact, they went further apart. I recall having asked Shastri about the differences between him and Kamaraj. His reply was: "I do try to keep close to Kamaraj, but there is something in his mind which I am at a loss to know." But the fact was that there were too many persons whispering in Shastri's ears, that if he wanted to be a "real No. 1", he would have to "deflate" Kamaraj.

At the time of Mrs Gandhi's first election, Kamaraj was once again in great demand. She entirely depended on him, and Morarji Desai rightly feared his opposition. Later it was proved that he was not a spent force, when he brought round the Syndicate, once positively hostile to Mrs Gandhi, to support her. History repeated itself for him. As soon as Mrs Gandhi was prime minister, she began ignoring him. Devaluation of the rupee, which Kamaraj regarded as a bigger debacle than NEFA, brought them almost to a parting of ways. So much so that when I asked her during a pre-election interview if the rumour about her differences with Kamaraj was correct, she said: "Obviously there are some interested parties. You see, here is a question of whom the party wants and whom the people want. My position among the people is uncontested."

Kamaraj's reaction to her observation was anger. He said openly the following evening: "What did she mean by the people wanting one person and the party somebody else?" But she never regretted what she said. In fact, when I met her for the first time after the 1967 General Election, she reminded me of her last interview by observing: "You put me in trouble last time. But, in retrospect, I think I said the right thing, and I have been proved right." What, probably, she had in mind was the defeat of the Congress stalwarts at the poll. Kamaraj had lost and so had Atulya Ghosh, Patil, and Biju Patnaik. The Syndicate was in disrepute because the big ones had been rejected by the people. It looked as if it really didn't count for much. From this, the conclusion drawn was that it hardly mattered (except for its nuisance value), which person it favoured for the party leadership. That is why, when it came to electing a leader, the Syndicate adjusted to the circumstances prevailing at the time.

The Congress had lost in six states: West Bengal, Orissa, Kerala, Punjab, Madras and Bihar. UP, Rajasthan and Haryana were hanging by the thread of a slender majority. New Delhi was agog with rumours that Congressmen in some states intended crossing the floor. This did take place in UP, Bihar, Madhya Pradesh and Haryana to give the Opposition short-lived ministries. The narrow majority of about forty members at the Centre made the leadership cautious, and the members somewhat independent and even defiant.

Even the top-most leaders agreed that some Congress MPs might defect. Jagjivan Ram's name was often mentioned, and a strong rumour swept the country that he might cross the floor with his "50 supporters". (There was no way to verify the number but that was the figure mentioned). It was said authoritatively that he had been offered the prime ministership. On the Opposition's behalf, Professor Humayun Kabir, who was once a Congress minister, did send feelers to Jagjivan Ram, but he did not respond favourably. He told me in an interview later that certain members of the Opposition approached him to cross the floor with his supporters. "Why should I?" he asked me. "I foresee a better future for myself in the Congress itself." His uncharitable critics said that Jagjivan Ram did not leave the Congress because he realized that very few members would quit the party with him.

Even the tenuous majority had not united the party. As soon as the constitution of the new Lok Sabha was formally announced, the candidates for leadership started entering the arena. Once again it looked like it was going to be Indira Gandhi versus Morarji Desai. She started with an advantage, because she was already the leader of the party. And she told the party members that what she wanted was a renewed verdict in her favour. Chavan was already on her side. He, in fact, had gone on record publicly that she must be re-elected as prime minister. Mrs Gandhi began by canvassing Kamaraj, who by this time had gone over to Morarji Desai's side. She later met Atulya Ghosh, Patil, C.B. Gupta, and many others. And then the ubiquitous round of confabulations, sterile and meaningless, began, as had been the practice in the past. Jagjivan Ram and Atulya Ghosh were among the first to talk to Kamaraj. Jagjivan Ram at one time thought that he might be a compromise candidate. He therefore decided to sit on the fence. Atulya Ghosh, discredited after the election, supported Morarji Desai.

But this time, Desai was cautious. He kept his counsel and did not tell anybody whether he would eventually contest the leadership. He had already been beaten twice. He didn't want to go wrong the third time. He was, therefore, determined not to tread on anybody's toes. He himself took the initiative of meeting Kamaraj. But what could Kamaraj do after suffering defeat in the elections? If it had been left to him, he would have made Desai prime minister. But by this time, Kamaraj did not count for much. He could make only a marginal difference; that was all. To him, Indira Gandhi's election looked almost a certainty. Morarji Desai was a strong candidate, but not against Mrs Gandhi. Kamaraj's assessment was that Desai would lose if he were to contest. Kamaraj's strategy, therefore, was to get Morarji Desai into the cabinet to keep a check on her. As usual, the Congress Parliamentary Party met and demanded a unanimous election. The members were, as before, reluctant to stand up and be counted. Moreover, the dominant feeling was that the party, like the leadership, had been weakened after several upsets in the election. Those who were left should stay together.

The bruised and battered Syndicate moved in once again. Mrs Gandhi did not think much of them. She told me in an interview: "You see, there is no doubt that the party bosses exert certain influence. It works both ways. That very influence alienates other people." So it was not an unmixed blessing, she added. Some MPs, however, did know their strength. Atulya Ghosh, S.K. Patil and Kamaraj, and with them, Sanjiva Reddy and Nijalingappa could pull a lot of weight. They, for their part, realized their limitations. That they were against re-electing Mrs Gandhi was an open secret but they were not so foolhardy as to ignore the fact that she had the largest following in the party. Her national image, and the fact that Chavan and Desai could not combine, constituted her real strength.

The Syndicate had no choice but to go along. The strategy planned was not to allow the situation to reach the point of contest so that all elements should remain together. In the name of unanimity, Mrs Gandhi and Morarji Desai were to be harnessed together in the cabinet. The Syndicate began emphasizing this, and most Congress MPs also lent their full support. The demand grew that Mrs Gandhi and Morarji Desai should meet, but this did not seem possible at that stage because each expected to win. Mrs Gandhi, the incumbent, made it known that a contest for leadership would mean a vote of no confidence in her. Desai's argument was that he should also get a chance to be the prime minister.

A campaign started building up that Mrs Gandhi be No. 1, and Desai, No. 2. When Desai was adamant about not accepting the Deputy's position, he was told that he could always throw her out from within. This argument did not cut much ice with him. Cautious and hopeful, Desai called on Kamaraj, who by this time had assessed the relative strength of the two candidates. His conclusion was that Desai might not win. He asked him if he would like to be No. 2 to Mrs Gandhi in the cabinet. Desai's reply was in the negative. He wanted to be prime minister since this was probably his last chance. Kamaraj did sympathize with him, but could not marshal enough support to make him win. He explained to Desai that his chances of winning were none too bright. Desai kept quiet. Kamaraj, however, got the feeling during the interview that bringing Desai to accept the No. 2 position might not be difficult; only, the position would need to be clothed with enough trappings. Sardar Patel was Deputy Prime Minister in Nehru's Cabinet; why not Desai in Indira Gandhi's?

Therefore, even when it looked like a contest, Kamaraj went on saying that he was making "some progress towards unanimity". He was positive that both Mrs Gandhi and Desai were afraid that their public image would suffer if either made a concession to the other; a face-saving formula would, he thought, be acceptable to both.

When Mrs Gandhi came to know about the working of Kamaraj's mind, she made it clear that she would not "buy" Desai's cooperation. I recall having asked her before the 1967 poll if she ever made an approach to Morarji Desai to join the cabinet. She said that no overture was ever made from her side, "but approaches have been made from his side". Desai denied that. There was no question of pre-conditions now. She made it known in public that a prime minister who sought somebody's cooperation on the condition that he or she would be offered a particular position in the cabinet, would be a weak one. She said she was keen to have unity, but without dictation or strings. Desai said he too favoured unanimity but it all depended "on whom and for what". It was shadow-boxing. And it looked as if both were heading for a clash.

Morarji Desai thought he was losing by not making an unequivocal declaration that he would contest. An erroneous impression was spreading that he might not challenge Mrs Gandhi after all. He was, therefore, the first to announce his candidature. Mrs Gandhi's reaction was immediate. She said that she was already the leader and her intention to contest should be taken for granted. Kamaraj had no choice but to fix a date for the election–March 13, 1967. But he did not give up his efforts for a rapprochement. He met both of them separately, and sent Desai's friend C.B. Gupta from UP to plead with him, and D.P. Mishra to Mrs Gandhi. Kamaraj's confidence in bringing them round was based on his assumption of their willingness to make up. He worked on this and successfully brought them nearer.

Desai offered to withdraw on the condition that he should be made Deputy Prime Minister with Home Affairs as his portfolio. Mrs Gandhi agreed to make him No. 2 in the Cabinet but refused to offer either the Deputy Prime Ministership or Home. She simply could not afford to annoy Chavan by taking away Home from him. Nor could she create doubts in the minds of her close allies by creating a post of Deputy Prime Minister. Chavan had been her staunch backer and had withstood all pressures and prizes from Desai's side. The young amateur crowd around her was also opposed to Desai being deputy prime minister because, as one of them put it, Desai would be a "Trojan horse in the Cabinet". They were spoiling for battle, and Dinesh Singh, her close supporter, had it down pat who would support whom. He gave Desai no more than 33 per cent of the votes of the Congress Parliamentary Party if it came to a contest.

There was a belated move on the part of Desai's supporters to confine the leadership vote to the Lok Sabha members. They said the Rajya Sabha was "packed" with Mrs Gandhi's nominees. The argument advanced was that all over the world, the directly elected House chose the leader. The Congress Parliamentary Party's strength stood at 428:275 in the Lok Sabha, and 153 in the Rajya Sabha. Their hunch was that Desai would carry with him the majority of the Lok Sabha members, but not if the Rajya Sabha members were also included.

A contest appeared unavoidable. Desai once again said that all was "in the hands of God". But this time he felt encouraged by the Syndicate's tacit support. He told all those who met him that Kamaraj was on his side. He began drafting a personal appeal to MPs, and prepared himself to contact them on the telephone. This time Morarji Desai did not blame the chief ministers for putting on the pressure, but picked on the business houses for having tried to buy votes to defeat him. No example was cited where money had been actually passed to an MP, but it was suggested that a member could cash his vote for as much as one lakh rupees. Desai reportedly said that some business houses were against him. The Opposition made capital out of this allegation. Whether it was true or not, many people believed it to be correct. It is quite possible that certain business houses took some interest in the election. In any democracy it was bound to happen. The fact that a majority of them were on Mrs Gandhi's side may also be true because the scales looked like they would tilt her way.

Kamaraj did not give up trying. Nor did some other leaders. There had never been such feverish activity before a leadership contest as was witnessed those days. Cars scurried back and forth between the houses of Mrs Gandhi and Desai. Kamaraj meeting Atulya Ghosh; Reddy meeting S.K. Patil; both meeting Kamaraj; then Atulya Ghosh, Reddy and Patil meeting Mrs Gandhi and Desai again; Jagjivan Ram meeting Desai; Nanda meeting Mrs Gandhi; Chavan meeting Kamaraj, and in turn meeting Mrs Gandhi. This never-ending round of meetings went on and on. Mrs Gandhi was willing to have Desai in her Cabinet but without giving the impression that there was a quid pro quo.

On the other hand, Morarji Desai could not just join the cabinet after having taken the whole issue to the pitch of a contest. There must be public evidence of a compromise; some arrangement whereby he could declare that he had, for unity's sake, stepped down to accept a position close to the prime ministership with the Home portfolio, against the No. 2 position with Finance. How to bridge the last bit of the gulf?

What looked like a stalemate did not deter Kamaraj. He thought of a *via media*: either No. 2 position and Home or the Deputy Prime Ministership and Finance. Mrs Gandhi did not agree to Home being taken from Chavan, her sheet-anchor. Nor would Desai accept anything less than the deputy prime ministership. About forty MPs aligned with Mrs Gandhi met at Asoka Mehta's house to say that she should not accept any pre-conditions. The Congress MPs' anxiety to have a unanimous choice was so evident that all leaders, whether D.P. Mishra on Mrs Gandhi's side or C.B. Gupta on Desai's, wanted a compromise.

Pressure or premonition worked. Morarji Desai sent word that he would not contest if he were given the deputy prime ministership and that it would be up to the prime minister to allot the portfolio. Mrs Gandhi accepted the offer and agreed to have Desai as Deputy Prime Minister. Some people said he would not be given any portfolio but that was not true. He was to be in-charge of Finance. For public consumption, it was announced that Desai would become the Deputy Prime Minister with "a suitable" portfolio. She did not want to give the impression that she had accepted a "pre-condition". Morarji Desai accepted the compromise formula. "My friends wanted me to do so," he rationalized later. And both heaved a sigh of relief: who could predict the outcome of a secret ballot?

It was obvious that the office of Deputy Prime Minister had not been properly defined. Kamaraj and the Syndicate were happy to leave it that way. Their purpose was to avoid a contest as well as to have Morarji Desai in the cabinet. And they had succeeded in doing so. But Mrs Gandhi's supporters were far from happy. The compromise formula was evolved late at night on the 11th of March. The following morning, the PM's house on Safdarjang Road was thick with doubts and difficulties about the scope of the office of Deputy Prime Minister. More than 30 Congress MPs met at Chavan's house and resolved that it should be made clear to all concerned, especially to Desai and Kamaraj, that the future Deputy Prime Minister would have no edge over other cabinet ministers, except that he would have second ranking. He would not–and could not–be another Sardar Patel.

Some of these MPs, including Mrs Gandhi's close supporters, who were referred to as the kitchen cabinet or the verandah cabinet (depending on the proximity to Mrs Gandhi) went to Kamaraj's house to emphasize that Desai should be Deputy Prime Minister by rank, but not in terms of power. Chavan and Jagjivan Ram rushed to Mrs Gandhi's house to ask what the duties of the Deputy Prime Minister would be.

Desai did not like the tone set at the meeting of the MPs. He went to Mrs Gandhi to register his complaint. At that time, Chavan and Jagjivan Ram were still sitting with Mrs Gandhi. To make herself quite clear, she said that the deputy prime ministership was only an office because he insisted on having that title; otherwise all ministers were equal. Morarji Desai did not come back happy from the meeting. But to a newspaperman, he said: "Surely I would not have joined the government if the attendant conditions were not suitable and acceptable."

Publicly, Mrs Gandhi said that the post of Deputy Prime Minister did not mean "any duality of authority". She made it clear that her authority would be "unfettered". She said that Desai had pledged "full and unqualified support" to her. But in the same breath, she expressed the hope that she would have the close cooperation of the deputy prime minister. She would not consult anybody in the formation of her cabinet or in discharging her functions. This was true; she never consulted Desai while constituting the ministry.

He, on the other hand, announced: "We must now work as a happy team." When a journalist asked Desai what had made him change his mind within 24 hours so as to accept the deputy prime ministership, he said: "Yesterday was yesterday and today is today." Asked what difference there was between Deputy Prime Minister and No. 2 in the cabinet, he said: "Certainly there is a difference, otherwise why the designation of Deputy Prime Minister? It carries a somewhat higher status and does give a different meaning." However, Mrs Gandhi's reply was that the difference was "only in name."

The third succession was over. There was no doubt that Morarji Desai had lost another chance—probably his last chance—to be the prime minister. But what could he do? And as he explained to me later: "How could I have defeated her when God was on her side?"

# Bilingualism

"You are a traitor," cried the excited Purshotamdas Tandon, addressing Govind Ballabh Pant, the then Home Minister, at the concluding sitting of the Parliamentary Committee* on the official language on November 25, 1958. "Even in UP, when I was the Speaker and you the Chief Minister, I had my doubts about your love for Hindi. Today I am convinced that you have none."

The Committee was considering the recommendations of the Official Language Commission** appointed

---

* Article 344 (4) of the Constitution provides that: "There shall be constituted a Committee consisting of thirty members, of whom twenty shall be members of the House of the People and ten shall be members of the Council of States to be elected respectively by the members of the House of the People and the members of the Council of States in accordance with the system of proportional representation by means of the single transferable vote."

** Article 344 (1) provides that: "The President shall, at the expiration of five years from the commencement of in 1955 to gauge the progress of Hindi over the past five years.

There was silence in the room. Members were visibly disturbed. Even the unflappable Pant showed signs of tension. All of a sudden his stick, which always rested on the side of his chair, fell on the floor. That was the only noise heard for some time until Dr A. Ramaswami Mudaliar, a Committee member from Madras, protested. Many others joined him, including a Hindi protagonist, Seth Govind Das, who had otherwise supported Tandon throughout the deliberations of the Committee.

Tandon did not relent but sat angry. Pant interjected: "I place India's unity before Hindi, and I am sorry if I have not come up to the standards of Tandonji."

Tandon had lost control over himself because the Committee had rejected by one vote his proposal to frame a "firm timetable" for the switch-over from English to Hindi by January 26, 1965, the date mentioned in the Constitution. The last "no" counted was that of a Communist member, S.A. Dange. This had tilted the evenly balanced scales. Tandon had expected Pant to vote for him to equalize the number of votes. As the Committee's Chairman, Pant could have exercized

---

this Constitution and thereafter at the expiration of ten years from such commencement, by order constitute a Commission which shall consist of a Chairman and such other members representing the different languages specified in the Eighth Schedule as the President may appoint, and the order shall define the procedure to be followed by the Commission."

his casting vote also, and Tandon expected him to do so—again in favour of Hindi. But he abstained, and the proposal fell through.

Pant could have done what Tandon wanted, only at the expense of Hindi itself. Tandon did not realize, however, that Pant was playing for higher stakes. He wanted the Committee to endorse the constitutional obligation to do away with English as the official language of the Union. The date of the switch-over—when or how—was only secondary. That was Pant's strategy all along.

In fact, his worry was to extinguish the embers of controversy that had ignited again. The very constitution of the Commission had an unsettling effect. Madras and West Bengal repudiated their constitutional obligation that the official language of the Union "shall be Hindi in Devanagari script" from January 1965. The West Bengal witnesses, including government representatives who appeared before the Commission, opposed the introduction of Hindi by that date. The chief ministers of Madras and Mysore also expressed the same opinion, and the Madras government wrote to the Commission that they would welcome an amendment to the Constitution to ensure the use of English after 1965.

Pant realized that the post-independence fervour to have one language as the focus of national unity had ebbed away. The criticism that Hindi had neither any cultural nor political pre-eminence over the other regional languages had become louder. There was now a concerted effort to discuss the entire language question *de novo*.

Persons like C. Rajagopalachari, who were once advocates of Hindi, had been alienated by what they characterized as the "vulgar haste" of the Hindi supporters to "impose" their language on others. K.M. Munshi, one of the framers of the Constitution and a champion of Hindi, had warned the zealots that "the pressure of propaganda as regards the time-limit should be relaxed in the interest of Hindi itself as well as the unity of India."

There was resentment that the Centre was bringing in Hindi "through the backdoor". The President's order dated May 27, 1952, authorizing the use of Hindi in addition to English for warrants of appointment of state governors and judges of the Supreme and High Courts, had created only a minor flutter. But a greater stir followed an order issued on December 3, 1955, allowing Hindi in correspondence with members of the public and international organizations, in administrative reports, official journals and reports to Parliament, government resolutions and legislative enactments, correspondence with state governments which had adopted Hindi as their official language, treaties and agreements, and government documents issued to diplomatic and consular officers and to Indian representatives at international organizations. The non-Hindi-speaking people, who had regarded the switch-over as a far-off possibility, genuinely feared that the Centre was quickening the pace of its introduction. In a country where the government is the biggest job-giver, this suspicion, however exaggerated, was not out of place.

On the other hand, those who supported Hindi wanted to jettison English even before the targeted date. They criticized the government for not doing enough to develop or spread Hindi. And there were all kinds of pressures on the Centre to introduce Hindi quickly in at least some spheres. The main argument for this was that some states were already imparting education in Hindi and it was unfair that students from these areas be asked to compete for government jobs in English, which they had not learnt or learnt only cursorily.

Pant realized that the atmosphere was built up for two conflicting demands—from the non-Hindi-speaking states for an indefinite postponement of the switch-over and from the Hindi-speaking states for a definite commitment for an early switch-over. Seven states had already adopted their regional language as the official language in place of English. It looked as though the remaining states would follow suit. The link between the different linguistic regions was already weakening.

English was still the only language stringing together north and south, east and west. But its standard was declining. The process of changeover to Indian language media in education and in administration had accentuated the difficulty in finding recruits who could discharge their duties efficiently in English.

A democratic government could not function indefinitely in a language which was understood by only a small fraction of the population. A common linguistic medium for communication among the different linguistic groups in India had to come from India itself; a country with its distinctive past and culture could not continue to function indefinitely through a foreign medium.

The protagonists of Hindi, who saw in the switch-over to the regional languages, indirect support for their cause, did not realize that this hurried change was really a threat to Hindi. The regional languages were taking the place which rightly belonged to Hindi. It was not realized that if and when Hindi came into its own as the only official language of the Union, it would not be able to push the regional languages out of the position only a link language should have.

Pant would often express these fears. But his main worry was how to end the daily challenges to the settled issue of Hindi as the official language of the Union. He could see that by not insisting on a definite date for the change-over, and not restricting the use of English, he could head off the demand for fresh thinking on the language question. He adopted this course even at the expense of annoying those who supported Hindi. In all the sittings of the Parliamentary Committee spread over 16 months, he leaned heavily towards the non-Hindi-speaking members. Never did he go against their wishes, especially their spokesman, Mudaliar. The result was that Pant was able to get the Committee to endorse the constitutional obligation of having Hindi as the official language of the Union.

As regards the switch-over date, he achieved a consensus to the effect that a complete switch to Hindi was not "practicable" by 1965. But by offering this concession, he made the Committee accept Hindi as the principal official language and English as an additional one. It was not easy, however.

Had the Official Language Commission given a categorical recommendation on the date of the change, most doubts would have been set to rest. Instead, it left a decision dependent on the preparations the government would make up to January 26, 1965. The ball was once again in the government's court.

What was worse was the dissenting opinion of the Commission's members from Madras, Dr P. Subbarayan, and from West Bengal, Dr Suniti Kumar Chatterji. They observed in their respective notes—at places the words used were the same—that Hindi had been adopted by the Constituent Assembly and not by a Parliament consisting of directly elected representatives of the people.

An erroneous impression was gaining ground that the Constituent Assembly had adopted Hindi by a majority of only one. This was the unkindest cut of all for Pant. He asked the Home Ministry to examine the facts. After studying the Constituent Assembly debates, the Ministry recorded the following note:

> It would seem that general agreement had already been reached as regards the adoption of Hindi as the official language of the Union, and also on the other important provisions of the Constitution relating to language, before the discussion of the draft chapters relating to official language was taken up in the Constituent Assembly. The main resolution was moved by the late Shri N. Gopalaswami Ayyangar. In the discussion that followed, claims were advanced by different members in favour of Hindustani (it received only 16 votes), Bengali and Sanskrit being made the official language in place of Hindi? But the question of numerals—Devanagari

or international—occupied most of the time and attention of the members.

More than a year later, on September 9, 1959, Pant himself said in the Rajya Sabha that "so far as my memory goes, and perhaps other friends who were there will endorse what I am saying, that this settlement, as it is now called, was really almost unanimously adopted. There was only one particular clause relating to international numerals about which there were a few dissentients. In other respects it was an agreed scheme that was adopted by the Constituent Assembly."

The facts are that before the language chapter was put before the Constituent Assembly, it was discussed at a meeting of the Congress Party members, then in an absolute majority in the Constituent Assembly. Jawaharlal Nehru, the then Prime Minister, proposed that Hindustani be adopted as the official language of the Union. His argument was that Hindi might introduce some communal feelings; moreover, Mahatma Gandhi always favoured Hindustani. At that meeting, Nehru's proposal was defeated by a majority of one vote. In the Constituent Assembly, the decision of the Congress Party was endorsed, without much fuss or opposition.

The Parliamentary Committee began its deliberations on the official language on November 16, 1957. At the very first meeting, the members were split into supporters and opponents of Hindi, with some sitting on the sidelines. Even the seats they selected confirmed that impression. Those who followed the most conservative line on Hindi, significantly sat on the left of Pant and inscribed their names in Hindi on the English nameplates the Home Ministry had placed in front of them. Among these members were Tandon, Dr Raghu Vira, Miss Maniben Vallabhbhai Patel and Govind Das.

Persons determined not to allow Hindi to gain ground sat on the right of the Chairman. Frank Anthony, an Anglo-Indian member was the most vocal among them. Mudaliar, Dange and B.S. Murthy, who helped Pant achieve a consensus in favour of Hindi, sat on the opposite side.

The Committee held 26 meetings, but there was hardly a sitting which was devoid of invective, accusations or denunciatory expressions. First, there was a controversy over the ambit of the Committee, whether it could consider only the recommendations of the Official Language Commission or its conclusions as well. Most members were not in favour of expanding its scope to include the conclusions. They took the view that the Official Language Commission did not consider the language problem in isolation but went beyond the terms of reference to study its ramifications in numerous fields of national activity. Findings on matters not covered by the terms of reference were, therefore, recorded as "conclusions" as distinguished from the "recommendations" relating to the terms of reference.

The members were content to discuss the recommendations since the Constitution had itself specified that "it shall be the duty of the Committee to examine the recommendations of the Commission". This clause was considered mandatory; hence only the recommendations were examined.

Later, Anthony shocked the Committee by insisting that its proceedings be made public. In fact, he began briefing the press, until, at the second meeting, Mudaliar complained: "Some of us have put a restraint by not even attending meetings where particular views were expressed, because thereby we would compromise our position as members of this Committee. I want to know whether we should still stick to that course and code of conduct or whether we may also avail ourselves of the opportunities, especially when pressure on us is very great, that our views should be explained to the public."

Pant said that he would like every member to impose on himself a "self-denying ordinance". Anthony opposed secrecy and said: "The *in camera* procedure would mean that about 20 persons, sitting behind closed doors, would decide this vital, highly controversial question for the whole country." He threatened to continue briefing the press. Pant's worry was that once the proceedings started appearing in newspapers, the members would play to the gallery and would not express their opinions frankly or accept a reasonable point of view. Public opinion would influence the deliberations of the Committee itself, apart from the law and order problem that a countrywide discussion would create.

Technically, the Parliamentary Committee's proceedings were not "privileged" because it was not a House committee. Although elected by the Parliament, it was not a normal parliamentary body and was under no obligation to report to Parliament. The report was to be submitted to the President directly. But, while framing the rules of procedure and conduct of business, the Committee laid down that its proceedings "shall be treated as confidential and it shall not be permissible for a member of the Committee...to communicate, directly or indirectly, to the Press or any other person information regarding its proceedings..."

Anthony was, however, able to persuade Pant to place the Committee's report before Parliament. But Pant made it clear that it was only a gesture, and even then he had to seek the President's formal approval to do so. It was pointed out that Parliament had no power to modify a single recommendation or amend a single word of the report.

There was yet another quarrel over what type of papers should be circulated among the members. The Home Ministry was picking out for circulation only those writings which supported Hindi and an early switch-over from English. At a Committee meeting, Mudaliar said: "I do not know on whose instruction particular papers have been circulated. Many of the papers, which are equally important and have equal validity and which contain equally valuable views, have not been circulated." Hirendra Nath Mukerjee, a Communist member, said: "We have found extracts from the *National Herald*. It was a capable editorial. I do not object to that at all but there must be some process of selection."

Some members asked for the resolution passed by the West Bengal Assembly and its proceedings in favour of retaining English. There was also a demand for the text of the speech of C. Subramaniam, the then Finance Minister of Madras, in which he had favoured the continuance of the *status quo*. The West Bengal Assembly had unanimously decided in 1957 that it could not accept Hindi alone as the official language and that the *status quo* should continue.

Pant agreed to the circulation of all the papers the members wanted to see. He added: "So far as the few papers that have been circulated are concerned, the gentlemen concerned wrote to the Secretary that these papers should be circulated among the members." This was not technically correct because some articles were planted in newspapers, so that when they appeared in print, they could be circulated.

For example, when the Committee began its deliberations, Rajagopalachari initiated a crusade against Hindi. Pant was unhappy. He feared that Rajaji's writings would vitiate the atmosphere and a settled question would be reopened. Could something be done to counter his propaganda? I ransacked the Press Information Bureau shelves and found a Hindi primer which carried a foreword by Rajaji pleading that the southern states learn Hindi. The reproduction of this foreword was bound to take the sting out of his attack. I was able to place the text with a local newspaper, which used it under the byline of one of its correspondents. It was then easy to circulate the reproduction among the members.

How did other countries where more than one language was current, decide which should have priority? Members asked this question repeatedly. Pant asked the Home Ministry to prepare a note on this at the very beginning of the Committee's meeting. The Ministry found that Switzerland had four national languages—German, French, Italian and Romansh. The first three were official and enjoyed "absolute equality". The Confederation used them in all official dealings with the Cantons, and the Cantons among themselves. All federal laws, regulations, notices and publications were issued in these languages. In Parliament, members had the right to speak in all the four national languages, but the proceedings were recorded only in the official ones. The medium of instruction in all primary and secondary schools was the official language of the Canton concerned.

In bilingual and trilingual Cantons, if the linguistic area was geographically distinct, the medium was the language spoken in a particular area. Even in bilingual towns there were separate schools for each language. In all schools, one of the national languages was a compulsory second language from the 5th standard to matriculation. Thus in the German-speaking Cantons, French was compulsory, while in the French-speaking Cantons, German was compulsory. The Italian-speaking Canton could choose either German or French as the compulsory second language. The universities were run by the Cantons, and the medium of instruction was the official language of the Canton concerned. In the Federal Court, any of the three official languages could be employed in proceedings. But a citizen had the right to demand that the judgment of a court be in the one he might specify.

In Canada, two official languages, English and French, were in use. In the national Parliament of Canada and in the House of Legislature of Quebec, both languages were used. Records and journals of the

Houses were also in both languages. In a Canadian court, a person could use either English or French. All publications of the Federal and Quebec governments were issued in both languages, and so were paper currency and postage stamps.

While the working language of the Federal government was English, letters written in French were also answered in it. The working language of the Government of Quebec was French, but letters addressed to it in English were answered similarly. A translation bureau was set up within the Federal administration, the duties and functions of which were to collaborate and act for all departments of the public services. In education, the medium of instruction was English and French, and there were universities in which the medium was exclusively English or French, although in each of them, arrangements existed for teaching the other language.

In Belgium, there were three languages—Flemish, French and German. Both French and Flemish were official languages and were used in government proclamations. Generally speaking, the problem was solved by the fact that a large number of individuals were bilingual or trilingual.

In the USSR, there were about 200 languages and dialects spoken by various linguistic or national groups. Among the more important languages were 16 or so. Russian had, in all respects, an outstanding position. The free development of all cultures and languages was not only allowed but actively fostered. Schools were opened, newspapers started, new literature produced, in languages where none existed previously. Within the national republics of the Union, it would seem that the regional languages found a great deal of scope.

In education, the regional languages were recognized and encouraged at appropriate levels. The Soviet government had taken special measures to equip them with scientific literature and personnel as far as possible.

Members of any nationality could speak in their own language in representative assemblies, including the Supreme Soviet, or in any court, and were entitled to address official authorities in their own language. In Moscow, in the Central Government, all instructions and decisions of state and judicial bodies, departments and ministries, were issued in Russian. All laws passed by the Supreme Soviet of the USSR were, however, published in the 16 important languages.

The *Gazette* of the Supreme Soviet was also issued in all these languages. In principle, a citizen had the right to make a written or oral statement in any language used in the Soviet Union, but Russian was found to be most convenient.

The language problem in China appeared in a very different light. While there were about 24 dialectal variations, the script was uniform. In terms of alphabetic writing, it might be said that the script had as many characters as there were words or expressions. The fact that there was an identical written script, even if there were variations in oral expression of it, resulted in situations in which two Chinese speakers could not make themselves understood to each other orally but could communicate in writing. Moves to convert the Chinese ideograms into an alphabet had been made for several decades and it seemed that a definite policy of alphabetization had now been adopted. In the ultimate analysis, the problem of Chinese language reform reduced itself to that of furnishing an alphabetical system of script to the language, in place of the ideographic system.

The Home Ministry's note served as source material, whenever any step to introduce Hindi was taken later. For example, the pattern of the Canadian Bureau of Translation within the Federal administration was adopted by the Centre after some years.

The first few meetings of the Language Committee were confined to the general observations of individual members. The cleavage between those who favoured ousting English quickly, and their opponents who wanted to retain it indefinitely, was clear from the very start. The Hindi supporters argued as if the adoption of Hindi was being discussed all over again. This encouraged the opponents still further to demand that the switch-over be deferred indefinitely. A few tried to utilize the opportunity to question the very status of Hindi.

From among those who supported Hindi, Tandon, who departed from his practice and spoke in English, said: "Since I was a young man, the one dream, the only dream that I had was that India should be strong, unified and integrated. Hindi, for me, is the most patent means of unification and integration." He wanted the switch-over on January 26, 1965, as provided in the Constitution, but did not mind if the date was extended by "a year or two" provided there was a firm timetable for replacing English by Hindi. His suggestion was that to accelerate the pace of substitution, a separate ministry of Hindi should be created at the Centre.

Voicing the other point of view, Mudaliar said: "The Indian Union has, necessarily, got to be bilingual during the transition. It is necessary in order to remove the suspicions and apprehensions, which are prevalent among the public in non-Hindi regions, that this perspective of prolonged bilingualism should be accepted by the Government of India and Parliament. These authorities should announce their readiness to make statutory provision for such bilingualism through the exercise of legislative power vested in Parliament under Article 343 (3)* of the Constitution.

Mudaliar accepted the constitutional obligation to have Hindi as the official language of the Union. But he wanted the change to be postponed "for a long, long time to come".

Anthony and Pramatha Nath Banerjee, a member from West Bengal, openly advocated the retention of English permanently. They, along with some other members, questioned the advisability of having Hindi as the official language of the Union. So divergent were the opinions voiced in the first two meetings that Pant told me: "I don't know how I am going to bring about unanimity. Sometimes I fear the Committee will break up before it submits its report."

---

* Article 343 (3) says: "In making their recommendations under clause (2), the Commission shall have due regard to the industrial, cultural and scientific advancement of India, and the just claims and the interests of persons belonging to the non-Hindi-speaking areas in regard to the public services."

Until now, Pant had been quiet. There was no harm in members letting off steam. But when he found some of them questioning the *raison d'etre* of Hindi, he intervened to say: "We are not writing on a blank slate today. The Constitution has adopted Hindi and many steps have been taken by the Government of India." The discussion was back on the rails again.

Mudaliar wanted the Committee to examine witnesses "so as to have our own views clarified and to know their views". He mentioned the names of Rajagopalachari and Morarji Desai. Both had expressed diametrically opposed views, the former coming out staunchly in favour of English and the latter for Hindi. Pant realized that if he were to allow a fresh examination of witnesses, the whole language question would reopen. This was the endeavour of many public men, inside and outside the Committee. For such occasions, he could use the Hindi fanatics. Govind Das was willing to oblige. He observed: "It is a very controversial matter and I am of the opinion that no fresh witnesses should be examined because there will be no end to it."

Pant himself was more tactful and said: "Unless you want to cross-examine them and to extract from them something which would make them modify their opinion or enable us to feel that what they have said is not exactly what they thought they were saying, I do not think it will be of gain because they have left no room for doubt as to their own attitude towards these matters."

Mudaliar said: "I do not think it will be proper to try to convert them to our views but what I wanted was to have the views clarified." One good thing about him was that if, after voicing his opinion, he found that he had very little support, he would not pursue the subject. And in any case, he was more concerned to see that the Madras government's memorandum—"It must be accepted as a fundamental rule admitting of no exception that Hindi and English should be available equally as two alternative media to be chosen at the option of the candidate"—was included for discussion. When Pant showed firmness on the question of witnesses, Mudaliar kept quiet, and the Committee settled down to business.

The consideration of the Commission's recommendations was like going up a precipitous incline. Not many members thought that they would have the stamina to scale all the heights. Pant saved the most difficult issue of when to switch-over to Hindi for the end. He thought the members would get used to travelling together and overcoming difficulties so that the date for the change would not present insurmountable difficulties. Pant took up the least controversial portions first.

The recommendation on coining new words was that "in adopting terminology, clarity, precision and simplicity should be primarily aimed at. Doctrinaire insistence on 'language purism' is deprecated". Raghu Vira, known as a purist, was quick on his legs and said that "adopting" in philological context meant taking one word without any marked change. "Adapting" meant taking a word from some foreign language with some change in form. Therefore, "if we could say 'in selecting the terms', it would be more appropriate".

One member interjected to say that "evolving" would be a better word. Pant was averse to altering the Commission's language. He realized that once he allowed a change, it would open the floodgates. He knew he would face real difficulties when matters of real importance came up for discussion. Therefore, sticking to the original text was preferable. When Raghu Vira persisted, Pant said: "We will see if we can find a more suitable expression."

Raghu Vira then said that the terms selected should be capable of becoming the basis of derivations. He said: "The derivatives would include nominal words, verbal nouns, action nouns, agent nouns, instrument nouns, adjectives, abstract nouns, etc, based thereon." He added: "For instance, if we take the word law, we should be able to form the adjective 'legal'; then we should have the word for 'legalization'; then, we should be able to form another word for 'legislate'; and from that the action agent noun, 'legislator'. If we have the agent noun 'legislator' it should have the adjective 'legislatorial' and other forms. So, the term should not be simply precise."

Interrupting Raghu Vira, Hirendra Nath Mukerjee said: "We all know that he has given us Indian equivalents of scientific and technical terminology in foreign languages, almost with a vengeance. For example, I find from the pamphlet *Modern Indian Languages* that *barna* (alphabet) is translated as *pinal.* My difficulty is about this kind of language. If we are going to have these equivalents in Indian language and teach our students and technicians, it would complicate the whole process of training at a period when the plan is in operation. We are working in the year 1958 and we have to have Indian equivalents of these foreign words.

Therefore, if we have language purism in a way Raghu Vira has done, it would complicate matters and make it more difficult to understand."

The real battle started when the committee came to the recommendation about the language qualifications for Central Government servants which mentioned "obligatory requirements of Government servants to qualify themselves in Hindi within a reasonable period to the extent requisite for the discharge of their duties".

Mudaliar said the Commission's recommendation had missed the real point: "We are not aiming at a national language but a language for the Union of the Government of India." He said that the Constitution does not contain a single reference to a national language.

M.P. Mishra, a member from Bihar, said that even in the Commission's report, the phrase "national language" had not been used. Mudaliar controverted this and said that the word "national" had been used more than once. He quoted from the portion on the propagation of Hindi among people in the non-Hindi-speaking areas: "This programme has to be stressed, for if large areas of the country are unfamiliar with Hindi, it can hardly attain the status of a national language."

Mishra did not give in and drew Mudaliar's attention to the Commission's explanation: "Since the place contemplated for the Union language and the official languages of the States, or the languages in the Eighth Schedule, does not exactly convey this context of meaning, we have avoided the use of the term 'national language' altogether. We sometimes refer to 'national language policy' but it will be seen that the meaning intended to be conveyed is entirely different, namely, the national policy regarding languages."

The discussion again meandered to the switch-over date of January 26, 1965—a Damocles' sword which was always hanging over the heads of the members. Pant said that as he had indicated before "there should be no rigid deadline". He repeated that the date mentioned in the Constitution was not mandatory "for all purposes because it gives Parliament the option to extend the period". Pant was anxious that the Committee should not get to discuss the target date, a point of controversy, until it had gone into the other recommendations.

It was starting from the wrong end because if the decision was to postpone the switch-over date, then there would be more time to make preparations for the introduction of Hindi. However, Pant had got away with the postponement of the debate on this crucial matter before and he wanted to do it again. His approach was that while discussing other recommendations, the Committee would have committed itself to so many steps that the switch-over to Hindi would become inevitable. The fact that it would not happen in 1965 was not really that important.

Mudaliar said that "as a preliminary" to the consideration of qualifications for government employees, "this committee should come to some conclusion as to when the transition is to take place".

Mukerjee said: "We could reopen the matter, and with all modesty and respect to everybody concerned, we could suggest that the target date should be given up at least for the time being and a fresh date given. I have seen in the papers that a former Congress Minister has suggested 1980 or so."

Tandon, who had been keeping quiet so far, said:

> Probably those of you who might have been the members of the Constituent Assembly might remember that originally, the time given in the resolution as framed was five years. Then there were talks and the date was put off; ten years were allowed and then ultimately to please all and to meet everybody's view, it was thought that 15 years should be given. That was given with the consent of those who belong to non-Hindi provinces. What Morarji Desai meant was that because such a long time had been given for the implementation of the constitutional requirements, therefore there had been so much controversy about it.
>
> These controversies would not have been raised if the thing had begun to be implemented very much earlier. What I mean to say is that this question of a new date only invites new controversies and puts off the implementation of the recommendations. That is not at all desirable. You should take up the recommendations honestly in the spirit of making a serious attempt to do away with the English language, a foreign language, as quickly as possible.

Murthy, always trying to take a middle course, said that the deadline of January 26, 1965 was vehemently opposed by the South; but there were others who were anxious to see that somehow 1965 be made the target date. If the Committee were to decide upon what facilities could be provided for those people whose mother tongue was not Hindi, "I do not think we would mind any date beyond 1965." Pant was able to close the discussion by saying, "1965 should not be regarded as the deadline. There should be no rigidity about it, and in a way, I am doubtful about the feasibility of our being able to stick to this deadline."

What ultimately divided the Committee was not whether Hindi was the national language to the exclusion of other Indian languages but whether Hindi could be introduced as a medium of instruction in administrative or military training establishments. There was agreement that "for some time it will be necessary to continue English" but that was where the unanimity ended. As soon as the introduction of Hindi was discussed, controversy erupted. Tandon and his supporters asked the Committee to recommend that "early steps should be taken to introduce Hindi as an alternative medium". The amendment of Murthy was that "suitable steps should be taken to introduce Hindi as a medium for all or some of the purposes of instruction".

Slightly different was Mudaliar's suggestion: "The introduction of the Hindi medium for all or some of the purposes of instruction may be considered and suitable steps taken." Both Murthy and Mudaliar were dead set against bringing in a word like "early", lest it should convey even an indirect suggestion to dilute the pre-eminent status of English. The Language Commission had been vague on this point and had only said: "It seems there has not been yet an overhaul of the linguistic media of instruction in some of the training establishments; and probably most of such training continues to be in English, although it may be susceptible to replacement, to some extent, by the Hindi medium." Why should the Parliamentary Committee go beyond this? That was the argument of the non-Hindi-speaking members.

The Committee met for days together without reaching any conclusion. Pant adjourned the sittings for a week to initiate behind-the-scenes efforts, but the deadlock continued. Murthy, a member from Andhra Pradesh, who was later rewarded and appointed deputy minister, did try to bring about a rapprochement. Pant vainly appealed to the members again and again to agree. Finally, like a defeated man, he said: "I cannot tell you how I deplore my failure (in not bridging the gap)." There was no choice except voting. Tandon's proposal was put before the Committee and defeated by three votes.

Hardly had this controversy subsided when a battle royal started on the medium for the entrance examination to the services. Murthy favoured the continuance of English. Tandon put forward the proposal to have both Hindi and English. Anthony was for English, or at best "Hindustani of Gandhiji's conception", and his preference was for a single medium, but in case of a change from the present medium "the prior approval of the State legislatures should be obligatory". Mudaliar, however, observed: "There is no use saying English and Hindi will be the medium. We have to see the situation when the regional languages have come into their own. Government will suggest that these regional languages should be the medium of instruction." The Madras Government's memorandum before the Committee had already suggested that competitive examinations should be conducted in the regional languages.

It appeared that there were very few to resist the pull of the regional languages. The discussion began moving in that direction. Practically none spoke of the danger of parcelling out people language-wise, after having divided them region-wise. And all the objection to the division twice over was how to effect moderation if the regional languages were to be the examination media. Mudaliar said that moderation could be handled only in a limited number of languages. Tandon asked: "How then will the examination be conducted?" The official Language Commission's solution was that "this might entail a region-wise decentralization of the entrance examination and, consequently, a quota system".

Tandon and other Hindi supporters were the first to agree to a quota system. Their only desire was to effect an early switch-over to Hindi, and they were willing to go to any length to achieve it. Pant vehemently opposed the quota system which he feared might one day bring in its trail a pernicious system like separate electorates. It was an unknown member, P.T. Thanu Pillai, a south Indian, who blocked the acceptance of this proposal. Thanu Pillai spoke out firmly against the quota system. He said that the principle, once accepted, would come to be applied to all fields, not the services alone. He said: "If I agree to the quota system, I shall be doing a great disservice to the unity of the country."

There was an applause after his speech—a rare thing for the Committee. Even the Hindi-speaking members found it hard to pursue the suggestion. Tandon conceded the principle was bad. The Committee directed the government to appoint an expert Committee to examine the practicability of introducing the regional languages, with specific instructions not to "bring in a quota system". The Home Ministry never appointed this Committee. The officials themselves came to the conclusion that the introduction of the regional language as examination media was not practical. Their belief was that once it was done there was no escape from a quota system. This is their fear even now.

The Committee continued its off and on deliberations for more than a year. The members quarrelled, made up, walked out, came back. Even in their differences, they had come to appreciate the thread of unity, running not only in that room but also in the polyglot country known as India. In the last days, their patience was at its tether. Tempers were frayed, and even the niceties of manner which marked the discussion in its earlier stages, were dropped. They had sat too long, had gone over the same ground too many times, and come to the same conclusions too often. The following conversation is typical of the jaded mood prevalent at that time. A discussion on the early introduction of Hindi in the administration was on.

Tandon: May I take it that Mr Murthy has withdrawn his amendment?

Murthy: All right.

Tandon: But you were arguing against it. You were appealing to us to drop the word "early".

Murthy: I want to be democratic.

Tandon: Who is aristocratic here? What is the meaning of democracy in these meaningless terms?

Anthony: I raise a point of order, Sir. I have been sitting very silently and listening to these fanatical views. Certain people have been calculatedly aggressive, rude and offensive to us, including you, Mr Chairman.

Tandon: I will request him to behave. Am I rude? What abusive language did I use, Mr Murthy?

Anthony: Certainly, I will raise a point of order.

Tandon: Mr Chairman, I raise a point of order. What is it? Do you know English? You improve your English. Mr Murthy, I leave it to you to tell me whether I have used any abusive words. There is a downright lie here.

Anthony: The only repository of truth is Tandonji and Dr Raghu Vira. Even the Chairman is telling lies!

Tandon: I am just talking to Mr Murthy to find out whether he has dropped the word "early" and I am putting the question to him and somebody drops in and says I am abusing. What is that? It is just like the ancient proverb "I tell lies to your face".

Murthy: I am very sorry I am the cause of this. I apologize to you, Tandonji.

Tandon: Not at all. I am so very sorry. I put the question to you and Mr Anthony says that I have been using abusive language. I would like to know which are the words which have meant any abuse.

Pant: I think Mr Anthony was somewhat impatient.

Pillai: It was an outburst of his collective impatience.

Even at the concluding session of the Committee, there was no dearth of accusations and counter-accusations. Tandon wanted to go through the proceedings to determine whether the report put together by the Home Ministry was accurate. Pant requested that at least the decision part be disposed of quickly. But Tandon replied: "I have to satisfy myself. If you want to adopt it, I shall not vote for it."

Pant, who had accomplished the miracle of having almost achieved unanimity on Hindi, did not want to spoil things through last-minute hurry. He allowed members some more time to express themselves. He said he did not want to push anybody. The technique worked and it was left to Pant himself to write the report.

The recommendation of the Committee, with the exception of Anthony, was that Hindi should be the principal language from January 26, 1965, and English a subsidiary one, with no target date for the switch-over. It was indeed a feather in Pant's cap.

Before the report was finalized, Pant sent the draft to Nehru for his comments. The use of the word "subsidiary" for English infuriated Nehru, who declared that this expression gave the idea that it was the language of "vassals". Pant backed up his preference for the word by sending Nehru various equivalents of "subsidiary" in English. That day I ransacked every library in Delhi to collect as many dictionaries as possible. In some of them "subsidiary" had "additional" as an alternative meaning.

Pant tried to argue with Nehru that the two words meant more or less the same thing. He also pointed out that the Madras government, in its memorandum after the Official Language Commission's report, had itself used the word "subsidiary" for English when it recommended: "It is possible, by 1965, to promote Hindi to the status of principal official language of the Union, if provision is made for continuing English as a subsidiary official language thereafter." Nehru did not agree with Pant. What was more, he was quite indignant and reportedly made some harsh comments. Pant thought over and over again about these remarks. That very evening, he had his first heart attack.

The final report retained the word "subsidiary" for English. But subsequently, the government quietly substituted "additional" and "associate" for it.

Once the report was out of the way, Pant, after recovery, decided not to have any further Commission or Committee on the official language. He had seen the very basis of Hindi questioned again and again in the Committee. Any further discussion, he feared, might challenge the constitutional obligation to have Hindi as the official language of the Union. This was too much of a risk to take.

Article 344 (1) said: "The President shall at the expiration of five years from the commencement of the Constitution, and thereafter at the expiration of ten years from such commencement, by order constitute a Commission." Both the Home and Law Ministries studied the Article again and again, and concluded that the word "shall" could be interpreted as "may". Therefore, the president was not bound to appoint a commission in another ten years. The suggestion was the Home Ministry's but the legal pundits buttressed it. Another commission which should have been constituted in 1960 was killed for all time to come.

Nehru commended the report as "quite a remarkable piece of work" and also praised Pant in the Lok Sabha for bringing together "people thinking quite differently". Maybe he felt guilty for what he said earlier. As far as Hindi was concerned, its fate had already been sealed for many, many years to come. In the Lok Sabha on August 6, 1959, about three weeks before the Parliamentary Committee's report was presented, Nehru had given an assurance that there would be no time-limit, and that the non-Hindi-speaking areas would themselves decide when to switch-over to Hindi.

This was probably inherent in the situation prevailing at that time. It was likely over-enthusiasm on the part of the supporters of Hindi which was endangering the unity of the country; it was possibly the genuine fear of the non-Hindi-speaking population that they would be shut out of jobs. Whatever the reasons, Nehru's assurance was timely and it forged another link in the country's unity. For the non-Hindi-speaking people, the assurance was like a safety belt in the swirling waters of Hindi.

Naturally, the pro-Hindi lobby was unhappy. A whispering campaign started against Nehru. Even Pant expressed his disappointment over the outcome. He told me one day: "Whatever I achieved in two years, the Prime Minister destroyed it in less than two minutes." He spoke to Nehru about this. Nehru in his speech on September 4, 1959, on the Parliamentary Committee report, tried to retrieve some of the lost ground. He said: "I had said that English should be an associate or additional language. What exactly did I mean by it? Well, I meant exactly what that means. That is to say, English cannot be, in India, anything but a secondary language in the future. In the nature of things, mass education will be in our own languages. English may be taught as a compulsory language—I hope it will be—to a large number of people. It cannot be to everybody but to a large number. It remains as a secondary language. But I say that Hindi, whenever it is feasible, comes into use progressively more and more for inter-State official work."

But the damage to Hindi had already been done. It was too late to retrieve anything. The non-Hindi-speaking areas considered that Nehru made the speech under pressure. That was not wholly incorrect. And they stuck to his earlier speech in which he said that the decision when to switch-over to Hindi would lie with the non-Hindi-speaking population. That remained so.

Pant never forgave Nehru for giving a blanket assurance to the non-Hindu-speaking areas. I recall that when the Parliamentary Committee's report was released to the Press, I also distributed the text of Nehru's assurance. The government statement on the report itself mentioned it. But Pant was very annoyed with me for having circulated Nehru's statement. He construed my act as an attempt to cloud the constitutional obligation to switch-over to Hindi on June 26, 1965. I told him that any newsman could have asked for the text of Nehru's assurance, and that I, a Government Press officer, was bound to give it. But Pant did not accept my explanation.

Once the Parliamentary Committee recommended that the attitude towards the changeover to Hindi should be "flexible" and "practical", it was a foregone conclusion that the target date would be discarded. The government proposed to amend Article 343 which said that "Hindi in Devanagari shall be the official language of the Union from January 26, 1965". The amendment was to provide for an indefinite use of English. But an unobtrusive sounding revealed that the Congress Party would split on this subject. The Opposition parties would also block an amendment to the Constitution, which would require a two-thirds majority of the House. The proposal was therefore dropped.

The Parliamentary Committee had suggested a legislation to continue the use of English "for as long as may be necessary" as "a subsidiary official language" for specified purposes. Some constitutional pundits pointed out, however, that there was no need to amend the Constitution to continue the use of English for an indefinite period; this could be done by the simple will of Parliament. Article 343 of the Constitution authorized Parliament to provide by law for the use of English "for such purposes as may be specified in the law". The way thought out was that a legislation be brought to continue the use of English from the appointed date, January 26, 1965, in addition to Hindi "(a) for all the official purposes of the Union for which it was being used immediately before that date and (b) for the transaction of business in Parliament."

This decision taken in early 1960 was not made public. The Law Ministry also advised the government that since English would continue to be used until 1965 for all official purposes of the Union, "it may not be wholly appropriate" to introduce a Bill for the continuance of English at that stage.

Later, the Madras Government enquired from the Home Ministry on January 17, 1961, what action had been taken on the resolution passed by the State Legislature that the *status quo* be maintained after the switch-over date. The Home Ministry replied that "the Government of India have decided to introduce, in due course, appropriate legislation in Parliament to implement the Prime Minister's assurance regarding the continued use of English for the official purposes of the Union, even after January 1965."

The legislation—the Official Language Bill—for the continuance of English was enacted in 1963. There was much commotion over the use of the word "may". The non-Hindi-speaking states wanted it to be changed into "shall". Nehru and Asoke Sen, the then Law Minister, assured the House that the word "may" meant "shall". This statement did not satisfy the non-Hindi-speaking states, but since the Congress was ruling all over India, Madras and other southern states acquiesced.

C.N. Annadurai, the Dravida Munnetra Kazhagam leader from Madras, made the same plea to substitute "shall" for "may" in the law permitting that English may be used in addition to Hindi beyond 1965. In his reply on April 17, 1963, Nehru said that while he was personally prepared to retain English as an associate or alternate language "until otherwise decided" by non-Hindi-speaking people, he did not see "how we can make this provision in the statute". Later when the sentiment became stronger in the south, a change of phraseology was demanded. The pertinent Clause 3 said:

> Notwithstanding the expiration of the period of fifteen years from the commencement of the Constitution, the English language may, as from the appointed day, continue to be used, in addition to Hindi—(a) for all the official purposes of the Union for which it was being used immediately before that day; and (b) for the transaction of business in Parliament.

By the time the Language Bill was passed, some states which had adopted Hindi as their regional language were anxious to introduce it for High Court judgments. The Bill authorized the Governor, after consulting the President, to allow the use of Hindi or the official language of the states, in addition to English, "for any judgment, decree or order passed or made by the High Court of that State".

To satisfy the Hindi-speaking population, the Bill laid down that the President "may appoint a committee" to review the progress made in the use of Hindi. But there was no mention of re-constitution of the Commission lest the entire matter be reopened.

When the Language Bill was discussed, MPs from non-Hindi-speaking areas reminded Nehru of his undertaking that he would leave it to them to decide when to switch over to Hindi. They wanted to amend the Constitution accordingly. The government promised to implement Nehru's assurance, but did not say when or how. There was, however, an influential section in the government which was not serious about it. But there were some who sincerely believed that such assurances were difficult to legislate. The passage of time was thought to be the best solution; no action was taken. Consequently the doubt about the real intentions of the Centre continued to exist in the minds of the non-Hindi-speaking population.

Meanwhile, there was a spurt of activity in the Home Ministry to train government employees in Hindi. This was encouraged by the Parliamentary Committee's recommendation for "preparatory measures for facilitating the changeover" and the memorandum of 44 MPs to the President, complaining about the slow introduction of Hindi in the administration.

A Home Ministry order was issued on July 30, 1960, making in-service training of administrative personnel in Hindi obligatory for all Central Government employees below 45 years on January 1, 1961. Employees below Class III, industrial establishments and work-charged staff were, however, exempted. The ministries were requested to release 20 per cent of their staff annually so as to train them in Hindi before the switch-over.

The Home Ministry was obviously not serious about this project because the Union Budget did not make provision for any large expansion of the Hindi teaching scheme. The amount asked for was Rs 8,54,200, and this included the salaries of clerical staff and peons.

It had taken about 12 years since independence to translate 28 manuals of office procedure, containing about 23,000 pages; approximately 70,000 to 80,000 pages had still to be done.

To imagine that government employees would be trained in Hindi by 1965 was only wishful thinking, not a reality. It had to be so, because the Home Ministry decided in 1961 to "introduce the use of Hindi, in addition to English, for noting on files as an experimental measure in selected sections in the Secretariat where the bulk of the staff have a working knowledge of Hindi." Expecting about half a million penpushers to transact business in Hindi in four years' time was indeed a leap of faith.

By the end of 1964, the Home Ministry claimed to have introduced noting in Hindi, in about 200 sections, with a substantial number of employees knowing Hindi. The number was inflated to a respectable figure by including sections dealing with translation work or with the issue of stationery, holding annual sports, and posting peons. There was no section of any consequence working in Hindi. In fact, nobody took it seriously and even training in Hindi was like a recess in school.

Despite the fact that practically no preparations had been made, a few days before the day appointed for the switch-over, the Home Ministry issued its ill-fated circular. It said that Hindi would become the principal official language of the Union on January 26, 1965, and that English would be an additional official language, but would be allowed to be used for all purposes. It also meant that correspondence between the Centre and the Hindi-speaking states—UP, Rajasthan, Bihar and Madhya Pradesh, and two Union Territories, Delhi and Himachal Pradesh—would be in Hindi. The other states were to continue to correspond in English. However, a Hindi translation was also to accompany a communication from Delhi.

Central Government employees would be at liberty to make notings in Hindi or English. Thus, a particular file might have some notings in Hindi and some in English. However, for the benefit of non-Hindi-speaking employees, an English rendering would be provided by the employee himself or by the translating unit each department would have.

The language of the Supreme Court would continue to be English under Clause I of Article 348 of the Constitution. But, the decision was that eventually Hindi would take the place of English. The circular also said that from January 26, all letters received in Hindi should be replied to in Hindi. Non-statutory notifications and statistics of births and deaths in the *Gazette* were being published in Hindi in addition to English. But now there would be a *Gazette* in Hindi as well.

In another circular, the Home Ministry said a beginning should be made in giving Hindi names to Central Government offices, organizations or institutions in addition to the English ones. To start with, Central Government offices constituted in Hindi-speaking states were to be given Hindi names. Thereafter, the process of changeover to Indian names would be carried on steadily. The Home Ministry also asked all the ministries to translate forms, rules and manuals into Hindi.

Madras was perturbed at the circular. After all, language touched the livelihood of the people, and they feared that their chances of employment would lessen now that Hindi had become the major language. Statewide agitation started building up in January–February 1965. The assurance of Nanda, the then Home Minister, that the introduction of Hindi would be so regulated as not to cause any hardship to the non-Hindi-speaking people, did not stop the agitation from spreading or becoming violent. One after another, five people killed themselves in Madras through self-immolation, after the pattern followed by protesting Buddhist monks in Saigon.

First, the government blamed the DMK for "exploiting the people's ignorance about the exact position on the official language". Later, the existence of the circular itself was denied. Then the Home Ministry asked the ministries not to issue any circular but await "comprehensive instructions on the subject". That was, however, never done; the Home Ministry had burnt its fingers so badly that it did not do anything in regard to Hindi any more.

The riots came to an end, but the confidence of the non-Hindi-speaking people was shattered beyond redemption. The Congress leaders from the south took it upon themselves to voice the fears of these groups. The trio, Kamaraj, Sanjiva Reddy and Nijalingappa (Atulya Ghosh also joined them) approached Shastri to emphasize that he should not hustle Hindi through, but should "uphold the declaration of Nehru". They left it to Shastri to devise ways of doing so. Annadurai wanted an amendment to the Constitution to keep the use of Hindi in abeyance indefinitely. Rajagopalachari wanted English to be "imposed" on the country for all time. This was not the position of Kamaraj and others. They were against "hurry", not against Hindi, which, Kamaraj said in a public statement, had been chosen to be "a common language to maintain the unity of the country politically and administratively". In fact, Kamaraj taunted Rajagopalachari for not being able to make even the General Council of the Swatantra Party—the organization to which he belonged—agree to the policy of English forever.

Shastri readily issued a statement that the switch-over to Hindi would be further slowed down, but he kept quiet about implementing Nehru's assurances. He was under great pressure from the Hindi lobby in Parliament not to agree to bilingualism for an indefinite period. Personally he favoured an early introduction of Hindi because, unlike Nehru, he felt more at home while speaking in Hindi. But sensing the mood of the south, he favoured an all-party consensus on the switch-over date. When no specific move to give legal shape to the assurances of Nehru was made, students in Madras intensified their agitation. By that time, schools and colleges in the State had reopened. And now the situation began building up to a climax.

The Madras agitation took a violent turn: in one day, on February 10, 1965, 19 people were killed by police bullets; two sub-inspectors were also burnt to death. Troops moved in trouble spots. Shastri decided to broadcast a policy statement on language to the nation. A Cabinet meeting was convened on February 11 to finalize the statement, which said that Nehru's assurances "will be honoured in letter and in spirit without any qualification or reservation". During the two-hour meeting of the Cabinet, Subramaniam, the then Food and Agriculture Minister, did not say anything except that he wanted legal sanction to be given to Nehru's assurances. He was, however, told that under the Constitution, such a step was redundant since English could be continued for an indefinite period without making any other legal provision. Apparently, this did not satisfy Subramaniam, who was emotionally upset by the disturbances in Coimbatore, his constituency.

Shastri was entering his car to go to Broadcasting House to issue the statement when one of his personal assistants came running to him with a news agency message. Subramaniam had resigned, and so had the Minister of State for Petroleum and Chemicals, Alagesan—a fellow Tamil. Shastri felt so unhappy that he was almost on the point of cancelling his broadcast. But the Home Secretary, L.P. Singh, who was at Shastri's house, pressed him to go ahead with it. That was one of the few speeches Shastri made, which sounded like it came from his heart.

The Madras riots continued unabated. Twenty more people died in a day. Vinoba Bhave, Mahatma Gandhi's disciple, started an indefinite fast to end the violence. The then President, Dr Radhakrishnan, advised Shastri to announce immediately the government's intention to bring in a law to incorporate Nehru's assurances.

Kamaraj, who rushed to New Delhi from Madras, repeated this view. He suggested a sort of bilingualism involving the use of both Hindi and English. Shastri decided to consult the state chief ministers and convened a meeting in Delhi on February 23. He favoured the proposal for a statute, but was reluctant to do this on his own.

The adverse reaction from Hindi supporters among the Congress MPs deterred him from doing what he felt was right. He was particularly afraid of Desai, who was saying that Hindi must be introduced as the official language of the Union immediately and that it was a mistake to have given 15 years for a switch-over. One incident in Parliament on February 17, 1965, served as a further damper. On that day, in the Lok Sabha, hardly had V.C. Shukla, now the Minister of State for Home Affairs, suggested that Subramaniam be persuaded to withdraw his resignation, when many Congressmen said "no, no" and some of them even demanded the acceptance of his resignation. Such was the mood of Hindi supporters.

Even before the chief ministers reached Delhi, pressure started building up in favour of legalizing the use of English for an unlimited period. The chief ministers of the southern states decided to jointly sponsor the proposal that the Centre legislate for bilingualism, without a switch-over in the foreseeable future. The chief ministers of the Hindi states were more anxious to continue Hindi as the principal language than to oust English. The Home Ministry was still sticking to its earlier stand that no fresh law was necessary to continue the indefinite use of English. Its argument was that one set of laws passed today was no guarantee that another set of laws passed tomorrow would not negate them. If the majority was in favour of continuing English, no law was necessary; but if the majority was against the use of English, no law was possible.

The chief ministers were not impressed by this reasoning, at least not those from the non-Hindi-speaking areas. They felt there was a genuine misunderstanding about Section 3 of the Official Language Act, which authorized the use of English. At the Congress Working Committee meeting, 24 hours later, Desai pointed out that to give legal expression to Nehru's assurances at that time would be to "surrender to violence", and he clashed with Bhaktavatsalam, the Chief Minister of Madras, who said this was a wrong impression. But the consensus was in favour of amending the Bill to give statutory shape to Nehru's assurances on the continuance of English as an additional language for as long as the people of the non-Hindi-speaking states desired. And this recommendation was made to the Central Government.

At this meeting, the chief ministers asked the Home Ministry to give "consideration" to the introduction of the regional languages as the medium for all-India and high Central service examinations. The word "consideration" is from the decision as recorded on February 24, 1965. This was strange. By that time, the introduction of the regional languages in competitive examinations should have passed the stage of "consideration". As far back as April 5, 1954, the

Working Committee had recommended: "Progressively, examinations for the all-India services should be held in Hindi, English or the principal regional languages, and candidates may be given the option to use any of these languages for the purposes of examinations."

Four years later, the Parliamentary Committee on Official Language asked the government to set up an expert committee to examine the introduction of the regional languages as alternative media for competitive examinations. As we saw, the Home Ministry never appointed the committee because Pant disliked the idea. He believed that it would lead willy-nilly to a quota system, destroying the all-India character of the services. More than that, it would bring down the standards of selection, because the criterion would be region, not merit.

At this meeting of chief ministers in 1965*, the quota system was very much on the cards. Brahmanand Reddy, Andhra Pradesh Chief Minister, formally proposed its acceptance in principle, leaving it to the Home Ministry to work out the details. Bhaktavatsalam reminded Shastri that the Centre had "already" expressed its "willingness" to give non-Hindi-speaking areas their due share, in case Hindi should become an alternative medium of examination. This stand was, however, different from what Kamaraj's regime had suggested a few years earlier. At that time, the Madras Government accepted that "Hindi and English should

---

* In the same year, the Union Cabinet decided not to adopt the quota system in services because it was considered "anti-national".

be available equally as two alternative media to be chosen at the option of the candidate". A few months later, in its reply to a questionnaire to the Official Language Commission, the Madras Government modified its stand and said it would be desirable to have the regional languages as media if possible.

But at that time, there was no talk of demanding or offering any special concession to non-Hindi-speaking candidates, should Hindi be introduced in addition to English as a medium of examination.

After the Official Language Commission submitted its report, the Madras Government changed its stance still further and said that "every regional language should be admitted as one of the alternative media for the Combined All-India Examination as soon as that language has been brought into use as medium of instruction in schools and colleges up to graduate level, and the problem of moderation should be solved as satisfactorily as possible by the Union Public Service Commission". This was more or less what the Official Language Commission had itself recorded: "As and when other regional languages become a medium of instruction in the universities up to graduation stage as Hindi has done, the admission of other linguistic media will have to be considered."

But then the Commission had left it to the subsequent commission to be appointed in 1960 to decide whether the regional languages had come up to the standard of being media for examinations. Had there been a second commission, this point would have been looked into. Now it was a question of pressure.

Soon after Hindi became the principal language of the Union in 1965, one candidate in the September examination of the UPSC answered his question papers in Hindi instead of English and prefaced his answers with the slogan: "Hindi mata ki jai." The UPSC was not moved by this emotional outburst and awarded zero to the candidate.

But the then Chairman, B.N. Jha, had his doubts, and believed that the candidate could go to a court and challenge the UPSC markings on the plea that no restriction could be placed on the use of Hindi after January 26, 1965, when it had become the principal language. He referred the matter to the Law Ministry for its opinion.

The Law Ministry justified the UPSC markings and observed: The UPSC was like a club framing its own rules of entrance. Just as the UPSC did not allow any candidate below the age of 21 or above 23 to sit for competitive examinations, it could similarly lay down that only English would be the medium of its examinations. The candidates had to fulfil that obligation to be able to compete, in the same way as persons wanting to become members of a club had to live with its by-laws. The zero was, therefore, justified.

The Cabinet met in early 1965 and decided in principle to permit all the languages mentioned in the Eighth Schedule* of the Constitution to be examination media.

---

* The Eighth Schedule lists 15 languages: Assamese, Bengali, Gujarati, Hindi, Kannada, Kashmiri, Malayalam, Marathi, Oriya, Punjabi, Sanskrit, Tamil, Telugu, Urdu and Sindhi.

English, which is not listed in the Eighth Schedule, was also to continue as an alternative medium. The scheme of examinations and the timing were left to the Union Public Service Commission. The Commission, however, dawdled over the problem unnecessarily. At one time it came up with the suggestion that only two languages, English and Hindi, be offered as the media of examinations.

The Home Ministry insisted on the implementation of the Congress Working Committee's resolution* that the UPSC examination be held in all regional languages. The UPSC still did not act until a hint was given to it in late 1968 that the government might be forced to "pack" the Commission to get the resolution on the introduction of the regional languages as media of examinations implemented. Under Article 309 of the Constitution, there was no limit on the number of members recruited.

The government had rejected more than once the UPSC's opinion that "in view of their past experience in these matters ... anything like effective moderation would be impossible" if examination media were all the regional languages. The Official Language Commission

---

* In 1968 both Houses of Parliament had adopted a Government Resolution on Language Policy which states *inter-alia* that "all the languages included in the Eighth Schedule to the Constitution and English shall be permitted as alternative media for the all-India and higher Central Services Examination after ascertaining the views of the UPSC on the future scheme of the Examination, the procedural aspects and the timing".

had left the decision to "the examining authority". The UPSC had a point that if answer books were answered in 12 or 13 languages, there would be a problem of maintaining any sort of comparability in the standards of markings followed by different examiners in different linguistic media. The Official Language Commission had itself pointed out: "It would be almost impossible to attain standards of dependable or convincing moderation if the competitive examination continues in the present form but is held through as many linguistic media as there are regional languages in the country."

Therefore, the UPSC at one stage suggested that only two languages, Hindi and English, be offered as the media of examination. But it had the wrong end of the argument. The point was not what was proper but what was feasible. Political pressures were such that there was no going away from regional languages. The Centre could not possibly disturb the hornets' nest once again.

The government no doubt proved its toughness and the UPSC had to announce that it would introduce from October 1969, regional languages and English as optional media for Essay and General Knowledge papers. But New Delhi did not stop to consider how a person who had received his higher education in the regional language and had been successful in the competitive examination through it, would be able to carry out his administrative duties at the Centre in Hindi and English, the two official languages of the Union.

This could have been possible if the knowledge of these two languages could be imparted at an early stage. Both the Radhakrishnan Commission and the

National Integration Council had suggested a high level of teaching and examination in schools and colleges. Such a step, it had been rightly argued, would prevent the isolation of universities functioning through regional media from the rest of the country and would facilitate the mobility of students and teachers.

But the government was in a hurry; it did not give time to all educational institutions to introduce Hindi. Instead of Hindi replacing English, the regional languages were to be allowed to take its place. Some people warned that haste may be destroying the country's unity. M.C. Chagla, the then Foreign Minister, resigned on this issue in mid-1967. He was not taking up the cudgels on behalf of English; his plea was for making haste slowly in switching from English to regional languages for higher education until an alternative language was ready to take over. In his view Hindi should serve as this link as the makers of the Constitution intended, but only after it had been sufficiently developed to be serviceable for purposes of all-India administration, higher education and judicial processes.

The government's explanation was that the Centre had no powers to stop the states from switching over to the regional languages. They had already done so, jettisoning English as soon as possible; the Centre was only facing the facts, however unpleasant and disturbing.

Where the government failed was in not making enough preparations. If Hindi and English had been taught effectively from an early stage, it would have been possible for officers recruited through regional languages to perform their duties at the Centre with efficiency. In fact, this—and the feeling that bilingualism should continue for some time—gave birth to the three-language formula: the mother tongue, English and Hindi. The Congress Working Committee also resolved that the three-language formula should be strictly adhered to and extended to the universities. But this was not implemented.

Instead, the question arose whether those whose mother tongue was Hindi needed to learn only two languages. It was laid down that they should learn an additional Indian language. Some Hindi-speaking States violated the spirit, if not the letter, of the decision by encouraging students to pick Sanskrit as the additional Indian language. This was far from fair because Hindi and Sanskrit were too akin to each other to be counted as two different languages. This issue has continued to simmer, and no solution has yet been found which is either practical or lasting. And in any case, the government is more anxious to please everybody than to have a clear-cut, definite programme or policy.

The solution to the bigger issue of switch-over to Hindi has, however, been found. But the Law Ministry had to prepare at least 15 drafts before an acceptable amendment to Section 3 of the Language Bill was approved by the Cabinet. The amended Section, as approved by Parliament, says:

(1) Notwithstanding the expiration of the period of 15 years from the commencement of the Constitution, the English language may, as from the appointed day, continue to be used, in addition to Hindi:

(A) for all the official purposes of the Union for which it was being used immediately before that day; and

(B) for the transaction of business in Parliament;

Provided that the English language shall be used for purposes of communication between the Union and a State which has not adopted Hindi as its official language, and between one State and another State where either of the States concerned has not adopted Hindi as its official language.

Provided further that nothing in this sub-section shall be construed as preventing a State which has not adopted Hindi as its official language from using Hindi for purposes of communication with the Union or with a State which has adopted Hindi as its official language; or by agreement with any other State, and in such a case, it shall not be obligatory to use the English language for purposes of communication with that State.

(2) Notwithstanding anything contained in Sub-section (1) where Hindi is used for purposes of communication

(i) Between one Ministry or department or office of the Central Government and another; (ii) Between one Ministry or department or office of the Central Government and any corporation or company owned or controlled by the Central Government or any office thereof; (iii) Between any corporation or company owned or controlled by the Central

Government or any office thereof and another, a translation of the same in the English language shall also be provided along with the Hindi text thereof till such date as both the staff of the Ministry, department, office, corporation or company aforesaid from which such communication is sent and the staff of the Ministry, department, office, corporation or company aforesaid in which it is received, have acquired a working knowledge of Hindi.

(3) Notwithstanding anything contained in Sub-section (1) both the English language and Hindi shall be used for—

(i) Resolutions, general orders, rules, notifications, administrative or other reports or Press communiques issued or made by the Central Government or by a Ministry, department or office thereof or by a corporation or company owned or controlled by the Central Government or by any office of such corporation or company.

(ii) Administrative and other reports and official papers laid before a House or the Houses of Parliament;

(iii) Contracts and agreements executed, and licences, permits, notices and forms of tender issued by or on behalf of the Central Government or any Ministry, department or office thereof or by a corporation or company owned or controlled by any office of such corporation or company.

Once again, before this section was finalized, there was a controversy over "may" used in Clause (1). "... the English language may, as from the appointed day, continue to be used, in addition to Hindi .... " The Cabinet Sub-Committee appointed to prepare a draft Bill for the Cabinet was stuck for days together on the use of "may". Subramaniam, who was back in the Cabinet after the assurance that Nehru's promise would be codified, insisted that "may" be substituted by "shall". The *via media* found was that in Clause (1), the proviso portion should contain "shall". Thus it was written "... provided that the English language shall be used for purposes of communication..." The section as such began with "may".

Again, Subramaniam was not satisfied with a general statement that English would continue to be used "for all the official purposes of the Union for which it was being used immediately" before January 26, 1965. He wanted the amended Act to mention specifically as much of official business as possible. Administrative and other reports, contracts and agreements, licences and permits, notices and forms—all were listed so that even when the switch-over took place, all these documents would continue to be available in English.

Thus, where the original Section 3 of the Act was confined to only a few lines, the amendment ran to more than two pages.

The main Sub-section (5) of the amended language legislation was that English would continue to be used as an additional language "until resolutions for the discontinuance of the use of the English language for the purposes mentioned therein have been passed by the legislatures of all the states which have not adopted Hindi as their official language and until after considering the resolutions aforesaid, a resolution for such discontinuance has been passed by each House of Parliament."

In other words, it meant that one state*, which was using English for administrative purposes, could use the veto to stall the switch-over to Hindi, even when all other states had agreed to do so. The Hindi-speaking states were not very enthusiastic about this provision, but none made it an issue.

The amended Bill would have been passed in 1965 itself. But first Pakistan's incursions in Kutch, and later, India-Pakistan hostilities occupied the government's attention. The introduction of the Language Bill was thus delayed. Later, the ruling party was busy with elections; and it was only in November 1967 that the Bill was passed by the two Houses of Parliament.

With the Language Bill, a resolution on the use and development of Hindi was also to be passed. This was meant to placate the Hindi regions because they were not at all happy over the veto given to non-Hindi-speaking states. The delay in the passage of the Bill resulted in the amendment of the resolution; by that time the MPs from the Hindi-speaking areas had joined hands. The resolution as it stood originally suggested that knowledge of both English and Hindi languages would be required at the stage of selection of candidates through the UPSC.

---

* Nagaland has adopted English as the official language since.

Now the Hindi lobby made an issue of this and wanted the knowledge of either Hindi or English to be compulsory. There were threats of defections. Two MPs, Mrs Sucheta Kripalani and Mrs Tarkeshwari Sinha—always looking for an occasion to build an opposition to Mrs Gandhi's government—mobilized Hindi- speaking members to demand an amendment to the resolution. They claimed that Madras State had held the government to ransom and, therefore, the Centre would only placate the South. Congress MPs were split as North Indians and South Indians. Disturbances started in UP and some other parts of Hindi-speaking states, and these exerted an extra pressure on New Delhi. Even the veto given to non-Hindi-speaking states, in the Official Languages (Amendment) Bill was sought to be re-discussed.

What ultimately forced Mrs Gandhi to give in was the reported threat of the UP Members of Parliament to withdraw support from her. Subsequently, in a press interview, I asked her if the report of the members' threat of changing loyalties was correct. She emphatically denied it. Kamaraj, with whom I checked, said that his information was that the UP members had put pressure on Mrs Gandhi. When I asked Chavan about it, he preferred to remain quiet. Most MPs from UP, however, still assert that it was "their ultimatum" that made Mrs Gandhi yield.

That Mrs Gandhi was exposed to strong pressure is evident; for at one time she was not willing to amend the resolution. But then, without consulting the cabinet or any senior minister, she agreed to the amendment. Chavan was informed of the decision only on the telephone. There was now no effective man from the south in the Cabinet to stall the decision.

The amended part of the resolution read as:

> that compulsory knowledge of either Hindi or English shall be required at the stage of selection of candidates for recruitment to the Union Services or posts except in respect of any special services or posts for which a high standard of knowledge of English alone or Hindi alone, or both, as the case may be, is considered essential for the satisfactory performance of the duties of any such service or post.

Other directives in the resolution, however, remained the same: the pledge to develop Hindi and other Indian languages, to accept the three-language formula, and to have regional languages as media of the UPSC examination.

The "Hindi or English" option put non-Hindi-speaking people at a disadvantage, because English was not their mother tongue, and, however proficient they might be in that language, they could not adequately compete with those whose mother tongue was Hindi. The then Madras Chief Minister, Annadurai, protested against it both to Mrs Gandhi and Chavan. He wrote a letter on July 27, 1968, to the home minister to suggest that Tamil and other regional languages should replace English at the Centre. The Government of India rejected the proposal on the ground that 14 or 15 languages could not become link languages because of the confusion this would entail.

The amendment to the resolution evoked opposition in non-Hindi-speaking areas on the ground that it placed unequal burden on them. The government examined a number of alternatives, one of which was to make knowledge of one more Indian language compulsory for candidates whose mother tongue was Hindi. But nothing has been finalized. The government is more than cautious now; it does not want to burn its fingers once again.

Following the Official Languages (Amendment) Act 1967, detailed administrative instructions were issued on July 1968. Among other things:

> (i) Efforts are to be made to use Hindi to as large an extent as possible for all types of correspondence with the States which have adopted the use of Hindi for the purpose of correspondence with the Central Government; and (ii) An employee is free to use either Hindi or English for noting and drafting and he is not to be required to provide himself a translation in the other language.

As days went by, the government became more realistic and more circumspect; it did not want to do anything which would revive controversies. The policy, even though not officially enunciated, was to continue bilingualism for an indefinite period, that is, the use of both English and Hindi; at the same time, making no effort to push Hindi. And even, if there was to be a change, the government would not come in; let a national consensus emerge. It appeared that New Delhi had learnt a lesson from the follies of its past.

# Devaluation

It was June 6, 1966—hot and muggy. Since it was a Sunday, most people were staying indoors. But all central ministers had been summoned to an urgent cabinet meeting. The only item on the agenda communicated to them that very morning was the "Reorganization of Punjab."

"Why on earth such urgency to discuss Punjab's reorganization?", one minister muttered as he entered the cabinet room. Others joined him in the protest. Only Asoka Mehta, the then Planning Minister; C. Subramaniam, the then Food Minister; Sachin Chaudhri, the then Finance Minister, and, of course, Prime Minister Indira Gandhi were keeping their thoughts to themselves. They had reason to: they were the only ones who knew what was coming.

The cabinet was to decide not on the reorganization of Punjab, but on the devaluation of the rupee. The ministers were taken aback; they were not prepared for it, despite all the rumours on the subject over many months.

Little did they know that the decision had been taken some weeks earlier. After her return from the United States in April 1966, Mrs Gandhi had reportedly communicated her intention to devalue the rupee to Sachin Chaudhri, who in turn had asked S. Bhoothalingam, the then Finance Secretary, to make necessary preparations for it. Asoka Mehta had also returned from Washington in early May after discussing the aid required to underpin this drastic step. He had talked to the International Monetary Fund (IMF) on the new rate of exchange for the rupee. For public consumption, his visit was connected with negotiations for World Bank loans.

In one sense, therefore, the ministers' approval was only a formality. The details had already been worked out; they were merely asked to read a note given to them and give their approval to it. Even Chester Bowles*, the then US Ambassador to India, had been told of the decision by L.K. Jha, the then Secretary to the Prime Minister, a day before, and informed that remittances to students abroad would be raised by 57.5 per cent and immediate arrangements made for increased payment. In any case, Bowles knew all along that devaluation was coming because America had been pressing for devaluation for a long time, through B.K. Nehru, then India's envoy in Washington.

Another person who knew about devaluation was T.T. Krishnamachari, former Finance Minister. Mrs Gandhi had met him a few days earlier in Bombay and had asked him to see her in Delhi. When told about devaluation, he evidently warned her against repercussions. Later, this became a point of complaint

---

* Bowles confirmed this during his talk with me on March 24, 1969 in Delhi.

by Morarji Desai who said that the Prime Minister had consulted one former Finance Minister but not the two others, meaning thereby, himself and C.D. Deshmukh.

Manubhai Shah was the first to raise his voice in the cabinet against the "cavalier manner" in which he had been bypassed in the initial stages. He was the Commerce Minister, directly concerned with exports and imports. Shah's objection was not to the procedure but to the proposal itself.

He had been told about devaluation three days before the cabinet meeting, but he had tried his best to stall the move. He was somewhat pacified when he was given the impression that the rupee would be devalued by about 15 to 20 per cent. He was furious when he came to know at the cabinet meeting that devaluation was to be to the extent of 57.5 per cent*.

Had all repercussions been thought out? asked Shah. Exchange earnings would not go up because traditional goods formed 75 per cent of the exports; their supplies were not elastic and the demand for them was not growing too rapidly either. Export of non-traditional goods was heavily subsidized already. Shah also argued that the slight fall in exports in 1965–66 was due to a shortfall in agricultural production on account of drought; the value of the rupee hardly entered into it.

Sanjiva Reddy, the then Steel Minister, and Jagjivan Ram, the then Railways Minister, also spoke against devaluation, but only briefly. Their primary concern was over how devaluation would affect prices. When

* The World Bank was itself pleasantly surprised over the extent the rupee was devalued.

assured that strict measures would be taken to control the price line—an oft-heard promise that could not be kept although made in all sincerity—they became quiet. Others were interested to have the matter out of the way quickly to save as much of the Sunday as possible.

Mehta and Subramaniam spoke in defence of devaluation, and some officials also joined in to lend support. They presented it almost as a panacea for India's economic troubles. The dichotomy of increasing imports and decreasing exports could be rectified only by making the rupee cheaper; in any case, the rupee already stood devalued because a US dollar fetched Rs 10 or more in the black market in place of its official rate of Rs 4.75.

Sensing that they had not convinced many ministers by painting a gloomy picture, the officials switched their line of argument. They now talked of the promise of 900 million dollars of untied aid available for spending on a very wide range of maintenance imports. This did impress some ministers who had been hard pressed to secure foreign exchange even for key sectors of the economy. The pause in US aid following the India-Pakistan war of 1965 had led to very sharp cuts in import allocations. Even before the war, the position was so bad that import licences had to be suspended for two months in May 1965.

Jha, one of the principal champions of devaluation, gave argument after argument to "prove" that India had lagged behind because a courageous step like devaluation had not been taken. By devaluing the rupee, the country would again be set on the right road. He and some other senior officials had sold devaluation to Mrs Gandhi by using phrases like "bold leadership" and "courageous step". They had no reason to believe that the same jargon would not sell with other ministers.

The cabinet's discussions continued for two hours, and would have gone on for more time but for the fact that some ministers wanted to go home for lunch. Mrs Gandhi, who had remained mostly silent, was at the point of adjourning the meeting, when Jha whispered in her ear that a decision had to be taken there and then. The Board of Directors of the International Monetary Fund (IMF), which had to give its formal approval to the new rate of exchange, would be meeting in Washington a few hours later; the cabinet decision on devaluation had to be communicated to them in good time. If the ministers were now to break for lunch, the entire schedule would be upset.

But Jha had perhaps another reason too; devaluation seemed inevitable, but who could guarantee the outcome of a continued meeting after a break? Some ministers were not entirely convinced of the need for devaluation but they did not seem to have any choice except to go along with Mehta and Subramaniam, who were providing eloquence to Mrs Gandhi's silence. All that she repeated again and again was that aid would not be available without devaluation.

The opposition of Manubhai Shah and a few others killed, however, the proposal of creating a fund of Rs 100 crores to compensate those who would be affected by devaluation. Shah said that such a fund would encourage all kinds of claims to be filed.

The official announcement on devaluation was made at 11 p.m. after receiving IMF's approval. But by the afternoon—soon after the state and deputy ministers had been "sold" on devaluation—the decision was an open secret. Fortunately, it was a closed day, and nobody could reap any advantage. Some journalists were personally briefed by Mehta during the course of the afternoon; he was particularly anxious to get good press. But he was to be disappointed. Barring one or two major dailies, all others deplored devaluation in no uncertain terms.

Looking back, some can say that devaluation of the rupee could hardly have been avoided. What else could a government, unwilling to cut its coat according to the cloth, do? The non-productive expenditure on administration—hiring more hands and opening more government offices—had increased enormously. When the Third Plan was drawn up, the assumption was that budget surpluses, after meeting current expenses, would provide Rs 410 crores* for plan investment by the Centre. In actual fact, there was no surplus but a deficit of Rs 642 crores. The steep rise in defence spending was one part of the explanation; another was the inflationary spiral touched off by persistent food shortage.

Export incentives and subsidies, which ranged from 4 per cent to nearly 100 per cent of the free-on-board (f.o.b.) value, and covered well over 70 per cent of India's exports, were bringing diminishing returns. On the import side, administrative controls had done all the paring possible but the effect was to provide windfall profits to those lucky enough to get a licence.

---

* A crore is equal to 10 million.

More importantly, India's aid-givers were unwilling to underwrite its payments deficit unless it first set its house in order by correcting the relationship between internal and external prices through a change in parity. The World Bank, which was a major source of assistance, was dragging its feet. Before giving further loans, it wanted New Delhi to implement the recommendations of a mission it had appointed in 1965 under the leadership of Mr Bell. He and the experts associated with him had examined India's economic problems as a preliminary to discussions on future levels of assistance and had reached four broad conclusions.

First, the cost of imports and the earnings from exports did not reflect the true value of foreign exchange; both were heavily undervalued. Until that was corrected, India's mounting payments deficit could not be tackled effectively. The second suggestion was that India's slender administrative resources could be put to much better use if New Delhi were to decentralize the decision-making process and concentrate on the things that really mattered. Implicit in this suggestion was a plea to leave many of the individual investment decisions to public and private entrepreneurs, with the Central planners confining themselves to guiding the economy through broad fiscal and other controls. An important and necessary corollary of the new strategy was the reliance upon the free play of market forces to allocate investment where it would do the economy most good.

Thirdly, it was suggested that India should, for a period, concentrate on consolidating the existing industrial base before going in for a further bout of expansion. In support of this argument, it was shown that capacity standing idle for want of materials and components (because available exchange was going into new projects) could contribute an increase of Rs 10,000 million in the national income over four years. Incidentally, the World Bank team was echoing on this point the conclusions presented in a study made by the US aid mission.

Fourthly, India was strongly urged to devote resources and attention to agriculture which provided the great bulk of wage goods to the working population. Unless farm output increased satisfactorily, the scarcities would push up prices to an intolerable level with grave consequences for political stability. Foodgrain prices in 1965–66 were 56 per cent above the level of 1960–61.

These suggestions, offered to New Delhi towards the end of 1965, evoked at first unfavourable, and even hostile, reactions. How could a country wedded to a socialistic pattern allow a free run to market forces? But gradually, there was a shift in thinking, accelerated by a change at the top when Sachin Chaudhri took over from T.T. Krishnamachari as Finance Minister at the end of December, 1965.

As it turned out, the exit of T.T.K. was to pave the way for devaluation. As long as he remained the Finance Minister, he stoutly opposed devaluation. He was conscious of the need to do something about the balance of payments problem, but devaluation was not in his textbook. The very word was anathema to him. His view was that devaluation would not help in making ends meet. Over the long run also, the essential task of building up the economy would receive a setback from "a sudden, sharp and indiscriminate increase" in the price of imports.

Shastri gave T.T.K. full freedom to save the rupee if he could and T.T.K. devised a number of steps as part of the 1965 budget to curb inflation by stimulating production, investment and savings. Excise duties were lowered on certain products to encourage higher output; the list, already long, of priority industries entitled to concessional treatments for direct tax purposes, was enlarged and rationalized. There were also schemes to grant tax credit certificates on increases in corporate income and on additional production in certain industries subject to excise duties. But things did not look up. Industrial production slowed down even more; the increase in 1965–66 was only four per cent compared to eight per cent or more in the earlier years of the Third Plan.

In mid-1965, as strong pressures were building up for devaluation, T.T.K. persuaded Shastri as well as other cabinet colleagues to stand firm. He, as Finance Minister, made an unscheduled broadcast on July 17 to scotch rumours, touched off by India's frantic efforts to secure aid to mend the critical foreign exchange situation. The following month he brought in a supplementary budget which sharply raised import duties, as well as excise duties on commodities with a high import content (as, for example, kerosene). He had earlier given added incentives to exporters, among them a tax credit certificate for export earnings. In other words, T.T.K. was prepared to encourage exports and discourage imports through means other than devaluation.

There have been suggestions that T.T.K. was forced out of the cabinet at the end of 1965 because he was unwilling to devalue. This was not correct. Shastri and T.T.K. came to a parting of ways when the Prime Minister decided to consult the Chief Justice of India informally about the charges the Opposition had made against the Finance Minister. T.T.K. said that if the Prime Minister were to do so, it would be tantamount to lack of faith in his integrity. Shastri said that it was in T.T.K.'s own interest that the highest judicial authority in the land should absolve him, and not the leader of the party to which he belonged. But T.T.K. remained unconvinced and submitted his resignation. And even before Shastri could get in touch with him, T.T.K. had announced his resignation in the Finance Ministry. Till today he has not forgiven Shastri for "driving him out" of the government and still calls him disparagingly "a little man".

Shastri himself was not sold on the merits of devaluation. But his approach was essentially emotional. He did not like the rupee to lose in value because it would create hardships for the public; in fact, when he took over as Prime Minister, his first official pronouncement was that he would try to reduce prices. All commodities were costing about a sixth more than three years earlier, while food, an item accounting for two-thirds of the family expenditure of some 70 per cent of the population, had gone up by about 35 per cent. He asked his secretary, L.K. Jha, formerly head of the economic affairs branch in the Finance Ministry, to devise ways to bring prices down. Scheme after scheme was prepared in the Prime Minister's Secretariat, and reams of paper used. There were dozens of meetings among officials. The end product was nil. Food prices went up by another 18 per cent in one year of Shastri's regime.

Shastri told me soon after the Indo-Pakistan war in September 1965 that if other steps failed to improve the economic situation, devaluation might have to be tried—but only as a last resort.

The hopes of a turn in the tide were dissipated partly by the Indo-Pakistan war in September 1965, and partly by the failure of the monsoon. Drought in several parts of the country put more pressure on the economy; foodgrains production dropped by almost 20 per cent in 1965–66 compared to the bumper harvests gathered in the previous year. The worst was the aftermath of hostilities: increased requirements for defence; relief and rehabilitation programmes in the border areas; dislocation of production; and last though not least, a pause in external assistance. Indeed, the prospect of achieving a non-inflationary balance in the Centre and state budgets was very dim.

Soon after the hostilities against Pakistan were over, T.T.K. addressed an urgent meeting of the cabinet and gave a frank account of the state of the nation. He painted a very dismal picture indeed. Nothing was right—neither production, nor exports, nor foreign assistance. And on top of it, imports were rising to the detriment of the balance of payments. The deficit on trade account alone had gone up by more than 50 per cent between 1961–62 and 1965–66. Foreign countries were reluctant to underwrite the growing gap.

The cabinet appointed a committee of four persons—L.K. Jha, S. Bhoothalingam, I.G. Patel and

P.C. Bhattacharya—to look for ways to rehabilitate India's economy. The committee was given a free hand to recommend any step—even devaluation, if the officials felt there was no other way out.

Morarji Desai, with whom I checked in early 1969, told me that the Finance Ministry files did not contain anything to indicate that Shastri had taken the decision to devalue the rupee in his lifetime. This was in contrast to what Asoka Mehta told me in January 1969. He said that "Shastri had decided to devalue the rupee in his lifetime. We only implemented the decision while he did not live to do so".

Mrs Gandhi is also reported to have said to some of her associates that Shastri had given the USA to understand that the rupee would be devalued. Again checking with the then US Ambassador, Chester Bowles, on March 24, 1969, I found that this was not true. Bowles told me that devaluation was inherent in the situation but Shastri never gave him or Washington the impression that he was ready to devalue the rupee. Bowles said that Shastri's visit to America was being finalized for early 1966 and it was difficult to say what the US President, Johnson and Shastri would have agreed upon between themselves.

No doubt, events were moving inexorably towards the inevitable step of devaluation. But conscious as Shastri was of public opinion, it is very unlikely that he would have gone to the limit of taking an unpopular step like devaluation. He always had his ear to the ground and had never done anything which would evoke unfavourable popular reactions. On devaluation, his attitude may not have been different. This is evident from the fact that he did not devalue the rupee in 1965 even when there were explicit hints from the World Bank and some foreign governments. In the cabinet meetings, he mentioned more than once about the "pressures" to devalue the rupee. He reportedly said: "I don't like others pressurizing us."

Shastri did not live long enough to see the findings of the officials' committee he had appointed to suggest ways to rectify the situation. The report made no specific recommendation; only several alternatives were placed before the government. One examined the consequences of maintaining the *status quo*. In that eventuality, it was pointed out, little foreign aid would be forthcoming for the Fourth Plan, then on the anvil. Nor would the World Bank offer any special assistance to meet the grave problems facing the country. The Western donors as well as the Bank had favoured devaluation; the officials argued there was no other major source of foreign exchange. As spelt out in an official apology, after the event, it had become "impossible for us to count on further assistance from international agencies" because of their belief that the value of the rupee was totally unrealistic.

The balance of payments had been under considerable pressure. For instance, in early 1965, gold had to be transferred from government stocks to the Reserve Bank to offset a steep decline in reserves. But this hardly helped; the fall in reserves continued right through the year. Another pointer to the rupee's increasing vulnerability was the rise in borrowings from the International Monetary Fund from $127.5 million at the beginning of the Third Plan to $325 million in March 1965.

The second alternative was to keep part of foreign earnings for certain "must" sectors like defence, food imports and remittances to deserving students abroad, and leave the rest to fend for themselves. Here the difficulty was in deciding the "core" requirements. How would one, for example, accept one student as deserving but not another? All kinds of pressures would work; nepotism and favouritism would have free play. Inherent in this alternative were controls, which were considered irksome and unworkable, because of the corrupt practices they brought in their trail. In T.T.K.'s days, the Ministry of Finance did not fight shy of controls; he was prepared for drastic measures to insulate the economy increasingly from outside influences to defend the rupee.

Making a distinction between core requirements and others, implied adopting the system prevalent in Pakistan. It meant that every commodity sold abroad would earn for an exporter's own use a fixed percentage of foreign exchange. This he could utilize either himself or sell in the market to reap a big margin via the bonus voucher system.

It was possible to devise alternative schemes, such as floating multiple rates. These schemes involved organized markets in which exchange was traded, and it was very likely that the rupee would have been far more depreciated in such markets than was really necessary. A floating rate might well have reduced trade with East Europe. It was also argued that a floating parity would keep alive speculation against the rupee continuing a situation of uncertainty inimical to aid and investment. The Finance Ministry became, overnight as it were, experts on Latin American countries which had tried the floating rate system without success.

The third alternative was devaluation. Even though the officials' committee did not specify which alternative to adopt, the case was loaded in favour of devaluation. The main argument was that untied, non-project aid brought immediate benefits to industry, which was beginning to grind to a halt in the absence of adequate foreign exchange for maintenance imports. Jha and Patel—always seeking an easy way out—had been all for devaluation from somewhere around 1964. As theoreticians, they felt that the only way to cope with the worsening balance of payments situation was to "increase the profitability" of export industries on a stable, long-term basis, and thus encourage larger investment in them.

Bhoothalingam got converted only after the Indo-Pakistan hostilities in September 1965. He did not see any other way out in face of the grave difficulties arising from the pause in aid and the unprecedented drought. The fourth official of the committee, Bhattacharya, just went along with the other three, but till his death he always swore against devaluation and asserted that he had opposed it. In fact, all officials, except Bhoothalingam to some extent, were to blame. Standing in the wings was Pitamber Pant, at that time an official in the Planning Commission, who had his eyes fixed more on 1984 than on the present. His responsibility was equal, if not more.

In fact, these officials on the one side and the two ministers, Asoka Mehta and Subramaniam, on the other, murdered the rupee. First they decided to devalue, and then went about finding reasons for doing so. Mrs Gandhi was taken in by their hypothetical assumptions and exaggerated expectations. Admittedly, the sad plight in which the economic situation was at that time, left her with few defences.

For many months before devaluation, the Finance Ministry had before it a report in favour of devaluing the rupee. This was by Jagadish Bhagwati, a young professor from Delhi University specially well-versed in international trade and monetary economics, who had been asked to suggest ways to strengthen the economy. His analysis said that the rupee had been devalued *de facto* because of props like export subsidies and other incentives; devaluation would only give *de jure* recognition, and there was no escape from that.

This was in many ways true. An economy which had seen the real value of the rupee plummeting since 1956 with the rise in prices was not able to bear the burden of two wars—against China in October 1962 and against Pakistan in September 1965. The policy of "Defence with Development" required discipline and sacrifice if it was not to be an empty slogan. The spark of sympathy which the Chinese attack had ignited in the heart of Western nations had built up hopes of massive aid. As soon as the guns were silent on the border, the last post of democracy in Asia was practically left to fend for itself. So much so, one of the armament factories promised by the USA and another by Britain remained paper schemes.

In India itself, the emotional upsurge witnessed during Chinese and Pakistani hostilities had conveyed a wrong impression of the people's capacity to bear with difficulties. The spurt in production—and hard work—lasted as long as the fighting continued. The nation quickly returned to the same old slow, phlegmatic pace—to the same internal squabbles.

Even the National Defence Remittance Scheme, introduced in the wake of the 1965 war, became an instrument for foreign exchange evasion. Under-invoiced export earnings were being remitted back to India under the scheme to qualify for its benefits. The Gold Bonds also had short-lived popularity; there were doubts raised even about some of the gold which had been made over to the government, one story alleging that smuggled gold had been legitimized in this manner.

The foreign reserves began to dwindle; one end of the candle was burning with the purchase of increased arms for defence (a country like France wanted cash down), and the other by the purchase of machinery, raw material and services for development. The reserves were running down; they stood at the end of March 1966 at just over $625 million. This was $100 million above the March 1965 level, only because $137 million had been borrowed from the IMF during the year. The adverse balance of trade was heavy—there was, on an average, an annual deficit of $1,000 million during the five years of the Third Plan.

The nation needed to be aroused to a positive response for bearing hardships and forgoing even dire necessities so that money could be set aside for development. What was required was a pre-1947 atmosphere, harking back to those days of vigour and vitality, of stout hearts and muscles, when all attention was focussed on making the British quit. The leadership could not generate that buoyancy of yesterday, that foolhardy determination or dedication to meet any situation for better or worse. It was not the nation which had gone effete but those who were at the helm of affairs. They were as bereft of ideas and ideals as they were unwilling to take risks. All that they wanted was to stay in power. Maybe, it is difficult to keep a nation in a straitjacket for a long time; maybe, democracy is handicapped in disciplining people. Whatever the reason, devaluation looked like an inevitable consequence of the condition in which the Indian economy stood in mid-1966.

The economic situation at that time could be summed up as under:

Total production of food had declined from 89 million tonnes in the 1964–65 bumper year to 72 million tonnes in the following year. Rice output dropped by 9 million tonnes or just under 25 per cent; wheat by almost 2 million tonnes or by a sixth; pulses by 2.5 million tonnes. Per capita availability of food was about 400 grams, the lowest since 1952. This was the situation despite heavy imports which were to add up to 10 million tonnes by the end of the year.

Foodgrain prices index in June 1966 was 167.9—the highest ever up to that point of time, against 140.5 in June 1965; 135.9 in June 1964; and 113.1 in June 1963. The general price level was up by 13.8 per cent in 1965–66 on top of an 8.8 per cent rise in 1964–65 and 9.4 per cent in 1963–64.

Prices of industrial raw materials were also at an all-time high; the same was the case with manufactures. The working class cost of living index in Delhi was 191 in June 1966 (100 in 1949), against 158 in June 1965.

Industrial output was on the decline. Growth was faltering in 1965 but came virtually to a stop in 1966. Over the whole year, the output of consumer goods increased by less than one per cent. Capital goods went up by 3.6 per cent but some sectors like railway wagons were specially hard hit. There was, in fact, a steep fall in production.

Steel production in January 1966 was in excess of demand, reflecting the slowdown in industry and construction. At Bhilai, 18,000 tonnes of pig iron were in stock while one lakh tonnes of steel ingots had accumulated at Durgapur.

Defence expenditures had increased from Rs 885 crores in 1965–66 to Rs 942 crores in 1966–67, a rise of Rs 57 crores or 8 per cent. On top of this, the India-Pakistan war was said to have cost Rs 100 crores.

Another pointer to the inflationary trend was provided by the sharp increase in net bank credit to government; it went up by Rs 518 crores between March 31, 1965, and March 31,1966, against Rs 288 crores in the previous year. In fact, inflation had become chronic; there was, to everyone's surprise, a rise in prices in 1964–65 despite a bumper crop.

In February 1966, there was yet another increase in the dearness allowance of government employees. This was to honour the commitment to neutralize every 10-point rise in the cost of living index. The Centre's bill went up by another Rs 25 crores, casting yet another burden on a budget already in deficit.

Government spending was getting out of hand under a variety of pressures. The budget for 1965–66 had assumed a deficit of Rs 3 crores, but the year ended with New Delhi in the red by Rs 165 crores. The gap between revenue and expenditure in states was even larger—almost Rs 190 crores.

Exports declined by 2.6 per cent from Rs 816 crores in 1964–65 to Rs 810 crores in 1965–66. The increase in world trade was passing us by. India's share in world exports fell from 2.1 per cent to 1. 2 per cent during the 1950s. World exports rose at 8.8 per cent during the first half of 1960s but India's exports at less than half that rate. "More important, a declining trend had set in. Exports had got stuck at a level of around Rs 800 crores in 1963–64 and 1964–65."

Washington, which was by then confident that New Delhi had no escape from devaluation, offered to relieve India of immediate difficulties. During his stay in Delhi in February 1966, Hubert Humphrey, the then US Vice-President, announced a loan of $50 million for immediate imports of fertilizers. This was welcome because it brought the aid freeze to an end. But he also reportedly made it clear that the disease from which the Indian economy suffered was more malignant than a small loan could cure. A wonder drug like devaluation might do. It was clear that Humphrey was not making just off-the-cuff remarks; the State Department had briefed him well. In any case, Mrs Gandhi was going to Washington; there would be all the time to bring her round.

An attempt had been made to revive the Indian economy through the budget presented on February 28, 1966. New Delhi announced that it was limiting development spending to existing schemes; no new projects were to be initiated with the sole exception of Bokaro. The aim was to hold down the rise in government expenditure to Rs 99 crores, compared with Rs 395 crores in 1965–66 and Rs 464 crores in 1964–65 (but in fact non-development expenditures were to rise by 19 per cent in 1966–67). Levies such as the tax on bonus issues; the capital gains tax on bonus shares; the equity dividend tax and the company profits surtax; against which investors had been protesting vigorously, were abolished, or appreciably modified. It was hoped to bring about a change in the investment climate, but in fact the all-industry index of share prices went down still further. This was probably a result of the 10 per cent rise in the general rate of tax on companies.

To mop up extra money, excise duties were increased on sugar, cigarettes, light diesel oil, fine varieties of cloth and a few other items. A flat special surcharge of 10 per cent on personal incomes was imposed to earn another Rs 25 crores.

The budget did not look like either stimulating savings or investment. In fact the rumour started that the devaluation of the rupee was only a matter of time. However, Asoka Mehta, while replying on behalf of Sachin Chaudhri, stated that there was no question of devaluing the rupee. Subsequently, a day after the budget was presented to Parliament, Bhoothalingam said at a Press briefing that "there will be no devaluation". The Ministry of Commerce in its annual report for 1965–66 released at about the same time, ruled out a change in the rupee's value on the ground that about 80 to 82 per cent of India's exports commodities moved at almost the international price and that only about 18 per cent required substantial assistance in the form of import entitlement or cash subsidy.

To some extent, the rumour of devaluation subsided, but it was openly said everything would hinge on whether Mrs Gandhi's visit to the USA brought the aid needed to tide over the situation. A ground swell of resentment against what was considered dictation on the part of Washington began sweeping the country and the Congress Party.

The Communists made all kinds of insinuations. For example, they said that Johnson had ordered Mrs Gandhi "to come to America" to get aid.

Mrs Gandhi took the earliest opportunity (March 1, 1966, in the Lok Sabha) to deny that aid was the primary reason for her visit to the USA. Foreign assistance was important and would be necessary for some time, she said, but if necessary "we can and shall do without it". This was one of those pious statements which every nation has to make to keep up appearances. None in the government at that time was even remotely thinking of doing without foreign aid, for that meant discipline and hardships. Devaluation was the line of least resistance because it was expected to bring massive dollops of assistance. Nobody was prepared to work hard.

Mrs Gandhi flew to America on March 26. Before her departure, it was clear that the days of Kennedy, when foreign aid was an integral part of US policy, had ended with his death. Johnson clearly made aid dependent on past performance. New Delhi did not object to the criterion but it happened to be prescribed at a time when its performance was rather bad. Johnson was said to be of the opinion that India must make greater use of private foreign capital and soften the country's myriad controls to encourage production.

Mrs Gandhi made a good impression in America, particularly on Johnson. Mehta, who met him after Mrs Gandhi's visit to the USA, said at a cabinet meeting that he did not believe in flattery but would say that Johnson had told him that Mrs Gandhi was the greatest woman on earth. Like a fatherly Texan, Johnson is reported to have said at a party that he would see to it that "no harm comes to this girl". He thought that the Bell Mission's recommendations, including devaluation, provided India with the best remedy for its economic ills. And when he found Mrs Gandhi coming round to accept these, Johnson was all out for aid to India.

In fact, it was an open secret in Washington at that time that Mrs Gandhi had agreed to devaluation. A senior Indian employed by the World Bank sought to postpone his return to be able to take back his dollar savings at the more favourable post-devaluation rate. Something had indeed happened behind the scenes, because the US State Department was more than co-operative. Even when Mrs Gandhi was still in Washington—March 30—Johnson sought the approval of the US Congress for 3.5 million tonnes of foodgrains for India and appealed to other countries to match the commitment. He was indeed keen to rescue Mrs Gandhi from difficulties. The message he sent to Congress was couched in strong emotional terms: "The facts are simple; their implications grave. India faces unprecedented drought. Unless the world responds, India faces famine."

Additional US food for India, $900 million in non-project aid, and the World Bank's agreement to consider additional project loans—these were the prizes which Mrs Gandhi earned after having accepted devaluation of the rupee. The import policy announced on April 1, 1966, had taken into account a "liberalization" of aid because licences were promised somewhat more freely than before.

The announcement of devaluation was received with concern and misgivings. People feared a sharp rise in prices even though Sachin Chaudhri, the then Finance Minister, said in his broadcast that "devaluation would provide a better corrective to the price rise". How? The claim was difficult to entertain, except that some more subsidies were in view, for imported foodgrains, kerosene oil and fertilizers.

But what shocked the people most was that the government, even after repeatedly contradicting the rumour that the rupee would not be devalued, had done so. In fact, Sachin Chaudhri had ruled out the possibility of devaluation at a press conference in Calcutta on May 16, only three weeks before the announcement. Every government must, of course, deny any intention to devalue up to the last possible minute, but when devaluation takes place, it has to pay for this in terms of a loss of credibility.

C. Rajagopalachari was about the only public figure to describe it as a "courageous act", but his Swatantra colleague, Minoo Masani, dubbed it a declaration of insolvency on the part of the Congress government. He warned of loss and hardship to a large number of people. For once, Masani and Krishna Menon were expressing identical views; Menon thought that devaluation would undermine the morale of the people and alienate them from the government. Among Congress bigwigs, R. Venkataraman, the then Industries Minister in Madras, said the decision was politically unwise and economically unsound. He said this on that very day; this left knowledgeable people in New Delhi in no doubt of what Kamaraj, who was maintaining a studied silence, was thinking. C.R. stood in strange company; P.C. Mahalanobis, a great champion of socialist planning was, also speaking of the great opportunities opened up by devaluation.

One reason for bitterness in the public mind was that devaluation was linked one way or another with aid. It was taken for granted that some arm-twisting had been done by the aid-givers. There was enough evidence to prove that it must have been so. An official note circulated among Congress MPs soon after devaluation admitted that "action could not be postponed as all further aid negotiations hinged on it". There were also hushed allegations that America had asked India to be less vocal on Vietnam. So vicious was the propaganda that Mrs Gandhi had to say at Pachmarhi (Madhya Pradesh) on June 11 that India could not be bought over—aid or no aid.

The Congress Parliamentary Party, which met three days after devaluation, expressed its unhappiness over the step but accepted it as a *fait accompli*. Nonetheless, anger and exasperation continued to simmer. The

Congress apart, resentment was deep throughout the country; both the USA and the World Bank came under strong criticism because the feeling was that devaluation had been carried out at their behest. The Communists were most critical; Dange called devaluation "an economic coup" and demanded the resignation of the government.

Finding that the denunciation was building up, Mrs Gandhi asked Central ministers to address meetings and broadcast speeches in defence of devaluation. Not all responded to her suggestion. The government's offices were asked to issue handouts to show how devaluation would help India. The indiscriminate plunge into publicity brought out the comical side of the government. The Council of Scientific and Industrial Research announced that "there would be a rush to buy Indian technology following devaluation".

There was a spurt in prices. The government talked of punitive action under the Essential Commodities Act; Food Minister Subramaniam openly mentioned the possibility of issuing an ordinance, and, as usual, there was the promise to set up a chain of co-operative stores (super bazars) and to secure for them consumer goods like soaps and toilet articles at production sources. The government was able to keep the price of these goods under check for some time by arranging the liberal import of ingredients from abroad. But this relief lasted only temporarily.

Once devaluation cleared the decks for assistance, Sachin Chaudhri started for Europe (June 21) to discuss aid. The donors had been appeased. Those who needed proof could see it in the resumption of US economic aid to India and the allocation of $900 million of non-project assistance by the Aid India Consortium within weeks of the devaluation announcement. But for the Indian public, the government had a supercilious pose. To press reporters, Chaudhri said before leaving: "I am not going to pick up aid; I am going to have discussions in different countries to see what would be mutually beneficial for the exchange of commerce and credit."

The Soviet Union was unhappy over devaluation. This was evident from the news dispatches appearing in Russian papers; editorial comment had, however, been avoided. Asoka Mehta was sent to explain the circumstances leading to devaluation. Manubhai Shah, who went to Moscow early in July to fix up a new basis for rupee trade contracts, was told by Kosygin that devaluation was a blunder.

However, the External Affairs Ministry denied that Moscow was concerned over devaluation. It was given out that there was "complete understanding" in Russia of the Indian action. Notwithstanding this so-called understanding, there was some very hard bargaining over new contract prices. In most cases, India's export prices had been quoted in rupees with no provision for automatic revaluation. Somebody had slipped up since Soviet export prices were protected by a specific provision covering any change in exchange rates. Shah persuaded the USSR to accept a 47.5 per cent increase in Indian export prices, but only after the matter had been taken up to the highest level.

The UK felt hurt because it had advised against devaluing the rupee. London had also promised to back India's case with the IMF for more standby credit to tide over the difficulties brought on by war and drought.

It was the promise of massive American aid and the theoreticians' plea that exports would increase which made Mrs Gandhi blind to the defects of devaluation. Both did not materialize. There was no impact on exports, either in 1966 or in the two subsequent years. One, it was too soon to expect results; two, a commodity like jute sacking could have reaped large dividends but Pakistan had also increased incentives to its jute exporters.

The nub of the Indian economic problem was low productivity, unutilized capacity and high costs. The government had magnified the problems arising from the foreign exchange shortage; the malaise ran much deeper. But the government had to have some peg on which it could hang its failures.

As regards US aid, India could import against non-project loans, whatever it wanted—components, raw material or technical know-how. It was a wide-ranging offer. In fact, Manubhai Shah flew back in a hurry from Geneva to have his say on import policy. He pleaded that an indiscriminate liberalization of imports would increase India's debts still further, and make the country more dependent on America. The proposal before the cabinet was to allow industrialists to import practically whatever they wanted on first-come-first-served basis. With the help of Sachin Chaudhri and Swaran Singh, Manubhai Shah was able to get some checks introduced to curb excessive imports.

The new import policy announced after devaluation, made 59 priority industries eligible for liberal imports.

These 59 industries accounted for over two-thirds of the country's total industrial output. The first set of licences were issued in record time—never had the government acted so speedily before. That was not all; supplementary licences were offered to anyone who ran through the first ones. Objections were raised against opening the floodgates from many quarters, but the government was helpless. Import liberalization was what the aid-giver wanted; this was, in fact, made a condition for giving $900 million.

With the passage of time, the criticism of devaluation became the criticism of Mrs Gandhi. Her opponents saw in devaluation an opportunity to discredit her and to dislodge her if possible. A whispering campaign began in the Congress Party that she was not upto the job. All failures were attributed to her leadership. Some charitable commentators said that she was misled by officials like Jha and Pitambar Pant, and ministers like Mehta and Subramaniam.

If there could be a watershed in human relationships, devaluation was the one between Mrs Gandhi and Kamaraj. After the announcement they began to go their different ways. Mrs Gandhi reportedly tried to mollify Kamaraj through T.T.K., but in vain. Kamaraj never forgave Mrs Gandhi for having devalued the rupee, and if he had his way, he would have seen to it that she was not the Prime Minister the second time in 1967.

Kamaraj questioned the economics of devaluation, but his main objection was to the "sense of humiliation" which the devaluation of the rupee had brought in its train. He had no doubt that foreign pressure had "debased" the rupee and that the government, headed by Mrs Gandhi, had "yielded".

Subsequently, Kamaraj explained to me that the refusal to devalue the rupee would have provided India with the much-needed ethos for a big effort at self-reliance. A country hoping to find a way to persuade the population to tighten its belts would have found in resisting devaluation, a point to rally the people. He said that he would have gone around the country to enthuse the masses with the argument that the people must unite behind the government since New Delhi had refused to devalue the rupee at the instance of foreign powers. If necessary, the Government should have resigned and sought first a verdict from the people. "I am sure the Congress would have swept the polls by making the refusal to devalue the rupee as its election plank," he said.

Even today, when he recalls those days, he says that a call to defend the rupee would have electrified the nation to immediate response. There would have been the same atmosphere as there was before independence—a determined nation preferring independence and honour to dictation and humiliation. The same old vigour and spirit of sacrifice would have been revived.

Morarji Desai's criticism of devaluation was less emotional; he believed that India had lost economically by reducing the value of the rupee. He prepared a note and circulated it among important Congress members. Desai argued that devaluation was the result of not taking "some timely steps". The 16 points which Desai made in his note said that the government should in no case undertake deficit financing for the next five years; both the centre and the state governments should henceforth have surplus revenue budgets; cut all current expenditure, including investments, by 10 per cent within the next four months; and stop all expenditure on community development. He wanted the services of the army to be utilized for productive tasks like distributing agricultural inputs.

Desai also urged similar discipline in other fields: general wage and dividend freeze for twelve months and increase of working hours in all factories and offices; every employer, engaging more than 50 persons, paying one-third of the wages in kind; and the government ensuring supply of basic necessities in sufficient quantities and at reasonable prices.

Among other suggestions Desai made, were to utilize the State Bank to provide timely credit to cultivators; reform of the credit policy so that export industry and trade as well as import substituting industries were not starved of funds; restrictions on credit to the private sector; fiscal incentives to all industries for increased production; heavy excise duties on all exportable goods to boost exports; and progressively make industries independent of imports.

It needs to be recorded that in public, Desai accepted devaluation as having become inevitable in the face of an 80 per cent rise in the general rise in the price level in ten years. In private, however, he was sharp in his criticisms but his sense of discipline prevented him—at least on this occasion—from pitching into Mrs Gandhi.

Mrs Gandhi thanked Desai for the note which she said the government would study to implement "as far as possible". This cliché, used in government offices, meant really nothing because the note became one of the many notes on devaluation—filed and forgotten.

Mrs Gandhi, on her part, had brought to the Working Committee meeting a note prepared by the government in defence of devaluation which acknowledged—for the first time—that the IMF had been for some time urging devaluation, and that World Bank economists were also of the same view.

Some proposals of Desai were worth implementing but his plea for a wage freeze evoked wide protest. Kamaraj, otherwise critical of devaluation, hotly opposed the suggestion. This gave Mrs Gandhi an added reason for brushing aside Desai's objections.

The note circulated among Congress leaders described the decision as the only alternative open in the circumstances. Surprisingly, the government was now talking less and less of the advantages of devaluation and more and more of the inevitability of the step taken. The note, however, warned that devaluation would have only a marginal effect on the country's budgetary position. And it was made clear that the need was to avoid deficit financing and to have fiscal discipline at the centre and state levels.

Once again, there were myriad economy boards, trying to find out how to cut government expenditure. An omnibus order was issued to all government offices to apply a cut of 10 per cent. Adept as government offices are at this sort of thing, they fulfilled the requirement by not filling vacancies. And as usual, the axe fell on some temporary peons and clerks.

The Congress Parliamentary Party, which so far had only a brief opportunity to discuss devaluation on June 9, had a real free-for-all debate on July 6. Outwardly, the criticism was about why the rupee had been devalued, but every harsh word was meant to be a stiletto pointed at Mrs Gandhi, and her "capacity" to lead the party. Her opponents thought that the attack on devaluation could be built up into an issue to "push her out".

H.C. Mathur, a member of the Administrative Reforms Commission, who led the attack, said that the Prime Minister should have consulted the party before deciding upon devaluation. This was not a step to be settled according to an individual's predilection; the future of the entire nation was at stake. He questioned the very right of Mrs Gandhi to decide upon such important policy matters without prior endorsement of the party's leadership.

"An ill-advised step" was the burden of criticism by many members. Ram Subhag Singh, the then minister in the Ministry of Railways, was violent in his attack. His argument ran like this: Indian planners lacked practical sense and it had become a fashion to import everything, whether it was required or not. For instance, along with the import of foodgrains under PL 480, India was made to import tobacco as well for which there was no need. He was particularly critical of ministers travelling abroad on the smallest pretext.

Humayun Kabir, a former minister, described devaluation as a "serious mistake" and urged immediate remedial measures. He did not think it would help in increasing exports substantially, particularly when the bulk of Indian exports comprised five or six traditional items which had an inelastic demand.

No doubt, the Congress Parliamentary Party was critical, but the real attack on devaluation—which by this time had become synonymous with the criticism of Mrs Gandhi—was made in the Congress Working Committee on July 19, 1966. At the previous session of the Working Committee about three weeks earlier, Kamaraj had left the discussion open because Mrs Gandhi was to leave for Moscow the following day. Morarji Desai's note had been circulated, but not quite read and even less digested. Now Kamaraj had all the time to let every critic have his say.

There was not a single member or special invitee who spoke in support of devaluation. The debate was vituperative and at times even personal. Sachin Chaudhri, the then Finance Minister who opened the discussion with the argument that devaluation was "inevitable", took the blame upon himself. He said he had advised the Prime Minister to devalue the rupee. Nobody took him seriously because by this time everybody knew that the chief architects were Asoka Mehta and Subramaniam. Kamaraj first asked Morarji Desai to make his comments. This was a clear indication that the scales were being loaded against devaluation, and Kamaraj would see to it that the decision was condemned in the Working Committee.

Desai more or less repeated what he had said in his note circulated at the previous meeting. This time, he tried to prove with facts and figures how post-devaluation measures had further "devalued" the rupee in the six weeks since the change. He said his fear was that another devaluation might become inevitable if nothing was done to strengthen the economy.

T.T. Krishnamachari, the former Finance Minister, who was a special invitee, made the sharpest speech. Being still close to Mrs Gandhi, he spared her but directed his sarcasm against Sachin Chaudhri. There were some digs against Asoka Mehta as well. T.T.K. startled the committee by a long and documented narration of the repeated but unsuccessful American attempts to put pressure on him when he was the Finance Minister. He went on to add that he, for one, feared that a second devaluation would be imposed on India in the near future. Desai interjected to say that the second round of foreign pressure might be on Kashmir.

The allegation that devaluation was forced on India by foreign pressure figured prominently. Chaudhri contradicted it again and again but after Desai joined issue with him on this point, he became silent. Patnaik quoted Schlesinger's book on Kennedy to show that devaluation was the first "gambit" of the USA in its attempt to interfere in the affairs of Latin American countries.

Mrs Gandhi kept quiet. In fact, her answers to all attacks on devaluation were just silence. But when Krishna Menon, a special invitee, ridiculed the argument that devaluation was a country's internal affair, she said that this view was first expressed by Brezhnev, the Soviet leader, when she had talked to him in Moscow a few days earlier.

Kamaraj's purpose clearly was to condemn devaluation—and indirectly Mrs Gandhi. He did not want to go beyond that. Therefore, no resolution was adopted. The matter was left there, with all members agreeing that there was no going back, and that strict economic discipline should be exercised to reap the maximum benefit from devaluation.

The criticism of devaluation—which the Congress Working Committee members leaked out almost verbatim to the press—did not augur well for a co-ordinated and concerted effort to pull India out of the quagmire. If anything, the quarrels in the Working Committee made it more difficult for the nation to accept devaluation or to close its ranks to make it a success. Some leaders might have settled their old scores with Mrs Gandhi but made no real contribution to the situation. The country felt still more nervous—and more insecure—after the devaluation than before.

When the Congress MPs discussed India's economic situation a week later, they took their cue from the Working Committee's discussions. The criticisms had a familiar ring: the government had gone under because of foreign pressure; Mrs Gandhi had been led up the garden path; certain pro-devaluation officials had bungled the situation. There was also an expression of strong dissatisfaction with the government for having allowed the economy to deteriorate unchecked over the years to a point where a drastic step like devaluation became unavoidable. Once again there was unanimity in concluding that devaluation had been a "most unwise step" to take.

However, at this meeting, there was an endeavour to accept the *fait accompli;* a feeling of resignation to an event from which there was no turning back. But what probably helped to set a conciliatory tone was the initial appeal made by S.K. Patil, the then Railways Minister, who presided in the absence of Mrs Gandhi (she had met him earlier to seek his support and this pleased him). Patil asked for unity and support. This at least mollified some of those members who were undoubtedly anti-Mrs Gandhi but did not want to show disrespect to Patil and his supporters.

The party also passed no resolution like the Congress Working Committee. But it was clear that Sachin Chaudhri and Asoka Mehta would, one day, have to pay a price for alienating the party. Soon after, Chaudhri was offered the UK High Commissionership. He, however, refused it. Later, the common man had his revenge, and defeated him at the polls. Asoka Mehta fell from Mrs Gandhi's favour, so much so that they were soon not on talking terms. Eventually he had to quit the cabinet in 1968. Nemesis caught up with him, even though it was two years later.

As far as foreign aid was concerned—even in the middle of July, six weeks after devaluation—it became evident that the American promise of massive aid on a long-term basis would not mature. Word received from Washington was that the US aid bill had to go before the Congress each year, and it was not possible for the State Department to make any prior commitments beyond the annual budget. Surprisingly, at the time of making all kinds of promises before devaluation, the U.S. officials never mentioned this basic requirement. And what about the Indian side? Why was it so gullible in accepting the assurances the officials gave?

On paper, devaluation should have worked. Bureaucrats had proved theoretically that exports would increase when a foreign buyer had found out that his money—dollars, sterlings or yens—could buy more things in India than before, and that imports would come down when importers had to pay more in rupees than before. Production in India would expand because, on the one hand, there would be an increased demand from abroad and, on the other, an additional effort to substitute indigenous goods in place of the imported ones.

Among aspects that these bureaucrats did not take into account was the failure of the monsoon. To their ill-luck, the rains once again failed in 1966. Drought engulfed several parts of the country. Depressed industrial activity called for a stimulus in demand. This could be done by pumping in more money. But the fear was that the prices would go up, particularly since a basic commodity like food was already in short supply. The government had done what it could to keep the foodgrain prices down through subsidies on imports. Making additional money available meant pushing up the demand for necessities still further.

The bureaucrats were also caught in their own toils because of the reliance they placed on subsidies to soften the rise in prices after devaluation. But who was to pay for the subsidies? More taxation was not possible because people were already complaining about the burden they were bearing. The rate of saving was coming down; an average person did not have any money to spare after meeting basic needs. More money had, therefore, to be created to finance subsidies on foodgrains, fertilizer or kerosene oil. Naturally, the availability of more money in the market was bound to affect prices of home-grown food which was not protected by subsidies, especially in a year of poor crops.

For devaluation to succeed, the first essential was that prices should not rise. Mrs Gandhi quite rightly focussed on this aspect at a press conference she gave on June 15 at which she talked of the powers taken under the Essential Commodities Act to regulate the prices of a variety of goods from matches to cycle tyres. She also announced plans for a chain of co-operative stores. Two days earlier, Sachin Chaudhri had announced that the government was appointing a Commissioner of Civil Supplies to watch over prices. But none of this helped; stability was scarcely conceivable when the creation of more money was a necessity, however unavoidable and unpleasant. Discipline, sacrifice and the cutting of government expenditure—these were some of the remedies. Devaluation could not succeed without them. And if such steps had been taken in time, devaluation would not have been necessary.

In other words, the basic issue was to bring the economy under discipline, which a weak and divided political leadership was unwilling to face. To be fair to Mrs Gandhi, it must be said that she did make some efforts in this direction. Within ten days of devaluation, she wrote to Chief Ministers—all of them were party colleagues—suggesting an overall cut in government expenditure. She followed this up with a telegram calling them to New Delhi for a conference on July 19 at which the requirements of economy were to be thrashed out more fully. But she did not reckon with the simple fact that chief ministers were not prepared to pay the political price involved in curtailing expenditure. After all, a general election was a few months away.

Since most Indian industries depended on imported materials to some extent, the price of finished products was bound to go up. The government, however, claimed that there had been a slower and smaller rise in prices after devaluation than before it. Amusingly, it was Manubhai Shah who voiced this official viewpoint in an answer to a Lok Sabha question, although he could scarcely have believed in it himself. The claim was based on the totally unrealistic official price index which showed a rise of only 3.4 per cent in the six months following devaluation, but others convincingly proved that the rise had been as much as 15 per cent. P.C. Bhattacharya, who was still the Governor of the Reserve Bank, was more frank; he confessed that "in spite of all that we have done, prices have gone up".

Lack of faith in the devaluation was expected, but not as wide and as persistent as was noticed after the announcement. The political leaders got funky. Some more steps, which were unpopular but had to be taken to benefit from devaluation, had to be dropped. If courage was needed, now was the time. The government lost its nerve. The result was the worst of both worlds.

The best bet of the bureaucrats was foreign assistance, and they expected a massive long-term commitment. But little did they suspect that the escalation of war in Vietnam would divert the attention of the USA from India and that foreign aid would be less and less popular with the Americans. Even Senator Fulbright, once a staunch supporter of aid, got engrossed in Vietnam as the war intensified. India was almost forgotten.

Once America faltered, other countries backed out. The most important consideration on which the bureaucrats had built their premises went awry. It is true that they could not have anticipated it, nor the second year of drought that cut national income and increased the food import bill. But neither the miscalculations nor the run of bad luck lessen the folly of devaluation, nor does it absolve the bureaucrats of the blame for having inflicted difficulties, and even indignities, upon the nation.

They can turn back and say that devaluation was an inescapable step, harsh and humiliating, but unavoidable. Subsidies and export incentives had already devalued the rupee; the step they recommended, meant only a *de jure* recognition of a *de facto* situation. And how could they have arranged foreign aid for the Fourth Plan without devaluing the rupee?

Only posterity will judge whether all they said—and did—was justified. Any nation faced with difficulties has to choose the alternatives available at that time. Those at the helm of affairs thought devaluation was the best way out. Was it?

# Full Circle

The telephone bell rang unusually long on September 24, 1968, in the office of the Minister of State for Foreign Affairs. The Soviet Ambassador to India, N.M. Pegov, wanted urgently an interview with the minister. No details about the business were offered, none asked. The meeting was fixed for the same afternoon.

Pegov was visibly agitated when he and his lean, well-groomed interpreter entered State Foreign Minister Bhagat's room. "Mr Minister, we are concerned to see the gist of the talks between the Soviet and Indian teams appearing in today's *The Statesman.*" He was referring to the joint consultations between India and the Soviet Union, the first of its kind, held in New Delhi a couple of weeks earlier.

The Ambassador insinuated that the Indian government had purposely leaked the details of the talks. This was by no means Moscow's first complaint to New Delhi about leaks. For example, once before, the Soviet Union had said that it would have to rethink supplying arms if news about them continued to appear in the press. Russia felt really embarrassed because it would scrupulously avoid mentioning the supply of arms to India while Pakistan cited details from the Indian press. Ultimately, the Cabinet decided to issue instructions under the Defence of India Rules, then in force, asking Indian papers not to carry stories about arms supply from the USSR, or for that matter from any country.

The stories stopped appearing in the press. But Pakistan continued to get information, down to the minutest detail. When a Pakistani delegation visited Moscow in early 1968, it gave to the Soviet Union a complete list of armaments Russia had supplied to India. Even spare parts were listed. Moscow drew the attention of New Delhi to the leak. While doing so, one top Soviet leader observed: "Why don't you have proper security?" Some time later, the same leader commented: "How is it that whatever we have supplied to Pakistan had remained a secret while the arms given to India become talk of the town?"

Mr Pegov's embarrassment over the news story on the talks was quite genuine this time because it was almost a verbatim report that had appeared in the press. Contrary to the versions handed out to the Indian public by both sides, the meeting between the two teams was far from happy as *The Statesman* article had correctly brought out. Initiating the discussion, Bhagat had given an assessment of India's domestic situation, particularly emphasizing the long lead the Congress still enjoyed over other Indian political parties; the latter had constituted rickety and make-shift coalition governments but had gone under. The reply of the Soviet delegation's leader, Firyubin, Deputy Foreign

Minister, was a three-hour dissertation on Soviet achievements—how it had successfully rebuilt a war-shattered country, and how the proletarian revolution had practically reached its goal of "to each according to his needs". The gaping Indian team assented in wonder.

During its stay in Delhi, the Soviet team had, however, sensed the angry mood of the people over Czechoslovakia and was therefore anxious to shore up Moscow's prestige as much as it could. The Congress Parliamentary Party had averred a split on a resolution Mrs Sucheta Kripalani, a senior member of the party, had sponsored. The resolution, which was supported by the non-Communist Opposition, wanted to condemn the Soviet Union for its aggression and to commit Parliament to the position that the Soviet Union and its allies had committed a clear violation of the UN Charter by their armed action. The House gave its approval on August 22, 1968, to the Prime Minister's bland statement on the subject which stopped short of censure and which merely said: "This House will no doubt wish to convey to the Soviet Union and its allies our view that they should carefully consider all aspects of the situation which has arisen as a result of the action by their armed forces, and its possible consequences." The House threw out Mrs Kripalani's amendment by 182 to 82 votes. Many Congressmen voted for the amendment despite the government's opposition.

There had also been differences within the Union Cabinet on the mild stand the Indian government took on Czechoslovakia. Morarji Desai, Deputy Prime Minister, and Ram Subhag Singh, the then

Communications Minister, had favoured an outright condemnation of the Soviet Union. Mrs Gandhi wanted to express only "regret" and she had her way. Swaran Singh, Defence Minister, supported her. His argument was that by condemning the Soviet Union, India would unnecessarily endanger its military supplies from the USSR. Asoka Mehta did not say anything in the cabinet when Mrs Gandhi's statement avoiding the phrase "condemnation" was finalized. But he resigned from the cabinet a day later. The failure of devaluation had devalued him, and he was looking for only an opportunity to quit.

Firyubin was apparently aware of these developments because he gave a long discourse on the Soviet action in Czechoslovakia. He reiterated in defence what had already appeared in the Soviet Press, alleging that West Germany and some other "reactionary powers" were trying to overthrow the socialist government in Czechoslovakia and establish a puppet regime in its place. The Warsaw Pact forces went in only to save a "socialist brother country from falling into the hands of imperialists". As soon as the danger was over, he said, the armed forces would withdraw. Without mincing words, he said that any country trying to go the Czech way would be dealt with in the same manner. Moscow would never allow the unity of the socialist countries to suffer or endanger the security of the Soviet Union, which had lost hundreds of thousands of citizens in the last war.

The Indian representatives listened in silence to Firyubin's homily, disappointed that he did not make even a passing reference to India's abstention in the

Security Council on the resolution condemning the Russian action in Czechoslovakia. There was a sigh of relief when the Soviet delegation did not bring up the private member resolution adopted by Parliament—with the Communists opposing it—on August 30, 1968, expressing support and sympathy to the movement by the Czechs to liberate and democratize the political life of that country. The Indian delegation was expecting this point to be raised because some days earlier the Soviet Ambassador had met the Prime Minister to seek a clarification about it.

The Indian delegation raised the question of the supply of Soviet arms to Pakistan. The arms deal with Islamabad had jolted New Delhi's confidence. In the past, whenever India had asked the Soviet Union about its policy on arms to Pakistan, the reply was that the question did not arise. For example, after the visit of then Pakistani Foreign Minister, Sharifuddin Pirzada, to Moscow in May 1967, Kewal Singh, who was India's Ambassador there, specifically asked whether Russia would arm Pakistan. Firyubin assured him that the Soviet Union was not supplying any arms to Pakistan. He however added: "Of course you know that we help you in a big way not only by supplying arms but also by helping in your defence production."

At the time of the Soviet arms deal with Iran, Kewal Singh called on Gromyko, Soviet Foreign Minister, to convey India's fear of a possible diversion of the supplies to Pakistan. The Soviet Foreign Minister said that the arrangements made with the Iranian government were such that there was no possibility of those arms going to Pakistan or being used against

India. In fact, before giving arms to Iran, the Russians had seriously considered the possible reaction in India. This, he said, was true of all Soviet policies relating to South and South-East Asia. Gromyko concluded by saying the Soviet Union would not do anything which would cast the slightest shadow on friendship between the two countries.

Again, when a Soviet MI-6 helicopter was sighted in Pakistan by a US correspondent, a Deputy Foreign Minister, Vinogradov, assured the alarmed Indian embassy in Moscow that the deal had no military or political significance whatsoever. The USSR had strong feelings of friendship for India and the sale of these civil aircrafts should not cause the slightest misunderstanding or doubt. Subsequently, Moscow gave New Delhi a list of "some non-combative weapons" supplied to Rawalpindi. When Kosygin met Mrs Gandhi briefly in Delhi while returning from Pakistan to the Soviet Union, he told her what arms Rawalpindi had asked for.

This time the Indian side was taking up with Firyubin the question of Soviet arms supplies on the basis of information it had from the horse's mouth. After a Pakistani military mission, headed by then Commander-in-Chief, General Yahya Khan, concluded his visit to Russia from June 28 to July 7, 1968, the Soviet Chargé d'Affaires in Delhi had met the Prime Minister to communicate Moscow's decision to supply arms to Pakistan. Actually, when S. Sen, the then Indian High Commissioner in Islamabad, informed New Delhi of rumours about the arms deal circulating in Pakistan, a query was raised with the Soviet Union. No reply came. It was only when Dinesh Singh, the then Commerce

Minister, took soundings in Moscow on his way back from a trip to Yugoslavia, that the Russians admitted the deal. Even at that time, Firyubin's reply to the Indian Ambassador in Moscow was: "Why should you worry? We are not giving missiles to Pakistan."

He gave a similar reply when Bhagat argued at the September meeting that the arms would make Pakistan still more intransigent and defeat the Soviet Union's efforts to bring India and Pakistan closer to each other. Firyubin said that it was strange that India was not objecting to the influence of either America or China in Pakistan but should ask the Soviet Union, a friendly country, to stand aloof. The Russian delegation claimed Soviet influence in Pakistan was already paying dividends. An example it cited was Rawalpindi's abstention on the resolution in the Security Council on Czechoslovakia.

Bhagat stuck to his point that Soviet arms had added to the tension in the sub-continent. Just as Pakistan had used US arms against India in the last conflict, it would use Russian arms in a future clash. Firyubin did not go beyond repeating that the Soviet Union would not allow such an eventuality to arise. America was thousands of miles away, "we are next door", he added. "And there is no one who can vitiate Soviet-Indian friendship."

This was the same reply which Mrs Gandhi had received when on July 10, 1968, she wrote to Kosygin to underline the strain which the supply of lethal weapons to Pakistan would throw upon India's close relations with the Soviet Union,

The letter was accompanied by an *aide-memoire* from the Foreign Office—making an appeal in the name of the strong and long-standing ties between Moscow and New Delhi. Mrs Gandhi urged the Soviet Union to give very careful consideration to the possible repercussions of arms supplies.

In his prompt reply on July 11, Kosygin assured Mrs Gandhi that his government continued to attach the utmost importance to Indo-Soviet friendship and that the Soviet Union would do nothing to undermine its very close and cordial relations with India. He made no direct reference to the reported Soviet decision to extend arms aid to Pakistan, but he repeated that even if Moscow decided to give some military hardware to Pakistan, it would be done in the larger interests of preserving peace in the region.

When Bhagat asked for details of the arms Russia proposed to "give" to Pakistan, Firyubin gave the laconic reply that information on this subject had been given to the highest quarters in New Delhi. It was made obvious that the Russian delegation did not want to entertain any further questions on the subject.

It was true, however, that when President Zakir Husain had visited Moscow just after the arms deal with Pakistan became known, he was given a list of the contracts signed with General Yahya Khan, now Chief Martial Law Administrator. Zakir Husain warned the Russian leaders against the likely growth of anti-Soviet feeling in India. But Moscow had considered all the possible repercussions in advance. The then Foreign Secretary, Rajeshwar Dayal, who accompanied the President, reported on his return to the government that the Russians had made up their mind and it was no use expecting them to change.

Russia reiterated that it would not give missiles. This was also not correct. The Defence Ministry's assessment was that, apart from spare parts for the tanks and MiGs Pakistan had bought from China, Moscow had promised to give Rawalpindi ground-to-air missiles some time in the future. A note the Defence Ministry then sent to Indian mission abroad, along with the policy directions of the External Affairs Ministry, reportedly said missiles formed part of the proposed supplies.

The logical consequence of Moscow's indifference to Indian opinion should have been a stern attitude on the part of the government. At a meeting of the Cabinet Sub-Committee on Foreign Affairs, the dominant opinion was in favour of the Opposition resolution in Parliament to deplore the Russian decision to give arms to Pakistan. But it was not considered proper for the government to say so in public, particularly when India's dependence on Russia for arms, trade and even capital goods was so great. It was argued that there was no resolution when the USA had given arms to Pakistan. Why not? However, at one stage; Mrs Gandhi toyed with the idea of appealing to Moscow to stop arms supplies to both India and Pakistan, but the Defence Ministry was against this approach because of the important equipment for the Navy and the Air Force outstanding under past contracts with India.

The government asked its envoys to emphasize that the supply of Soviet arms to Pakistan would increase tension in the sub-continent and that Islamabad would ultimately use them against India. There was no word of condemnation or criticism of Russia. If anything, there was a suggestion to the envoys to guard against any unfavourable reaction to the Soviet Union.

The same trend of thought ran through the series of talks which the Prime Minister had had with different groups and individuals, including some editors. These meetings were held soon after the first publication of the news of the arms deal and before the opening of the monsoon session of the Lok Sabha in July 1968. Mrs Gandhi said to her visitors that India should not bother about what the Soviet Union did or did not do. "Ours is an independent policy," she added. Asked why New Delhi leaned backwards to align with Russia, she said: "This is a wrong impression spread by interested parties." Without doubt, there was unhappiness and disappointment that friendly Soviet Union should have decided to arm unfriendly Pakistan. But, at the same time, there was a deliberate effort not to do or say anything which would annoy Moscow.

When the Prime Minister talked to junior ministers on this topic, she asked them to be "responsible" and "unemotional" in their comment. Some of them demanded a lessening of dependence on the Soviet Union for military hardware; two Ministers of State went to the extent of suggesting that India should manufacture the nuclear bomb. Mrs Gandhi's advice was for restraint and caution. Her argument was that a strong posture did not necessarily mean condemnation of the Soviet Union in public.

The nation's anger was deep and wide, and public criticism, strident and unrestrained. "We didn't expect it to be so vehement," a Soviet journalist told me. And then when he got heated during the arguments we had, he said: "What did you do when the USA gave arms to Pakistan? What can you do?" I did not argue further. I felt humiliated.

Therefore, while talking to Firyubin during the India-Soviet consultations, in September, Bhagat was quite conscious of the fact that Russia had made up its mind. He wanted only to reiterate India's opposition. In fact, it was Kashmir which was very much on his mind, and he specifically asked the Russians if their government had changed its policy. The Indian side was keen to obtain a reiteration of Moscow's stand since 1955, that Kashmir was an integral part of India.

But the only reply that Firyubin made was that the Soviet Union was in favour of direct talks between the two countries. Pressed further to say how Russia would vote if Pakistan were to raise the issue again in the United Nations, Firyubin confined himself to repeating that Moscow would always suggest bilateral talks. There was no direct reply to the question of whether the Soviet Union would use its veto against Pakistan in the Security Council. The Indian delegation made many efforts to get a fresh commitment, but the Russian representatives stuck to their reply that they would favour bilateral talks and that there was no change in their stand.

In fact, after the Soviet Union communicated its decision to supply arms to Pakistan, India had made discreet inquiries from Moscow to find out whether there was any change in its policy on Kashmir. New Delhi had been assured that there was none. Subsequently, in a letter written in July to Mrs Gandhi, Kosygin had referred to Kashmir as one of the problems to be settled between India and Pakistan. It was true that Kosygin had said nothing more, but the use of the word "problem" was considered significant because Russia had never before described Kashmir as a problem. Incidentally, this letter also mentioned that India should settle with Pakistan on the Farakka barrage*. Later, when Moscow was told India's point of view on the barrage, the Soviet Union said that it was not going into the merits of the case but only wanting to lessen the points of friction between the two countries.

Firyubin did not bring up the Farakka barrage during his talks with Bhagat. But he did ask questions on China. The Russian delegation said it looked as if Peking and Delhi were coming together. The Indian delegation's reply was that there was no such likelihood, and it was for all to see that Peking had not lessened its hostility towards Delhi.

The Soviet reference may have been to a statement made by Mrs Gandhi to the Foreign Correspondents' Association in New Delhi on September 5, 1968, in which she had indicated her interest in resuming a dialogue with China. Actually, her suggestion for an initiative was not altogether new.

Since Mrs Gandhi held out an olive branch to China—she did so unambiguously at her press conference on

---

* India was building the Farakka barrage to utilize water in the Ganges to flush the Hooghly, the river sustaining Calcutta. Heavy silting is making the Calcutta port increasingly difficult to access. Pakistan's contention is that the tail end of the river flowing through its Eastern wing should be assured an adequate supply. What is adequate is a matter of dispute.

January 1 although she had been hinting at this even earlier—Moscow has felt uneasy about New Delhi's policy towards Peking. What surprised the Soviet Union most was that India should speak of making up with China even after the abuses and humiliations which Peking had showered on India. India, in Soviet eyes, is not following a steadfast policy towards China. Some people in Moscow fear that anything can happen any day; India may one day leave the Soviet Union high and dry.

Mrs Gandhi subsequently denied during a talk with some editors that she ever said that Peking's attitude towards New Delhi was softening. Explaining, she said that all that she had said was that India was prepared for talks with China to remove any misunderstanding that New Delhi was being intransigent in its stand towards Peking.

For some months—but more so after the Arab-Israel war which brought home to India the dangers flowing from the convergence of US-USSR policies—the idea of unfreezing the position vis-à-vis China had been discussed in the Foreign Office. When M.C. Chagla was Foreign Minister, he thought of posting back an Ambassador to Peking. But before the Ambassador could be nominated, the officials of the Indian Embassy were the victims of the cultural revolution. The proposal was dropped. In fact, China's continuing animus was evident from the liberal support it was giving to the hostile Nagas and rebel Mizos in arms and military training.

The Indian delegation at the Bhagat-Firyubin talks came back with a mild riposte: it had heard of moves for a rapprochement between the Soviet Union and China. The Russian delegation denied this: if proof was required*, it said, New Delhi had only to listen to the abuse Peking showered on Moscow every day; it was filthier, they said, than that hurled at the Indians.

There was also a discussion on West Asia, and the Soviet delegation made no bones about saying that India was less pro-Arab than before. The Russians also expressed opposition to regional pacts or defence arrangements in South-East Asia and advised New Delhi to stay away from them. On Vietnam, they wanted the American forces to quit immediately and leave North and South Vietnam to come to a settlement within the framework of the Geneva Agreement.

Before the representatives of either side got up to go, Bhagat said that he would like to raise two more points. One was about the misrepresentation of Indian frontiers in Soviet atlases. These were the same publications which were proscribed on November 15, 1962, when the Chinese aggression was in progress. Some maps in the Soviet atlases had shown large portions of the State of Jammu and Kashmir and practically the whole of NEFA as part of China. Bhagat said that while New Delhi

---

* The possibility of a border clash between the Soviet Union and China in Manchuria was disclosed to me by Denis Healey, the British Defence Secretary, when I met him in London on January 7, 1969. When asked if the withdrawal of the British from South-East Asia would not encourage the Chinese to fill in the vacuum, he said that China would have to watch its border with the Soviet Union because very soon they might clash there. And this took place on March 2.

had accepted the Moscow version of the Sino-USSR border, the Soviet Union was still showing the same Sino-Indian border as in Peking's maps. This question, he said, had often been raised in Parliament, much to the embarrassment of the government. The second point was that the Soviet radio, Peace and Progress, continued to make anti-Indian propaganda and abuse Indian personalities.

On the merits of Bhagat's first complaint, Firyubin said that Russian surveyors were responsible for drawing the maps; their attention had been drawn to India's complaints; the current complaint would be noted once again. As regards to the broadcasts by the Peace and Progress Radio, Firyubin said that when the Indian press and political parties like the Jana Sangh abused Soviet leaders and defamed the Soviet Union and the system obtaining there, some reply had to be given to rebut those "lies". He said the Soviet Embassy in Delhi had given him a pile of press clippings, all against the Soviet Union. On the other hand, no Soviet paper was allowed to attack a friendly nation like India.

I recall when I was in Moscow in 1965, I was asked the same question: "How is it that your papers criticize the Soviet government, when we don't criticize yours?" I was at pains to explain that the Indian press was absolutely free; it criticized its own government as vehemently as the Soviet Union or other countries. The Soviet journalists remained unconvinced.

The Indian delegation however made the point that while the Indian Press was independent, the radio station was owned by the Soviet government. To this, the Soviet delegation's reply was that the station had been started to give fitting replies to abuse of the Soviet Union. Firyubin, somewhat petulantly, asked if there was any other point India would like to raise. The meeting ended on that note.

The Soviet chagrin at the leakage of these discussions in *The Statesman* article was understandable; it took away—as stated earlier—the general impression of the talks having been "friendly and cordial" as the joint communique had suggested. In reply to Pegov's protest, Bhagat denied that the government had inspired the leak. The government's embarrassment and unhappiness at the reproduction of the gist of the talks was conveyed to the newspaper. A few days later, a Soviet journalist reproached me for having carried the despatch. He said: "It is India which will lose by alienating the Soviet Union; and let me tell you that such write-ups can create an unbridgeable gulf between the two countries. I hope you are aware of the economic and military assistance we are giving you." And then he added: "This attitude has made us befriend Pakistan."

Probably this was his personal opinion but, ironically, a Russian journalist first told me about the likely change in Soviet policy towards Pakistan as far back as 1965. That was during June when Lal Bahadur Shastri, the then Prime Minister, was on an official visit to the Soviet Union. The Russian journalist said: "You know it is in the interest of India that the USSR should befriend Pakistan so as to get it out of the Western military blocs like CENTO and SEATO." "Not at the expense of India, I hope," I replied. "No, no, how can you think so? We are your brothers."

I noted the word "brothers" because it had a familiar ring. At the time of Peking's attack on India, Moscow had used the same word for the Chinese to explain why it was reluctant to support us, mere "friends". However, later, Moscow came to our side and placed the blame squarely on China for attacking India. In his report to the Central Committee of the Communist Party of the Soviet Union (CPSU) in February 1964, one of the foremost theoreticians of the party, Suslov, said: "It is a fact that when the Caribbean crisis was at its height, the Chinese Government extended the armed conflict on the Sino-Indian frontier."

He added that "while allowing relations with India (which as everybody knows is not a member of military blocs), to deteriorate sharply, the Chinese leadership at the same time actually leagued with Pakistan, a member of SEATO and CENTO, which are threatening the peace and security of the Asian peoples." Thus once again, official Soviet pronouncements made it clear that opposition to military blocs, anti-colonialism and peaceful coexistence were the factors binding India and the Soviet Union, and prompting it to side with India even against a Communist country.

In fact, India was an important factor in the Sino-Soviet dispute. In answer to the Chinese criticism of the Soviet stand on the Sino-Indian border conflict, *Pravda* asked pertinently whether the Chinese antagonism was motivated by "hostility towards the first socialist country or the desire to discredit the policy of peaceful coexistence consistently pursued by the Soviet Government..." After giving support to the

Indian stand, namely, its acceptance of the Colombo proposals* and the desire to resolve peacefully its dispute with China, the editorial issued a warning about "reactionary forces in India", who were trying to "push India off the road of neutralism and to draw her into Western military political blocs".

Russia's open clash with China made Khrushchev think in terms of developing contacts with the peripheral countries and of seeking accommodation with them despite the fact that they were all "capitalist" and "members of military alliances directed against the Soviet Union". Pakistan, Turkey and Iran were all her neighbours. The clash with Peking made him more realistic, and for once, a hard-boiled Marxist was pragmatic. Therefore he began building bridges between Moscow, Ankara and Teheran. Khrushchev was particularly anxious to make up with Rawalpindi because, apart from its dependence on the West, it was also drifting towards Peking. However, he did not want to do anything which would annoy Delhi. He had departed from Stalin's thesis that there were no basic differences between bourgeois-led governments like India and Pakistan and had publicly commended India's role in ending the wars in Korea and Indo-China at the 20th Congress of the Communist Party of the Soviet Union (CPSU) in February 1956. He also referred to the policies of non-alignment and peaceful coexistence practised by countries like the "Indian Republic, the Burmese Union and a number of other States".

---

* The Colombo proposals are discussed in the last chapter.

Some say that Nehru's death was the watershed in India-Soviet relations. This is quite possible, because Moscow's anxiety to have a dialogue with Pakistan was quite obvious shortly after Nehru's illness in Bhubaneshwar. The Soviet Union had confidence in socialist Nehru, but not in his successor. After his death, Moscow was quite serious and persistent in befriending Pakistan. However, while Khrushchev was in power, he saw to it that every move Moscow made to get nearer to Islamabad was explained to Delhi. The Soviet First Deputy Premier, Kosygin, who had come to Delhi to represent Moscow at Nehru's funeral, assured Shastri that the Soviet Union's approach to India and Pakistan would remain quite different, so long as India remained non-aligned and Pakistan continued to be a member of Western military alliances.

When Khrushchev was pushed out of office in October 1964, a change in the Soviet policy towards the sub-continent was made easier since Kosygin had no personal commitments to the old posture. The start of the new regime in Moscow, no doubt, coincided with the replacement of the Cold War by a more sophisticated form of international rivalry, which obliged the Soviet Union, as it did other powers, to reshape her policies. But nowhere was the shift so noticeable as in her attitude towards Pakistan. Moscow was seriously worried over Islamabad's increasing ties with Peking, besides its continuing dependence on Washington. An invitation was sent to President Ayub for an official visit which Z.A. Bhutto, the Foreign Minister, had tried vainly to arrange several times before.

President Ayub's visit in April 1965 brought into focus Moscow's new policy which culminated in the supply of military equipment to Pakistan three years later. At that time, only economic, trade and cultural agreements were signed. But one visible effect was the disappearance from the Soviet press, of frequent criticism of Pakistan's political and economic policies. After Ayub's visit, a correspondent of APN, a Soviet news agency, said: "The Soviet Union and Pakistan have much in common in their approach to key international issues. The public of the Soviet Union treats with deep understanding the efforts by the people of Pakistan towards strengthening the country's sovereignty and developing the national economy and culture."

Shastri's visit came close on the heels of Ayub's. The air was thick with rumours that Moscow did not want to put all its eggs in India's basket and had therefore begun wooing Pakistan. At least when Shastri landed at Moscow airport, it looked like that. There was Kosygin, the Soviet Prime Minister, at the airport, and a guard of honour to click its heels. But there was no crowd, none all the way to the *dacha* where Shastri was to stay. All India Radio, however, broadcast that evening that the reception was warm and enthusiastic.

The explanation given to me for Moscow's coolness, as an Indian correspondent covering Shastri's visit, was that Nehru's name was a byword in Soviet homes; he therefore drew large crowds, while Shastri was relatively unknown. But the other point a Soviet journalist made unwittingly had more weight. He said the Soviet leaders wanted to assess Shastri before extending full support to him. This turned out to be correct because after "a favourable talk" with Brezhnev, the Secretary of the CPSU, Shastri was cheered by hundreds of people wherever he went. Kosygin accompanied him to Leningrad. Even at midnight, when Shastri arrived at the railway station to board the train, there was a large appreciative crowd to bid him goodbye.

Other formalities apart, it did take some time before the Soviet leaders opened up. For example, when at the instance of Washington, Shastri asked for Moscow's good offices to stop the fighting in Vietnam, his hosts were reticent at first. Later, they confided in him and said that America must stop aerial bombing to begin with. Shastri said that America had done so before but there was no response. Brezhnev said: "Nobody noticed it. Let them really stop it and see the results."

When the discussions turned to Pakistan, it was obvious that the Soviet leaders wanted to befriend Ayub, but not at the expense of India. They went to some length to explain to Shastri that all that they wanted to do was to wean Pakistan away from the CENTO and SEATO military pacts, just as they were trying to do in the case of Iran as well as Turkey. Kosygin reportedly said that by "retrieving" Pakistan from the influence of America and China, the Soviet Union was in fact helping India, because, as a friend, it would try to persuade Pakistan to make up with India. He assured Shastri that the friendship with Pakistan did not mean any loosening of ties between "the two brothers", India and the Soviet Union.

The thread was picked up by Brezhnev, who went to the extent of saying that India and the USSR should not stand on formalities, and that their leaders should meet every now and then to discuss mutual problems. "After all, it is only a five-hour flight, and we should in fact be spending a long weekend in each other's country for relaxation," he said.

The Soviet assurances to Shastri included the fulfilment of its obligation for the sale of defence equipment to India, and its readiness to undertake further supplies. Doubling of trade was promised. From a mere $2.29 m in 1953, the volume of trade rose to $86.28 m in 1957–58 and $253.7 m (both ways) in 1964, and to over $350 m in 1968. The total trade between the two countries would go up to a much higher figure when the wagons deal, now under discussion, was concluded. By March 1968, India had received Soviet credits and loans totalling $1,393 m on easy terms of repayment. The aid already committed by the Soviet Union to India's Fourth Plan totals approximately $460 m (Rs 346 crores).

Pakistan's aggression in the Rann of Kutch was very much in the mind of Shastri. He wanted the Soviet Union to commit that Kanjarkot, Chhadbet and Biarbet formed "part and parcel" of India. The Soviet attitude was to sympathize with India in private but to avoid condemning Pakistan in public. The Soviet press refrained from criticising either side, while Kosygin said that the Soviet Union was "not interested in discord and disagreements but friendship and cooperation between liberated states". He appealed for a ceasefire to be followed by a negotiated settlement. Significantly, no distinction was made between liberated states that were non-aligned and those who were aligned.

To Indian journalists, Kosygin said that, "it would be better if the *status quo ante* is restored in the interests of peace." He said that India and Pakistan should not allow "imperialists" to drive a wedge between them.

Shastri was, however, told that Soviet support for India on the Kashmir issue was to continue. But he was asked to spell out specifically India's position on the Pakistan-occupied territory called Azad Kashmir. The Soviet leaders reportedly complained that they had not been informed about India's offer to accept the ceasefire line as a permanent boundary in Kashmir, which had been made during the Swaran Singh-Bhutto talks in 1963. The insinuation was that India, not the Soviet Union, was seeking an understanding with Pakistan, even at the expense of weakening its stand on Kashmir. And they made it clear that they strongly opposed the suggestion of an independent Kashmir, which to them would become "a hotbed of Western spies and reactionaries".

Shastri appeared satisfied with the Soviet explanation. He told me that if Russia could wean Pakistan away from China and also minimize her dependence on the West, "we should welcome this". Once the Soviet leaders found Shastri amenable, they came into the open to mend their fences with Islamabad.

In his report to the 23rd Congress of the CPSU in early 1966, Brezhnev referred to the "traditional, time-tested friendship with India". But he also said that the Soviet Union was paying "attention to improving relations with such major Asian countries like India and Pakistan which can virtually be considered our neighbours as well."

Mentioning India and Pakistan in the same breath was strange. The implication was, however, clear: the Soviet Union had placed India along with Pakistan in the group of states at its periphery, without making any distinction between India, a non-aligned country, and Pakistan, still a member of SEATO and CENTO. The Soviet Union declared that the improvement in relations with Pakistan would not be at the expense of India, but a certain, inevitable qualitative change was implied.

Contrary to this posture of neutrality, the Soviet Union was earlier openly siding with Indonesia, which was pursuing a policy of confrontation against Malaysia. Both were "liberated" states. The obvious Soviet explanation was that Malaysia was the thin end of the wedge of Western imperialism in South-East Asia. What was not so clearly stated was that Indonesia was following internal and external policies which the Soviet Union found ideologically more acceptable, even though they were not in keeping with the policy of peaceful coexistence among neighbours.

The Tashkent Conference*, held after the hostilities between India and Pakistan in September 1965, gave concrete proof of the Soviet stake in peace on the sub-continent. Kosygin offered Soviet good offices for arranging a meeting between Shastri and Ayub Khan for resolving "all disputed problems including questions connected with Kashmir" as early as September 4. The plea was reiterated after the ceasefire after Moscow

---

* For more details, kindly read the author's book: *A Tale of Two Countries—The Study of Indo-Pakistan Relationship.*

had sounded out New Delhi informally. Shastri agreed because, as he explained to some editors in Delhi before leaving for Tashkent, it was difficult for India to retain for long Haji Pir and Tithwal vantage positions in Kashmir, in the face of the Security Council's unanimous resolution asking India and Pakistan to go back to the positions they occupied before the hostilities. The best thing would therefore be to ask for the conference and make Pakistan commit to "certain things" while "conceding" withdrawal from the territory occupied by India.

On the very first day in Tashkent, it was evident that the Soviet Union favoured withdrawal of Indian troops from the Tithwal and Haji Pir areas as part of the disengagement previously envisaged in the UN Security Council's resolution of September 20.

The Russians, however, conceded that the implementation of the resolution was linked with the "withdrawal of armed personnel" including infiltrators. But there was a tendency to put on India rather than on Pakistan the responsibility of liquidating the infiltrators. It was contended that since Pakistan was unwilling to take the responsibility, India was at liberty to deal with the infiltration in the manner it liked.

The Kashmir question unhinged the discussion on the very first day. Swaran Singh, leading the Indian Ministerial team, and Z.A. Bhutto from the Pakistan side, could not agree upon a formal agenda because of Pakistan's insistence on discussing the Kashmir issue. Kosygin pressed Shastri to agree to the discussion, because, according to him, Ayub had also to cater to and modify public opinion in Pakistan.

Shastri did not want to link Kashmir with the discussions at Tashkent lest Pakistan should believe that the hostilities had forced India to seek the solution of an 18-year-old "dispute". At Kosygin's insistence, there was a discussion on Kashmir but both sides reiterated their earlier stand.

Not finding any solution for Kashmir, Kosygin offered to Ayub after Shastri's approval, a marginal change in the present ceasefire line in Kashmir as a permanent boundary between the two countries. Ayub did not seem to reject the offer at that time and gave the impression he would consider it some time later.

The Soviet Prime Minister wanted India to withdraw from Haji Pir and Tithwal in implementation of the Security Council resolution. Shastri insisted first on Pakistan agreeing to a no-war pact, but later he wanted a declaration that it would withdraw all armed personnel (meaning thereby infiltrators) from Kashmir. At one stage, when Ayub was reluctant to agree to an undertaking on armed personnel, the conference looked like ending in a fiasco. Kosygin tried to persuade Shastri not to press the point but the latter would not budge. He reportedly told Kosygin that if he wanted a concession on the point, he would "have to talk to another Prime Minister of India". Later Ayub came round.

The Tashkent Declaration signed on January 10, 1966, did specifically say: "The Prime Minister of India and the President of Pakistan have agreed that all personnel of the two countries shall be withdrawn not later than February 25, 1966, to the positions they held prior to August 5, 1965, and both sides shall observe the ceasefire terms on the ceasefire line."

The words "all personnel" were taken by the Indian side to include armed infiltrators. The Pakistan spokesman at Tashkent however, denied this interpretation, adding the armed infiltrators were not sent by Pakistan and that Rawalpindi did not own the responsibility of ousting them.

Russia was all along maintaining parity between India and Pakistan. The reception arrangements indicated this. There were an equal number of flags of India and Pakistan displayed in Tashkent streets. Banners in Hindi said: "Welcome friends from India." With the same prominence, banners in Urdu said: "Welcome friends from Pakistan." Indian journalists were housed in Tashkent Hotel on one floor, while Pakistani journalists were accommodated on another with equal comfort and facilities.

In the formal opening speech at the meeting Kosygin maintained parity. Twelve times India's name came first and twelve times Pakistan's. And so much so that at a cultural programme organized at Tashkent, even some Indian songs were announced as Pakistani songs to ensure that the two sides had an equal number of items.

In March, 1969, when Moscow got worried over Ayub's future, it sent its Defence Minister, Marshal Grechko, to tour Pakistan on a fact-finding mission. But parity was maintained between India and Pakistan. Grechko first went to New Delhi and returned to the Soviet Union; once again he flew to Rawalpindi and then returned to Moscow.

Marshal Grechko did discuss at Delhi the conditions in Pakistan, even though earlier, D.P. Dhar, India's Ambassador to the USSR, had been told how distressed the Soviet Union felt over the troubles in Pakistan. Marshal Grechko had been probably asked to maintain a pose of neutrality. And immediately after his return, General Yahya Khan was given a clean bill of health. *Pravda,* in an article published on April 1, 1969, under the name of its Karachi correspondent, signified Russia's full sympathy with the problems General Yahya Khan was faced with. It was obvious that the Soviet Union, once having gone close to Pakistan, was not willing to be niggardly in support even though what Pakistan had was a naked military dictatorship smothering the flicker of freedom which shone only for a while.

In Delhi, Grechko took most of his time during his interview with Mrs Gandhi in telling her how serious the Sino-Soviet clashes on the border were. Moscow was anxiously awaiting some word of sympathy or support from Delhi. This must be so because some Soviet journalists visited newspaper offices in New Delhi soon after the clash to find out if the Government of India had issued any instructions not to play up the border clashes between Russia and China.

In the recent past, New Delhi has been convinced more than before that Moscow wanted to treat India and Pakistan on par. In the middle of March 1969, the Deputy Chief of the Staff of the Soviet Navy, said in Pakistan, at a dinner given by the Pakistan Navy Chief, Vice-Admiral Ahsan, "A powerful Pakistan Navy would be a powerful pre-condition for peace in this part of the Indian Ocean." New Delhi enquired from Moscow about the meaning of "a powerful Pakistan Navy". Instead of being on the defensive, the Soviet

Union's reply was that India had received from it, arms many times more than Pakistan. And it was argued that while the arms supply to India was being given unconditionally, it was not so in the case of Pakistan.

Marshal Grechko's reported observation in Pakistan—again in the middle of March 1969—that Pakistan should be strengthened against its "enemies", was first confirmed by the Soviet Embassy in Pakistan. In reply to a query by the Indian High Commission in Pakistan, the Soviet Embassy confirmed that Grechko said those words. At that time, the Soviet Ambassador was away. When he returned, the embassy retraced its steps and said that Marshal Grechko's remarks had been torn out of context.

Somewhat baffled by the contradictory statements, Mrs Gandhi sent a letter to Kosygin through Dhar, our ambassador in Moscow, in the middle of April 1969, to emphasize upon the Soviet Union that the theory of keeping the balance between India and Pakistan was wrong because India was many times bigger than Pakistan and had wider commitments to meet. The supply of the additional Soviet arms to Pakistan would make her still more intransigent and further lessen the chances of implementation of the Tashkent Declaration. The only effect the letter had was a feeler for a visit by Kosygin to reassure New Delhi that the Soviet arms would never be used against India and that the Soviet Union would itself see to it that it was never done.

These gestures, however flattering, have not rehabilitated New Delhi's confidence in Moscow. Even though Delhi has been repeatedly assured by Moscow that it is not balancing the strength of Rawalpindi. India suspects that the Soviet Union is arming Pakistan and also giving other assistance as for the establishment of an atomic reactor in East Pakistan to do so. Had New Delhi not been dependent on Moscow for arms, it would have reacted more adversely and might have moved away from the Soviet Union as happened in the case of the USA when it started giving arms to Pakistan. At present—or until India achieves self-sufficiency—New Delhi has no other choice. Moscow knows it.

Dr Zakir Husain's death came very handy to Kosygin. Apparently, he came for the funeral but his real purpose was to assure Mrs Gandhi that the Soviet Union would never allow Pakistan to use Russian arms against India. However, he could not take the plea that Moscow had given only defensive weapons because New Delhi knew of the supply of Soviet tanks to Pakistan.

But to comfort New Delhi, Kosygin said that the Soviet Union was willing to offer as much equipment to India as it wanted. The offer, however generous, could not be accepted beyond a point because India had to pay for the arms it was to buy. He refused to change his policy towards Pakistan, and was quite frank about it. When Delhi newspapermen asked him about the gist of the talk, he merely said that they should ask Mrs Gandhi, who, according to him, would be "truthful". This word was not to the liking of the Prime Minister's Secretariat and various inquiries were made about whether he actually said so. He had.

Up to October 1964—when Khrushchev was removed from power—the attitude of the Soviet Union towards non-alignment was positive. The domestic ideological stance of the individual non-aligned country did not come in the way. Referring to the conference of the non-aligned countries held in Cairo in October, 1964, a *Pravda* editorial commended the contribution of non-alignment to the victory of the principle of peaceful co-existence, and the complete elimination of colonialism. The Soviet lead was followed in the East European countries. The then Czechoslovak Foreign Minister stated in the Czech National Assembly that the policy of non-alignment was "objectively in line with our policy of peaceful co-existence. It is also helping to unify the peace-loving forces". The Polish press comment was that the Cairo conference was a "milestone on the road of the Third World's political emancipation" and a "major contribution to the struggle for peace". The Polish Communist Party paper *Trybuna Ludu,* wrote that non-alignment was "convergent with the policy of the socialist countries".

With the exit of Khrushchev, differences emerged among the non-aligned. Now the Soviet ideologists were arguing that non-alignment also meant socialism, and seriously questioned the path India was following. In fact, the change towards India was born of the Soviet leaders' conviction that it was essentially a bourgeois country, as far from socialism under Nehru's successors as Pakistan. There was only one difference. New Delhi, not being a member of any military pact, was more non-aligned than Islamabad, but nothing beyond this. Both were following the same capitalist path of development with only marginal differences. Viewed from the point of orthodox Communist ideology, it was logical to equate countries like India, Pakistan, Turkey and Iran.

A subtle difference between non-alignment as a political stance and as an economic philosophy was sought to be made in the joint statement issued in May 1965 at the end of Shastri's visit to the Soviet Union. Non-alignment was stated to be serving the "noble goals of preventing war and consolidating peace, easing world tensions and developing international cooperation". Economic policy as such was interpreted as the people's right "to choose and develop the political, economic and social systems which they consider best suited to their aspirations".

Now, criticism of the Indian economic system also began appearing in the Soviet press. In an article entitled, "A Critique of Mahatma Gandhi's Social Teachings", in the Russian journal *Voprosy Filosopfi*, in 1965, the concept of *sarvodaya* was subjected to a critical examination. It was labelled "petty-bourgeois socialism". Criticizing Gandhi, the article said he had preached "class cooperation" and he tried to conceal "intra-Indian class contradictions" by reference to organizing function of the exploiters, of the inability of the working people to govern the State and of "the naturalness of inequality". Gandhi's concept of *sarvodaya* was called "nothing but an idealized antiquity..."

The article was reminiscent of Stalin's days. Against this, the Soviet ideologists commended the "socio-economic reforms which are being carried out in the

UAR, Burma, Algeria, Mali, Guinea, and several other countries" which are "spearheaded against imperialism and its pillar within the country—feudalism—and anticapitalism."

At the 20th Congress of the CPSU in February, 1956, Khrushchev had grouped together the Indian Republic, Burma, Indonesia, Afghanistan, Egypt, Syria and other states which stand on a position of peace. He had offered to support "those countries which do not allow themselves to be drawn into military blocs..." and proposed strengthening "the bonds of friendship and cooperation" with them. But in 1966, the CPSU Central Committee grouped the non-aligned countries into two categories: those who were "fighting for the social progress of their country" like the UAR, Algeria, Syria, Burma, Guinea and Mali, and the others like India.

New Delhi noticed this distinction and asked for a clarification. Kosygin told the then Indian Ambassador, T.N. Kaul, that undue political importance should not be attached to slogans. But later, events showed that this distinction had been deliberately made.

In the CPSU Central Committee's May Day slogans for 1967, the same practice was followed, with India again figuring after the UAR, Syria, Algeria, Burma, Guinea, Mali, Congo (Brazzaville), Laos and Cambodia. The people of these countries were said to be "building an independent, national, democratic State and are struggling for a socialist path of development". As for Laos and Cambodia, their people were "waging a courageous struggle for freedom and independence against foreign interference!" For India, it was hoped that the "traditional friendship and cooperation" between the people of India and the Soviet Union would be strengthened.

In his report to the 23rd Congress of the CPSU in early 1966. Brezhnev said that countries like the UAR, Algeria, Guinea, and Mali were undertaking socialist measures like driving out foreign monopolies and confiscating or nationalizing feudal estates and capitalist enterprises. He said the Soviet Union had "established close, friendly relations with the young countries steering a course towards socialism. Naturally, the further these countries move towards the objective they have chosen the more versatile, profound and stable our relations with them become". India had gone several rungs down. He said the "CPSU Central Committee and the Soviet Government" were paying attention to "improving relations with such major Asian countries as India and Pakistan which can virtually be considered our neighbours as well".

The Soviet Union was, quite clearly, investing non-alignment with a new content. According to its ideological theoreticians, "the most purposeful and resolute followers of a non-alignment policy are those States whose governments carry out profound social and economic transformations and enlist the services of broad democratic circles in the management of the State". Thus non-alignment, which mainly meant abstention from bloc politics, was now linked with the internal economic and political development of a state, contrary to the basic principles of "non-interference", an essential ingredient of peaceful co-existence.

In fact, Moscow went still further. The crisis in Kerala in 1959, where the Communist government was deposed, was passed over by the Soviet press in comparative silence. Of course, Khrushchev was in power at that time. Even after his removal, the official Soviet policy, as interpreted to India, appeared to be the same. In December 1964, Deputy Foreign Minister Firyubin gave the Indian Ambassador the Soviet government's views regarding the arrest of Left Communists in India during the Chinese aggression. He said the Soviet Union respected the "sovereign right of an independent country to maintain its security, law and order. We are Communists but we do not wish to export revolution or to make plots against sovereign countries". But things changed in 1967. A *Pravda* article on October 18 expressed anxiety over the resistance encountered by the West Bengal Ministry "in the implementation of progressive measures". The resistance was from "monopoly circles". The article quoted journals like the CPI organ, *New Age,* to the effect that "behind every poisoned pie in our country, one can see the hand of the CIA, and the reactionary conspiracy in Calcutta was not without that either".

Earlier, in 1965, R.A. Ulyanovsky, Deputy Chief of the International Department of the CPSU Central Committee, wrote a book entitled *The Dollar and Asia.* In it, he sought to show India's steady "shift" from its proclaimed goal of socialism to a policy of class collaboration with American "monopoly capitalism and imperialism". The main import of the book was that, contrary to New Delhi's declared policy towards foreign investment and on building up of the public sector by curbing foreign and Indian monopolies, the government actually resorted to a "programme of active collaboration with it". Pointing this out as a departure from India's avowed policy of socialism, it said that the "official socialism proclaimed in India expects to get along without nationalizing foreign property". There was also pointed criticism of India's programme of joint ventures in Asia and Africa. It was mentioned that though the "export of capital from India is formally prohibited, the equal participation of Indian firms with foreign firms in the capital of newly formed firms in other Asian and African countries, is allowed".

Judging the government's economic policies by the Communist yardsticks of class and ideology, the author stated that the "entire policy of the Indian national bourgeoisie and its ruling circles, with regard to foreign capital, as before, bears a deep imprint of class limitation. This policy has never been radical and it had always suffered from excessive moderation". Ulyanovsky accused India of hypocrisy and opportunism, and said that the government, by "giving private foreign investors guarantees against nationalization on the one hand, and widely accepting socialist assistance on the other", tried to "utilize the relations between the socialist community and the imperialist camp to their advantage and to receive maximum economic aid from both sides". For this attitude, the author saw the explanation in the "class nature of India's ruling circles".

Up to this point in his book, Ulyanovsky confined himself to the general term "India's ruling circles", but felt it necessary to be more specific when he referred to a United States-India conference held in Washington in May 1959. This conference was attended, among others, by the Indian Ambassador to the United States, Chagla, who was reported to have observed that "India is the battleground" of a "great and decisive battle" being waged in the world "between dictatorial and democratic methods of solving the problem of poverty" and that if "democracy fails in India, freedom will be the casualty over the whole of Asia and Africa". Interpreting this speech, Ulyanovsky stated that "anti-Communism is manifested not only by the Right-wing parties of India. It is also inherent in influential groups of the National Congress and among many in the ruling circles". Chagla's speech "with its clearly pronounced anti-Communist essence was, as it were, a blend of the ideology and policy of the extreme feudal and pro-American elements and reactionary groups of the Indian bourgeoisie ready for compromise with the ideology and policy of US imperialism itself".

There were other articles also in the Soviet press in the post-Khrushchev period, which reflected the new trend. They referred to countries which "merely proclaim socialist aims" and of "national leaders who identify socialism with more or less democratic social reforms under capitalist development". Among the examples mentioned were "Indian democratic socialism", "African socialism" and other varieties. According to these articles, the Indian ideologists drew an "idyllic picture of the peaceful growing of capitalism into socialism through voluntary renunciation by the ruling classes of their riches and privileges without any aggravation of the class struggle".

Soviet writings also began attacking the Indian Government openly for following "deliberate anti-Communist policies". According to Soviet authors, India was apparently aligned with the "imperialists" in some ways. The earlier Soviet concept of "national democracies"—countries which were newly independent and under the leadership of an enlightened national bourgeoisie—was replaced by the new concept of "revolutionary democracies". Again, it was only countries like the UAR, Mali, Guinea and Burma, which merited the new epithet. According to the Soviet definition, only they, among the newly independent, followed the path of non-capitalist development.

Articles in various journals implied that India was not following a socialist path, nor was she trying to resist foreign interference. On the contrary, it was alleged that the Indian government had resiled from its avowed position on socialism and had given way to monopoly capitalism, which was colluding with foreign capital.

A Soviet expert recently wrote that, "as long as economic dependence on imperialism is not ended, as long as a country has not won emancipation in this respect, it is impossible to speak of the complete and final victory of the national liberation revolution". Shorn of verbiage, it means that the Soviet Union does not recognize former colonies as truly independent so long as they remain within the orbit of the world capitalist economy. The existence of pre-capitalist elements in the economies of the former colonies, the extremely low living standard of the masses, the narrow domestic market, the difficulty of mobilizing financial and material resources, the lack of managerial and technical personnel—all these are held to necessitate active State participation in the solution of economic problems.

According to two *Pravda* correspondents, Belyaev and Bwilatsky, a great deal had been done in India to introduce the principle of the state sector as a vital factor in the economy. They noted with satisfaction that 12 per cent of the national income was contributed by this sector. Even under the adverse conditions of a "mixed economy", industrial output had increased by 2.5 times in the years of independence. But they were alarmed to find that the state-sponsored development of the metallurgical, ship-building and oil extraction and refining industries, did not give rise to panic among the capitalists of India, who were not interested in developing non-profitable but essential industries. Apart from this trend, the *Pravda* journalists found other causes for complaint in the development of the state sector. Its existence had not prevented the "rapid development of monopolies in a number of economic branches". Finally, they noted the charges of poor management and corruption levelled at the state sector. They saw this as a "problem of national specialists who are still in shortage" and a problem of poor pay in the state sector compared with the private sector. They warned that "the economy of a country, which tries to solve its problems by developing the State sector, without restricting the growth of monopoly capital, will inevitably experience acute contradictions—sooner or later resolved by an inevitable clash in politics".

This thinking of the Soviet Union was ventilated by Skachkov when he visited India in December 1968.

He reportedly told the Prime Minister that the Tatas had excelled in performance over the Soviet-built steel plant at Bhilai because partisan civil servants tended to favour the private sector. He, for one, would nationalize the entire steel industry.

When Skachkov met D.R. Gadgil, Deputy Chairman of the Planning Commission, he inquired: "Mr Deputy Chairman, how did you come from the Soviet Union?" Gadgil replied: "I flew by Boeing." "You travelled by an American plane. Why do you prefer them? Why do you not buy our planes?" said Skachkov. The reference was to the planes which IAC was to buy to expand its service. The expert committee appointed by the Government of India to go into the types of planes to be purchased, had preferred a US plane. When the recommendation came before the cabinet, Dinesh Singh, the then Commerce Minister, had it shelved until the offer for a Russian plane had also been scrutinized thoroughly.

The real aim of Soviet participation in India's industrialization was believed, in Moscow, to have been to create "a growth in the size of the working class and enhancement of its social role". This industrial proletariat would not only create conditions for social progress but also force the national bourgeoisie—the vacillating Congress leadership—to take part in the "anti-imperialist and anti-feudal struggle". These elements would later join up with the comparatively unorganized peasantry to reach the culminating point of the national liberation struggle in a peaceful transition to socialism or communism. Believe it or not, this is what the Soviet Union expects.

Another point of difference between Moscow and New Delhi was on the signing of the treaty on non-proliferation of nuclear weapons sponsored by the USSR and the USA. Although the treaty was somewhat different from its original draft, it still did not satisfy New Delhi. India's objection was that the treaty sought only to prevent the non-nuclear countries from acquiring or manufacturing nuclear weapons or nuclear explosive devices while permitting the existing nuclear countries to develop and stockpile more weapons. Again, the treaty required only the non-nuclear countries to undertake certain obligations—not to manufacture, acquire or receive nuclear weapons or explosive devices, and to expose their nuclear reactors and other facilities to international inspection and safeguards. The nuclear powers were not required to assume corresponding obligations. They were free to proliferate weapons, and their nuclear reactors and facilities were immune from international inspection and safeguards.

Furthermore, the treaty prohibited non-nuclear countries from developing explosive devices for peaceful purposes. The sponsors of the treaty contended that a nuclear explosive device was indistinguishable from a nuclear weapon. India felt, however, that distinction could and should be made between explosive devices that were used only for peaceful purposes and others that were used for testing weapons.

The Soviet Union tried its best to make India sign the treaty. But for the intervention in Czechoslovakia, which made the Soviet Union draw back from any action which might alienate Indian opinion further, it would have stepped up the pressure to make the government yield. It may still do.

More recently, the Soviet Union had been having its doubts about the ruling party, Congress, itself. In an article on India's impending elections in 1967, the Soviet journal, *New Times* said that the prestige and influence of the Congress Party had declined considerably. The main reason attributed for the decline was that the "capitalist path of development, which India has followed since liberation, has not improved the lot of the people". It quoted Congressmen as having said that India was receding from socialism. By way of criticism of the Congress election manifesto, the article said that even an issue like the nationalization of banks was formulated in an "evasive" way. This manifesto was contrasted with the election manifesto in 1962 "framed with the participation of Jawaharlal Nehru". The implication was clear—after Nehru's death the Congress had started losing its socialistic zeal. It went down further, after the death of Shastri when the "Right wing" in the Congress tried to preclude the inclusion of "radical" Congressmen in the government and there was a "special effort to install former Finance Minister Morarji Desai, a prominent Right winger, as head of government".

But at times, Moscow believed that Desai might become Prime Minister. There was, therefore, no attack on him. When Kosygin met him in Delhi in January 1968, he was believed to have remarked that according to the general impression, Desai had no liking for the public sector. Desai disputed this and said: "This is the propaganda made by the Communists in India." He added: "Otherwise, show me where I have been anti-public sector." At this meeting, Desai told Kosygin that the Communists in India had extra-territorial loyalties and that the Soviet Union should insist that they look towards Delhi instead of to Moscow. "You don't like internationalism," was the reply of Kosygin. Desai had the last word: "Internationalism, yes, but not at the expense of nationalism."

There is no knowing the extent to which ideology plays a role in Soviet calculations regarding foreign policy; probably very little. Otherwise, why should the Soviet Union woo Iran and Turkey? (bourgeoisie countries by any standards). It is obvious that for Russia, like other countries, national interests come first. Ideology operates only when there is no such consideration.

Take the Soviet Union's confrontation with China. Both Moscow and Peking are claiming the frontiers of the 19th century, when the two were under the yoke of the Czars and imperial dynasties. The Communist brotherhood had not been able to resolve the differences which the reactionary regimes before the revolution had created by grabbing each other's territory. Now, without any ideological compunction, both the Soviet Union and China, motivated by national considerations, are claiming the "old and real boundaries", unmindful of the red blood the revolutionaries on both sides would spill in the process.

There is no yardstick to measure the change in the Soviet policy towards India. At least some recent pronouncements by Soviet leaders tend to suggest that external policies, especially the attitude towards the developing countries, are being influenced by ideological considerations. This may not be true because national interest comes first in the case of Russia. Moscow is trying, however, to give the impression that ideology is the main reason. In his report to the Joint Jubilee Meeting of the CPSU on the occasion of the 50th anniversary of the revolution on November 4, 1967, Brezhnev outlined the basis of Soviet relations "with the young national States". He said that the extent and the concrete forms of these relations depend on the general political course which a particular State pursues. "We have closer economic and political ties, closer relations with countries which in their development are heading towards socialism." That meant that the Soviet ideologists were anxiously questioning whether India had not moved considerably away from its professed ideals of "socialism" and "progress".

But there was never any compact between India and the Soviet Union, even at the height of Indo-Soviet friendship during the time of Nehru and Khrushchev, that India would pursue the brand of socialism that would appeal to the Soviet ideologists. On the contrary, this friendship and cooperation was based on the understanding of their mutual differences. Speaking before a visiting Soviet delegation in 1959, Nehru had said: "There are some things in India I have no doubt, which probably you do not approve of. There are some things in the Soviet Union which we cannot approve of. But these are minor things because we have different approaches, but the basic thing is the regard for each other..." Obviously, Moscow has moved a long way from that concept.

# China's Invasion of India: A Diary

October 20, 1962

Home Minister Lal Bahadur Shastri looks anxious about the happenings on the Sino-Indian border. The war has begun; the Chinese have attacked the Thag La ridge this morning. Attacks have also been made on the Ladakh side. But the newspapers play it down; they give more prominence to a crisis in the UP Congress over a land tax proposal before the State Legislature.

"If only we were better prepared," Shastri says. "I don't mind approaching any power for help to fight the Chinese." It appears he made a similar suggestion at the Emergency Committee of the Cabinet (ECC) which has been meeting almost every day to take stock of the situation. Apparently, he has been overruled. "Panditji does not want to bring in the big powers," Shastri says, and he sounds unhappy. Nor is he pleased with Prime Minister Nehru's statement on October 12 at New Delhi airport that Indian forces have been ordered to throw the Chinese out of NEFA. Shastri fears it will complicate matters still further. "We must gain more time to prepare. Panditji trusted the Chinese too much. We are the ones who, in fact, introduced Prime Minister Chou En-lai to the non-aligned powers in Bandung."

Some ministers demand severance of diplomatic relations with China. Nehru is not in favour of this "extreme" step. He wants "some bridges" to stay between the two countries, because he is still convinced that China's aggressiveness is a passing phase. By severing diplomatic ties, Sino-Indian relations might reach the point of no return. He does not want to do that—at least, not yet.

The Home Ministry has reported that the police posts established on the Ladakh border are not tenable. They will fall to the very first onslaught by the Chinese. I remember the former Home Secretary, B.N. Jha, telling me that it was "a bright idea" of B.N. Malik, the Director of Intelligence, to establish police posts "wherever we could", even behind "Chinese lines", so as to "register our claim" on the territory. "But," he added, "Malik does not realize that these isolated posts with no support from the back, will fall like nine pins as soon as the Chinese push forward. We are unnecessarily exposing the policemen to death. Frankly, this is the job of the Army, but since they have refused to man the posts until full logistic support is provided, we have placed the policemen."

The posts run in a zig-zag line; 41 of them have been established, a few policemen here and a few of them there, sometimes like islands in the multitude of Chinese predators.

A message received from Prime Minister Khrushchev says that he hopes the conflict which has arisen between India and the People's Republic of China will not develop, but will be solved by peaceful means on a mutually acceptable basis in the interests of the Indian and Chinese peoples, and of conserving and consolidating world peace. In a reference to Western attitudes as reflected in press reports, he says: "They were trying and are trying by all means and methods to sow the seeds of hostility between two great Asian powers, to weaken the traditional friendship between the Indian and Chinese peoples and provoke a conflict."

## October 21, 1962

The massive Chinese attack and our puny efforts to cope with it were now plain for all to see. The government has decided to play down the news of reverses which were pouring in endlessly. It was treating it like the 8th September intrusion in NEFA, which was officially described as the "appearance of some Chinese forces in the vicinity of one of our posts".

I remember the first time I heard of the Sino-Indian border dispute was in the Union Home Ministry in early 1957. I was complaining to a senior official about the East Pakistan border bristling with dangers. He feigned ignorance. But his one remark, even though cryptic, was significant. He said: "Why Pakistan alone? You will have trouble with China very soon."

He did not elucidate, but in reply to my insistent queries he did add that there were vague reports of China building a road* through Sinkiang. The Ministry of External Affairs had been informed of the reports many times.

A couple of weeks later, I was sitting with the same officer when he told his private secretary to put certain papers in the "Border File". I asked what "Border File" meant. He explained that since the Ministry of External Affairs refused to entertain information about China's inroads into Indian territory, this was straightaway filed. Nehru got enraged even at the mention of a border dispute with China.

Laughingly, he remarked that "in our Ministry, when somebody does not want to deal with a subject for a long time, he says: 'Put it in the Border File'". I was to hear this euphemistic description of inactivity often after that.

Another time I heard the border problem discussed threadbare—when Chou En-lai called on G.B. Pant, the then Home Minister, in April 1960. Pant had the habit of writing down his main speeches and briefs and then delivering them "extempore". That time also, there were scores of papers typed and re-typed, meetings with the Foreign Secretary, and much poring over maps till Pant

---

* Mr Lakshman Singh from UP was the first person in 1954 to inform the government about the building of the Aksai Chin Road. As our Trade Representative, he used to visit Tibet every year. His contacts were wide, and he met some labourers who had worked on building the road.

could remember the names of even remote rivulets. The Pant-Chou meeting, arranged at short notice, was meant to remove the impression then spread by the pro-Peking Communists that Nehru felt personally hurt by Chou En-lai's actions and was, therefore, somewhat adamant about the terms for any settlement. The Prime Minister also wanted to show that he was not alone in taking decisions on the border issue. His Cabinet colleagues had to be carried along, and all of them felt rather strongly on the issue. Probably there was also some pressure from the party, which wanted somebody other than Krishna Menon, the Defence Minister, to be associated with the discussions. The reputation of Pant was that of a shrewd person, a hard nut to crack.

I recall that before hostilities broke out a "solution" of the border issue was suggested by Menon, but he was overruled by Pant. Menon had told Chen Yi, China's Foreign Minister, that India might accept Peking's suzerainty over the area in Aksai Chin, where it had built the road to link Sinkiang and Tibet as well as over a ten-mile trip to serve as a "buffer" to the road. In exchange, China must officially accept the McMahon Line and India's rights to the rest of Ladakh. China had reportedly accepted this and so had Menon, who apparently had talked to Nehru before going to Geneva. But Pant reportedly stood in the way and had the government withdraw its offer through an informal resolution in the cabinet. Even leasing out the Aksai Chin area was not acceptable to the ministers. "We can never trust the Chinese again. Sardar Patel* was quite right in warning us against them."

* See Annexure 1.

So this was the stance of Pant when Chou En-lai and ten other persons accompanying him came to 6, King Edward Road, where Pant was living. I had never seen Pant waiting more anxiously for a meeting. He wanted to prove his mettle in External Affairs as he had done in Home Affairs. The drawing-room had two rows of chairs facing each other. We sat on one side, with the big sofa left to Pant (surprisingly, he did not spread himself out as he usually did), and on the opposite, sat Chou En-lai and his team. There was not much time wasted on pleasantries and Pant came straight to the point. He reeled out the names of hills, rivers and passes as if he had known them all his life.

Starting from the Ladakh side, Pant tried to establish the watershed theory that the point from which water flows to either side, is the dividing line. This line could not be straight, he argued, and would naturally swerve from one side to the other, depending upon the flow of water. Chou En-lai spoke very little, with the help of an interpreter he had brought along. Until then, my impression had been that the dispute was only about the Ladakh side, but Chou En-lai twice or thrice questioned the validity of the McMahon Line. Pant began with the presumption that the McMahon Line was a settled fact, but Chou En-lai did not accept this. He made it quite clear that the McMahon Line was open to interpretations.

Chou En-Iai explained how important for China was the road it had built to join Sinkiang with Tibet. Without that road China had no way of reaching Sinkiang, he argued. Pant's reply was that India was ready to guarantee safe and free traffic between Tibet and Sinkiang but would not part with its territory. Chou En-lai kept quiet, but he did hint at consequences fraught with danger. It was clear that the two sides stood quite apart.

At that very meeting, it became obvious that some scrutiny of the different claims would be necessary. Finally an official team was appointed with S. Gopal and Jagat Mehta as members for the Indian side. Gopal went all the way to London to get material to support India's case. He was happy to have got some material but there was some other which the British government did not part with although it made photostat copies available. The Chinese tried their best to sabotage this project but the Mountbattens were a great help. The story that the Chinese tried to snatch some material from Gopal in mid-air is not correct. He contradicted this when I later asked him for confirmation.

At that time in India also, there was a rummaging through old files to pick up any word that might go in support of India's case. Then there were all types of "incorrect" maps available in Delhi. The report was that China was collecting them to controvert India's case. Getting wind of this, the Cabinet decided to bring in a Bill to proscribe all those books and maps which would question the integrity of the border. Their publication was regarded as indirect help to China. The government itself withdrew several official maps and books, which did not indicate meticulously a curve here or a bend there or which left the boundary undefined. Many maps of the Survey of India and books of the Publications Division were withdrawn, and there was a circular sent to return all such material. Officers personally looked into almirahs and nooks and corners to surrender "all the incriminating stuff".

It was a load of material which Gopal and Mehta carried to Peking. But photostat copies of the entire data were prepared and left in Delhi lest "theft" or some other "happening" might destroy the valuable evidence.

I got a hint of how little was expected of the officials' meeting from the Ambassador of a pro-Peking East European country, even before the officials' team left India. I was only the Home Ministry's PRO, and had no other *locus standi*, but it was obvious that the East European Ambassador who invited me for a chat at his chancery wanted me to convey the gist of the talk with Pant. At the very beginning of this conversation, he said that the opinions he would express were the views of his and other Communist countries, and he specifically mentioned Russia. His proposal was that India should accept a package political deal, getting recognition for the McMahon Line in exchange for giving over control of some areas in Ladakh. He said that the areas demanded had never been charted, and nobody could say to whom they belonged. What was being claimed to be India's was what had been forcibly occupied by Britain. No power could honour the imperialists' line, nor should India insist upon it. Whatever be the odds, China would never part with control of the road it had built because that was the lifeline between Sinkiang and other parts of China, he argued.

The Ambassador said that Nehru, left to himself, would have agreed to this. But he was under great pressure from the Rightist forces and was, therefore, taking "an uneasy posture" on the border issue, the Ambassador said. Were he to stand firm and face the anti-Left forces, he could end the opposition, which the envoy described as a storm in a teacup. He also criticized India for having given asylum to the Dalai Lama. According to the Ambassador, this act of New Delhi had aroused suspicions in the mind of China; it now felt unsure of India's intentions and suspected that India regretted its earlier act of accepting the suzerainty of China over Tibet.

I asked him whether he thought war could break out between India and China. He said he feared such a possibility, and added, "Anything can happen when relations deteriorate and when forces get arrayed against each other." As a warning, he mentioned that India should know that the Chinese forces were far more experienced and more powerful than India's.

Mrs Indira Gandhi was said to have remarked after the Chinese attack on India that she and her father found some faint signs of Chinese aggression over the border issue in 1954, when they visited Peking. But, as she reportedly explained, the choice was between postponing economic development, which her father thought was the immediate need, and stepping up expenditure on defence, which he believed could wait for some time. It was a difficult choice to make, she said, but her father did believe that China would not attack India that soon, though "we were definite that it would come some day".

## October 22, 1962

The press is told that the Chinese have suffered heavy losses, on the NEFA front, and newspapers lap it up. The Cabinet, however, is horrified at the speedy advance of the Chinese forces. A few, particularly Nehru, still expect Peking not to proceed too far and to stop before long. But most ministers have no such hope. They insist that the nation should be told the facts. But it is agreed not to raise a scare in the country. At the same time, Nehru is to make a broadcast to the nation to build up public support. All political parties, including the Communists, are to be approached for cooperation, and Mrs Indira Gandhi is to appeal to women to prepare to meet the Chinese aggression.

One regret that stretches all the way to the top levels is that the Intelligence Department failed to give timely warning* about the enemy's build-up. It is evident that the Chinese have been planning the attack for many days. Had there been prior intimation, the Army would have fared better. One bit of news conveyed to Delhi from the front is that Peking settled some time ago hundreds of "soldier-peasants" along the McMahon Line in the Eastern sector so that they would be on hand at an opportune time.

Defence Minister Krishna Menon is nobody's favourite, except Nehru's. Shastri makes no secret of

* The Intelligence Bureau, with which I checked facts, said that it had warned the government in time about the possibilities of a Chinese intrusion, but no precautionary measures were taken.

his dislike for him. He has told me that all ministers freely speak against Menon behind Panditji's back. They think Menon has let the country down. Shastri says that Morarji Desai had asked him to tell Panditji to drop Menon from the Cabinet. Shastri is himself of the same mind but does not want to hurt Panditji at a time when he feels let down by China.

Many Congress MPs, particularly U.N. Dhebar, former Congress President, Hare Krushna Mahatab, Deputy Leader of the Congress Parliamentary Party, and Mahabir Tyagi, are amassing brushwood to put around the stake for Menon. At a small party meeting, there is open talk that Menon must be punished for not having prepared India for defence and for misleading Parliament about the threat to NEFA. Many persons have criticized even Nehru, but fearing that the gist of the discussion would reach him, they have decided to tell the press that both, "Parliament and the Prime Minister", have been misled.

I have told Shastri that Menon has said at a mammoth meeting in Bombay, that Chinese aggressors would be thrown out. "This will not stop the campaign against him," has been Shastri's reply. "Panditji had told Menon to improve his image. I don't think this will help him."

Nehru has told his colleagues that he would be writing to the heads of State to acquaint them with the full story of the Chinese attack. He has already met the Soviet envoy, I.A. Benediktov, said to be quite high in the Soviet hierarchy, to explain India's point of view and to seek Moscow's assistance in solving the border dispute. The USSR Ambassador's reported reply is that he would convey India's feelings and its desire to enlist the good offices of the Soviet Union for asking China to stop aggression. But he is doubtful if they can do anything at present when their hands are full with the Cuban missile crisis, which according to him, has become rather serious in view of America's "active interest".

Ironically, New Delhi has received a cable from the Indian delegation to the UN, seeking instructions on how to vote on a resolution which the USSR has submitted to seat China. And, as before, the delegation has been asked to support the resolution.

## October 23, 1962

The cabinet has decided to reject the Chinese offer, and once again ask Peking to restore the *status quo* prevailing at the beginning of September. The Prime Minister is to send a reply to make it clear that the conditions that Chou En-lai has put forward in his letter, would restore neither India's "dignity" nor "self-respect", both of which the Chinese attack has injured.

I am also told that the reply is meant to emphasize that Nehru and his colleagues are united in their policy on China. This apparently has become important because there have been rumours that some cabinet colleagues disagreed with Nehru on how to tackle Peking. One has only to probe a Congressman to hear a mournful condemnation of Nehru and Menon. Outwardly, they go on saying, "Panditji ki jai."

A message of sympathy and support, which the UK Prime Minister, Mr MacMillan, has sent, has touched Nehru. He has immediately written back: "My dear friend ... Grateful for your message of sympathy and support in the difficult situation. We have, throughout the last five years of Chinese aggressive intrusions, sought to resolve the differences by peaceful talks and discussions but the aggression started by the Chinese from September 8 and the invasion by vast armies along various parts of India since October 20 have left us no choice but to resist. Your kind message and the assurance that you will do everything in your power to help us have further heartened us in our determination to resist this blatant Chinese aggression."

Through J.K. Galbraith, US envoy in Delhi, who was away from India when the Chinese attack began but rushed back immediately, Nehru has sent a message to President Kennedy. Apart from going over in the message, the series of acts of aggression committed by China, Nehru wants American understanding. His request is for small arms.

The non-alignment policy is also under attack. Even ministers say: "We have no friends. By sermonizing to everybody on what to do or not to do, we have alienated all. And the non-aligned countries are afraid to stand up and be counted." Nehru is still not prepared to ask for any direct help from any foreign power, although such is the demand of many ministers and important party leaders, the Congress and other.

With the fall of Tawang, which the government announced as "a withdrawal according to plans", the talk of pinning responsibility on Krishna Menon for the reverses has become louder in Congress circles. Many Congress MPs are angry with Nehru, and some make no secret of it. But he is too big for them. Nehru is in the know of the storm building up against Menon, and he has asked Shastri to talk to some important MPs to explain how China, not Menon, had let India down. Shastri, however, had no heart in the effort. He himself thought that Menon was "the villain of the piece." "Left to me, I should drop him straightaway", he said.

Nehru himself assembled some of the critical Congress MPs to appeal to them that "this was no time for a post-mortem". Explaining his earlier statement that "adequate arrangements" had been made to protect NEFA, Nehru has said nobody thought that the Chinese would throw in 30,000 troops. "This can happen in a totalitarian State but not in a democracy", which has to make every possible saving for welfare purposes. Not that it convinced the MPs. But there was no choice but to accept what Nehru said. They knew that the people, however aggrieved or hurt, were still behind him. However, some of them wanted an early session of Parliament and Nehru has agreed to the suggestion.

## October 24, 1962

Our Chargé d'Affaires in Peking, A. Bannerjee, has brought Chou En-lai's letter for Prime Minister Nehru. The letter's contents run like this: "It is most distressing that border clashes as serious as the present ones should have occurred between our two countries. Fierce fighting is still going on. At this critical moment I do not propose to trace the origin of this conflict. I think we should both look ahead. We should take measures to turn the tide."

The three proposals which Chou En-lai suggests to stop the border fighting are: (1) Pending a peaceful settlement, the armed forces of each side should withdraw 20 kilometres from the "line of actual control" and disengage. (2) If India agrees to the proposal, the Chinese government is willing to withdraw its frontier guards in the Eastern sector of the border to the north of the "line of actual control". At the same time, both China and India should undertake not to cross the line of actual control, that is, the traditional customary line in the middle and western sectors of the border. Matters relating to the disengagement of the armed forces are to be negotiated by the officials of the two sides. (3) In order to seek a friendly settlement, talks should be held once again by the Prime Ministers of China and India, and for that purpose, the Chinese Premier would be ready to go to Delhi for talks.

The letter contains cliches like "Sino-Indian friendship", "Asian-African solidarity" and "Asian peace".

The letter, if anything, is too late. A pool of blood lies between the two countries at the border, and any kind of settlement. Nehru feels hurt because he had regarded Chou En-lai as a friend, and, as he admits before a colleague, nothing in his political career has grieved him more than the Chinese perfidy. Nevertheless, Chou En-lai's letter is considered conciliatory in tone. Some ministers think that if China is willing to make up with India by withdrawing from all Indian territory except the Aksai Chin area, some settlement is possible, "though we should never trust them again."

New Delhi intends communicating the gist of Chou En-lai's letter to friendly nations to keep them in the picture. The Ministry of External Affairs will contact a few of their representatives in India to explain the "line of actual control", a phrase which, the government fears, will be twisted by China.

According to Peking, the "line of actual control" means the line now held by the Chinese. In the past, Peking has been nibbling at Indian territory, and has occupied large chunks. To advance a few hundred kilometres and then offer to withdraw 20 kilometres is hardly a constructive proposal. A withdrawal of 20 kilometres would be tantamount to the Chinese vacating aggression partly and the Indians withdrawing another 20 kilometres into their own territory. Nehru says: "This is a demand to which India will never submit, whatever the consequences, and however long and hard the struggle may be."

This looks like a long fight because the Chinese Army is advancing in all sectors.

## October 25, 1962

The Prime Minister has written a letter to President Nasser, more or less on the lines sent to other foreign heads of state. It says: "As you are generally aware, China had, by military action, forcibly occupied about 12,000 sq. miles of Indian territory in Ladakh in the western sector of the boundary over the period of the last five years. Despite this unilateral and forcible occupation of Indian territory, we, because of our dedication to peace and peaceful methods, did not precipitate a clash but made proposals for a meeting of the two governments. While exchange of notes for the finalization of these talks was going on, China, on September 8, suddenly marched her forces into India in the Eastern sector across the highest mountain ridge, which constitutes the boundary in this particular area, to spread the conflict further and seize more Indian territory by force. We had to make arrangements to resist this further aggression by China. Even then, we maintained a defensive attitude and continued to send notes to China asking her to correct the situation created by this latest aggression and withdraw her forces to her side of the international frontier in the Eastern sector to create an atmosphere for talks and discussions. We made it clear at the same time that if this further aggression continues, we will have to resist it."

Nehru says: "It is the Government of China who are not only refusing to undertake talks and discussions for easing of tensions and for settling differences between the Governments of India and China on the boundary question, but are creating further tension and conflict in another section of the boundary, namely, the Eastern sector, by pushing its forces across the frontier into Indian territory and mounting concerted attacks on Indian defence forces. The responsibility for the new incidents and the loss of Indian lives rests squarely on the shoulders of the Chinese authorities, who must bear full responsibility for the consequences. If the repeated Chinese professions of a desire to resolve the differences peacefully by discussions had any meaning, it is still open to the Government of China to direct their forces south of the Thag La ridge to return to their side of the boundary, that is, to the northern side of the ridge. The Government of India cannot and will not permit intrusion and aggressive activities against Indian defence forces in Indian territory to go unchallenged."

Nehru points out that the Chinese, for reasons best known to them, mounted a concerted, well-planned attack in the early hours of the morning of October 20 at several places in the eastern as well as the western sector with massive forces and with heavy offensive equipment—though they continued to say that they were border guards—and have in the last four days advanced into Indian territory, both in the eastern and western sectors, the advance in various areas ranging from 30 to 50 miles, and are still advancing despite stiff resistance from our limited armed forces in these border areas. These are the facts of China's blatant aggression which is an attempt to endorse territorial claims by military might.

Nehru says India is prepared for discussions if a suitable climate is created, restoring the *status quo* as it was prior to September 8. There is a clear hint to Nasser that "friends like you could give advice to the Chinese".

## October 26, 1962

Nasser has reportedly acted promptly on the advice. The Indian mission in Cairo reports that Nasser has sent messages to many African and Asian countries, including Indonesia, Burma, Ceylon, Afghanistan, Morocco, Guinea, Mali and Algeria, to use their good offices in bringing about a settlement of the Indo-China border dispute.

Nasser is said to be doing his best to stop the Sino-Indian hostilities. His Ambassador has talked to Chou En-lai in Peking. The Chinese Prime Minister has repeated his three-point proposal communicated to

Nehru through Bannerjee on October 24. But more than that, he has accused India of having fired the first shot. Chou En-lai has requested Nasser to strengthen Asian-African solidarity in view of the American threat of nuclear war starting from the Caribbean Sea. Chou En-lai also has sent a letter to Nasser and this has been transmitted by our ambassador in Cairo, Azim Hussain, to New Delhi. The letter says:

> The Chinese Government has always stood for peaceful settlement of Sino-Indian boundary questions through negotiations. Contrary to our expectations, the Indian Government has at three consecutive times in the last three months rejected Chinese Government proposals for negotiations, and following that, Indian forces launched massive general offensives against Chinese frontier guards both in the eastern and in the western sectors. The armed conflict on the Sino-Indian border is entirely forced upon China by the Indian side. Nevertheless, the Chinese Government has not abandoned its efforts for a peaceful settlement of the Sino-Indian boundary question. It is convinced that the boundary question cannot be settled by force. It issued on October 24 a statement putting forward three proposals. I ardently hope that Your Excellency … will use your influence to promote the materialization of these proposals.

Meanwhile, Nasser has heard from some of the non-aligned countries he had contacted. None is willing to take any initiative; in fact, they have some reservations about the merits of India's case.

The Prime Minister has written to Mr Khrushchev. The letter says:

The Government of India share the desire of the Government of the USSR to do whatever they can to resolve the differences between the Governments of India and China on the border question by peaceful talks and discussions in a spirit of understanding and cooperation. They have throughout these last few years made serious attempts to resolve these differences by peaceful means.

The Government of India appreciated the position of the USSR and the cautious stand taken by them on the India-China border differences. That is why the Government of India did not so far place the merits of the case before the Government of the USSR. It was only a few days back, on September 18, that our Foreign Secretary, on hearing about your Ambassador's interest in this matter, talked to him about the background of the case and the latest developments and gave the Ambassador copies of notes exchanged between India and China on the latest clashes in the Eastern sector of the boundary.

As Your Excellency is aware, our policies ever since our attainment of independence have been conditioned by our historical background and thinking. We have been strictly non-aligned, taking attitudes on the merits of each question. So far as the relations between India and the Soviet Union and even between India and China are concerned, the Government of India have never been, and will never be, influenced in any way by the views or attitudes of other Governments. The Government of India is, therefore, surprised at the references in the USSR Government's note to those "who are interested in intensifying world tension, who wish to line their coats by military clash between India and China", to "forces of reaction and war" and "imperialist circles" and how they "dream" in their sleep of ways of disturbing the friendship of the Soviet Union with India and with China.

China-India relations have deteriorated because of certain things done by China in her relations with India in the last few years. The present crisis has not been of the Government of India's making, but has been forced by deliberate aggressive moves made by the Government of China to alter the *status quo* of the boundary unilaterally by force instead of seeking a solution by talks, discussions and negotiations. It would be appropriate in this connection to state the following facts:

(i) Till 1954, i.e. about five years after the formation of the Government of the People's Republic of China and the establishment of their control in Tibet, there had been no trouble of any kind on the India-China frontier. On the contrary, the governments of India and China negotiated an Agreement on Trade and Intercourse between India and the Tibet region of China, under which the Government of India, on their own initiative, gave up various extra-territorial privileges exercised by the Government of India in Tibet which had come down from British times. This was done in a spirit of understanding to establish friendly and cooperative relations between two sovereign and independent countries, removing all traces of colonial traditions of the past.

(ii) The Government of India had no doubts about the customary and traditional boundary confirmed by treaties and agreements of the past; and this boundary was known to the Government of the People's Republic of China. There were inaccuracies in Chinese maps regarding this boundary and these were brought to the notice of the Government of China as early as 1954 and on several occasions afterwards. We were always given to understand that they were old maps which had not been revised.

(iii) The presence of Chinese forces in the area of Aksai Chin along the Sinkiang-Tibet caravan route came to the notice of the Government of India for the first time when the Government of China published a map of their projected road. An Indian patrol which went to the area in the course of its normal rounds was detained by the Chinese border forces and, on enquiry, the Government of China informed the Government of India: "According to the report of the Chinese local authorities in Sinkiang, frontier guards of the Chinese Liberation Army stationed in the south-western part of Sinkiang discovered in succession on September 8 and 12, 1958, two groups of Indian armed personnel at Tahung-Liutan and Kezrekirekan on the Sinkiang-Tibet road on Chinese territory". This communication was dated November 3, 1958.

(iv) By the beginning of 1959, the Chinese forces had moved further west and as mentioned in the note of the Government of the USSR, an armed clash took place at Kongka Pass when the Chinese border forces opened fire, killed 9 Indian personnel and captured the rest.

(v) Even after my meeting with Premier Chou En-lai in April 1960 and during the subsequent discussions of the officials of the two sides, the Chinese aggressive moves continued. By the middle of 1961, the Chinese border forces were nearly 70 miles south-west of the Sinkiang-Tibet road where they were in 1958.

(vi) Due to these aggressive intrusions by Chinese forces, the Government of India were compelled to take certain defence measures to halt the Chinese advance. While taking this action, the Government of India at the same time expressed their desire for talks and discussions to remove the border tension prevailing in these areas and made various proposals throughout last July, August and September. The Chinese responses to these approaches were negative and disappointing. The Chinese even refused to consider discussion of measures to correct the situation created by their unilateral alteration of the *status quo* of the boundary. Instead, they insisted on India accepting the precondition that the Chinese forces could not be asked to withdraw from the areas they had occupied over the last few years in the region of Ladakh.

(vii) It is pertinent to mention that according to the Chinese notes it was the Chinese frontier guards which detained the Indian patrol party in September, 1958, at the north-western end of the Sinkiang-Tibet road. Chinese notes received during the last few months again refer to Chinese frontier guards who are now manning a series of posts nearly a hundred miles south-west of where they were in September, 1958. Surely, the India-China frontier cannot be mobile and vary from year to year in accordance with the progress of Chinese forcible intrusions.

(viii) While notes regarding the scope of these talks and discussions were being exchanged and even dates and places were being specified, the Chinese forces crossed the Thagla Ridge, which constitutes the boundary between India and China in the Eastern sector, and intruded into the north-west corner of North East Frontier Agency of India. The Government of India had to take measures to meet this further attempt to alter forcibly the *status quo* of the boundary.

(ix) The Agreement concerning the McMahon Line, which is the name by which the boundary in this sector between India and the Tibet region of China is often called, merely formalized what had been the traditional and customary boundary between the territories of India and Tibet. It was a well-recognized and long-established boundary which was not "created", but only confirmed by a treaty in 1914. The local authorities and inhabitants of the area, as well as the governments of the two sides had for centuries recognized the validity of this boundary alignment, and even the People's Government of China, after they established their control in Tibet, proceeded on the basis that this was the boundary. The same watershed boundary, represented by the McMahon Line of 1914, between Burma and China, has recently been once more accepted in the treaty between the governments of Burma and China.

(x) Any talks or discussions, whether they are regarding preliminary measures to relieve tension or substantive discussions, are, of course, without prejudice to the position of either party regarding its claims in connection with the boundary. But there is no convention or precedent in international practice which justifies forcible occupation of territory without a declaration of war; and this is what the Government of China have done over the period of five years since 1957 in Ladakh, and have been doing now since the beginning of September in the north-west corner of the Eastern sector of the India-China boundary.

The Government of India agree that these border questions are difficult and complicated and have to be handled with patience to arrive at reasonable solutions. They have acted all along in this spirit even after the forcible occupation of about 12,000 square miles of Indian territory by the Chinese in the Ladakh region. They only took limited defensive measures to stop further Chinese intrusions and asked for talks and discussions to consider what measures should be taken, by agreement between the two governments, for restoring the *status quo* of the boundary and easing tensions in the area, prior to discussion on the question on merits. The Government of India laid down no pre-conditions of any kind. It is the Chinese who, through their Foreign Minister, stated that no one can make the Chinese withdraw from the Ladakh area that they had occupied during the last few years. It was this pre-condition about which notes were being exchanged when the Chinese thought it fit to cross the well-known India-China boundary in the Eastern sector and commit further aggression into India. Consistent with her self-respect and dignity, India had to take such action as it could to resist this new intrusion.

On the very morning on which your Ambassador handed over the note of the Soviet government to me, the Chinese mounted a well-concerted and premeditated attack on our defence posts in the Western as well as Eastern sectors of the boundary and are advancing further into Indian territory. You will agree, Mr Prime Minister, that this blatant use of force by the Chinese to annex such territory as they can is at complete variance with the policy regarding exercise of patience and settling differences in a spirit of cooperation and understanding counselled in the Soviet government's note. The Chinese chose to launch their carefully organized large-scale and vicious attack on Indian defence posts south of the McMahon Line, which is the international frontier and which had been quiet and peaceful for all these years, and also on our defence posts in the Western sector, on the very day on which you, Mr Prime Minister, were making sincere efforts to have the boundary differences between India and China resolved peacefully.

There is a reference in the note to the talks which our Defence Minister Shri Krishna Menon, had with the Soviet Ambassador in Delhi on September 15 and October 8. You will appreciate, Mr Prime Minister, that these talks had taken place after the recent aggressive intrusion by China south of the international frontier into the north-west area of the Eastern sector of the boundary. Even then, the Defence Minister pointed out, in the context of the great patience and forbearance shown by the Government of India at Chinese aggression in Ladakh during the last few years, that India would certainly have to resist if the Chinese continued this new aggression in the Eastern sector. Surely, neither you nor any of India's other friends would want her to submit to the arbitrary and blatant use of force by any power, however strong.

It is not India who is attempting to settle the dispute by the use of force. China had already, by military action, forcibly occupied the greater part of the disputed area in the Western sector, that is, in Ladakh, over the period of the last five years. Despite this unilateral and forcible occupation, India, because of its faith in peaceful talks and discussions, did not precipitate a clash but made proposals for a meeting between the representatives of the two countries. While the exchange of notes for the finalization of these talks was going on, China in the beginning of September suddenly marched her forces in the Eastern sector across the highest mountain ridge—the Thagla Ridge—which constitutes the boundary in that particular area, to spread the conflict and seize Indian territory by force. I agree with Your Excellency that this is a very dangerous path, but it is China which is following this path.

I can assure you, Mr Prime Minister, that so far as the Government of India are concerned, we are wedded to paths of peace and to the policy of settling outstanding differences by talks, discussions and negotiations.

All our past traditions and policy have clearly demonstrated our love of peace and our abhorrence of war. We have not set foot on an inch of Chinese territory, but have remained on our own territory which has been in our possession for a long time past and which has been clearly shown in all our maps as well as in our Constitution as being part of the Indian Union. It is true that this Indian area now occupied by China is mountainous and sparsely populated. But that does not lessen our undoubted claim to it. Politically, by treaty and tradition, it belongs to India and has all along been treated as such. Our literature for two thousand years or more is full of references to it as part of India and our people, nurtured in this literature and old tradition, are greatly attached to it. It has been and is a part of India's life and heritage. No country with any self-respect can accept a claim which is contrary to history, treaties and its own traditions, more especially when this is accompanied by aggression.

We know that China is a great and powerful country. We have sought, in the past, friendship and cooperation with it, and pleaded its cause before the United Nations and elsewhere. It has been a matter of great surprise and regret for us that in spite of our friendly attitude, the People's Government of China has committed gross aggression on our territory and has carried on a propaganda against us which is vituperative in the extreme. You will appreciate, Mr Prime Minister, that India could not have acted otherwise than it did in challenging the Chinese claim which had no basis, and in protesting strongly against their aggression. Even so, we have been prepared for discussions which might lead to a peaceful settlement, but how can we have any discussions when actual and new aggression is continuously taking place, and vast Chinese armies are moving further into our territory? Any discussion can only be worthwhile if a suitable atmosphere is created for it. We, therefore, proposed that the first thing to do was to create that atmosphere by the Chinese government restoring the *status quo* as it was prior to September 8. We could then consider what further agreed steps should be taken to correct the situation created by the earlier unilateral alteration of the *status quo* of the boundary and to ease the tensions, preparatory to the substantive discussions of the differences regarding the boundary.

## October 27, 1962

The Prime Minister has received a cheering reply from Kennedy to a message sent through Galbraith and a letter written on the same lines to other world dignitaries.* Kennedy's letter says:

> Your Ambassador handed over your letter last night. The occasion of it is a difficult and painful one for you and a sad one for the whole world. Yet there is a sense in which I welcome your letter, because it permits me to say to you what has been in my mind since the Chinese Communists have begun to press their aggressive attack into Indian territory. I know I can speak for my whole country when I say that our sympathy in this situation is wholeheartedly with you. You have displayed an impressive degree of forbearance and patience in dealing with the Chinese. You have put into practice what all great religious teachers have urged and so few of their followers have been able to do. Alas! This teaching seems to be effective only when it is shared by both sides in a dispute. I want to give you support as well as sympathy. This is a practical matter, and if you wish, my Ambassador in New Delhi can discuss with you and the officials of your government what we can do to translate our support into terms that are practically most useful to you as soon as possible. With all sympathy for India.

Compared to this reassuring note is the bad news from the front. Lt General Kaul, whom Shastri refers to as "Panditji's weakness", is down in Delhi with some ailment. The Chinese are advancing without

* Kennedy was indeed happy to have received Nehru's letter, and sent him a very affectionate reply. But later when the US President came to know that Nehru had sent him the same letter which he addressed to other world dignitaries, Kennedy's response was less effusive.

meeting any meaningful resistance. The stories reaching Delhi are that the officers have got too used to a life of inactivity and luxury and are unable to enthuse the *jawans* by showing initiative or valour. There is a hiatus in the living standards of the two and even at the height of 7,000 feet, the officers want hot water bath and commodes which the *jawans* are required to carry for them. Nehru has also heard about lack of contact between the civil and the military. Shastri has also been asked to fly to Gauhati and Tezpur to co-ordinate the efforts of the state government and defence personnel.

## October 28, 1962

All VIP planes have been pressed into service and so Shastri and his staff caught the morning courier service. There was none at Gauhati airport to receive us. A local official gave a message on behalf of the Assam Chief Minister that the State Cabinet was in session at the Circuit House and waiting for Shastri to join the deliberations. He drove straight to Circuit House. The first topic of discussion was the creation of a Home Guards Force. The state government had not yet passed the Bill to do so. For some technical hitch, it was diffident to issue an ordinance. Military representatives present at the meeting wanted to requisition all jeeps in the tea estates and elsewhere but the state government was reluctant to allow this in view of the adverse repercussions the step would have. A senior official explained the rules and procedures required to take such a step. It was a marathon meeting and continued for more than three hours. At last the state government agreed to the requisitioning of jeeps. Even at a time when the enemy is fast advancing towards Assam, red tape has not lessened.

It was rather late when we started for the Tezpur military barracks where Lt General Harbaksh Singh was waiting for Shastri. It was pitch dark but as we took a turn we saw a small hut decorated with earthen lamps. Shastri remarked: "I did not realize it was Diwali today." He looked pensive for a moment and then laughingly addressed me: "I made you miss sweets."

Lt General Harbaksh Singh had a big map on the wall opposite him. Surprisingly at that late hour—it was about 10.30 at night—both Shastri and the commander looked fresh and earnest. They went straight to business. After explaining the position of our troops and what had happened in the past few days, the commander said that the immediate needs were jeeps and warm clothes. He regretted that the *jawans* could not be supplied with the necessary winter clothes; there were not enough jeeps to take them up the hills, and, therefore, hundreds of them had to walk 40 to 50 miles to reach their posts. This exhausted them, but there was no demoralization. Lt General Harbaksh Singh told us how one of the *jawans* at Tawang killed several of the enemy troops with his slow .303 and then bayoneted five, one after the other, before he was shot through the head. Another instance was that of a brave engineer who blew up a bridge as well as himself to slow down the pace of enemy troops.

## October 29, 1962

Lt General Harbaksh Singh was at the airport to bid us good-bye. A company of *jawans* had been flown to

Tezpur and were getting ready to walk all the distance from the airport to Bomdila, about 50 miles. They looked cheerful and raised the slogan "Jai Hind" when they saw Shastri. He talked to some of them. Most of them were from Punjab but one was from Shastri's home town, Allahabad. All of them wore khaki cotton dress. He realized how essential was the supply of warm clothes.

When Shastri shook hands with Lt General Harbaksh Singh before departure, he said: "Commander, are you hopeful you will now halt the Chinese?" He replied: "Hopeful? I am confident." That evening we heard in Calcutta that Lt General Kaul was back at his post. Shastri remarked: "I wish General Harbaksh Singh had been kept on. He looked every inch a soldier."

Canada's response to India's request for arms has been rather quick. Ottawa has informed Delhi about the kind of military equipment available, and one item mentioned is the Caribou transport plane, capable of landing and taking off on short runways in rough terrain. This would probably lessen the walking distance for the *jawans*.

America is also flying in a substantial quantity of arms and equipment. The only problem about these armaments is that it must be a long time before the *jawans* learn to use them effectively. However, Army Headquarters in New Delhi feels that only a few days would be required to master them.

The mode of payment to America is yet to be determined, but neither Washington nor New Delhi seems worried about this. The urgent problem is to get the arms to the front because the outmoded .303 rifles have been found totally inadequate against the "human wave" attacks by the Chinese, who are equipped with automatic weapons.

There is no response yet from the Soviet Union to India's request for arms. One vague report reaching New Delhi's top official circles is that Moscow would first like to know how far Nehru would resist the demand to remove Menon. Nehru's impression is that the Cuba situation has probably made it necessary for the Soviet Union not to fall out with China, and therefore, it is reluctant to give arms.

## October 30, 1962

Nehru seems to have waited too long for the Chinese to make "some conciliatory gesture". The border situation is worse. Except in Ladakh, everywhere else the Chinese are cutting through Indian defences like knife through butter. Pressure inside the Congress Party is building up in favour of asking America and Britain for help. Some MPs are in touch with the envoys of the two countries in Delhi and report that they are keen to offer help but will not until the Indian government specifically asks for it.

The people, who feel horrified and helpless over the performance of the Indian forces at the front, have been given the sop that some armaments have been received from abroad and more are expected. This is true, but the fact is that very little has been done to buy or procure arms. Maybe, Nehru is conscious that the big powers will ask for a political price. Maybe, he still expects

Peking to "behave". Maybe, he awaits the miracle of a settlement even at this late hour. But the time is ticking away—and the Chinese are advancing.

The news from Moscow is not very encouraging. The USSR believes that the three-point proposal offered by the Chinese Prime Minister is "constructive" and "aimed to end the conflict". New Delhi is asked not to postpone peace by putting any "prior conditions" and Zorin, the Soviet Deputy Foreign Minister, has told our representative at the UN more or less the same thing. India should not stand on prestige but initiate negotiations on the basis of what the Chinese have offered.

Shastri has told me that it would be difficult for Panditji to save Menon for long. "I have heard members saying that Panditji will have to go if he does not drop Menon. The entire Cabinet, except K.D. Malviya, is against Menon and one can see how bitterly most ministers feel. The State Chief Ministers are against retaining him, and most of them have informed Nehru of this.

Nehru has decided to talk to some irritated MPs to lessen their anger. But they are in a nasty mood, and it is obvious that he would have to do something more—at least move Menon from the Defence portfolio.

America's Ambassador to Pakistan, McConnaughly, has rushed to Rawalpindi to meet Mohammed Ali, the Foreign Minister. At India's initiative, he is asking Ali to give an undertaking that Pakistan would not attack at this time. New Delhi's information is that the

US envoy has spoken forcefully about the dimension and seriousness of the situation and has expressed the hope that Pakistan will not embarrass India. He has argued that the outstanding issues between the two countries should remain frozen during the time India was engaged in fighting China.

Mohammed Ali has reportedly said he could not give the official viewpoint without consulting President Ayub. Mohammed Ali's personal view is said to be that he, for one, is quite clear about the seriousness of the situation. The Chinese are a greater menace than the Russians. India has nothing to fear from Pakistan. Mohammed Ali has said that President Ayub has already received President Kennedy's message not to do anything which would in any way distract New Delhi's attention. Mohammed Ali has also mentioned that a similar request had come from Prime Minister MacMillan.

He however says that once Kashmir is out of the way, both countries can jointly stand four square against the common threat from the north. Pakistan's fear is that if India were to contain China through massive aid from the USA, it may use what it receives from them, against Pakistan. Mohammed Ali argues that Pakistan will have no grouse against "its allies"—a phrase which he repeated again and again while talking to the US Ambassador—if they give to Pakistan matching military aid "so that the balance of power remains unchanged."

For whatever reasons, Mohammed Ali has mentioned to the US Ambassador that India has received no support from even non-aligned countries.

## October 31, 1962

At long last, Nehru has had to bow to the Congress Party's mounting criticism against Krishna Menon and move him from the Defence portfolio. He has been given Defence Production instead, and Nehru himself has taken over the operations side. A laconic announcement issued from Rashtrapati Bhavan does not say anything except that Nehru has taken over Defence and that Menon will continue to be in the Cabinet as Minister for Defence Production.

The announcement has not evoked any enthusiasm because it is considered the change is only on paper. Shastri says that it would have been better if Panditji had given Menon some portfolio other than Defence Production. MPs would not be content with the change which, to some of them, might mean only a change in nomenclature, but no clear break with the past.

Those who know Menon will testify that designations have not stood in his way in the past. Nonetheless, quite a few Congress members feel satisfied and think the curtailment of Menon's authority is preliminary to his exit.

Among the non-aligned countries, the UAR has been most active in finding some way to end the hostilities. Cairo's four-point plan is: (1) An immediate ceasefire; (2) Reversion by India and China to the positions they held on October 20 before the fighting; (3) Creation of a "no man's land" between the troops of the two sides; and (4) Negotiations to resolve the border problem.

New Delhi's interpretation is that "the positions held on October 20" means the line prevailing on September 8; in other words, India will get back Dhola and Khinzemane on the McMahon Line. New Delhi is in favour of accepting the UAR proposals if a ceasefire is followed by the withdrawal of Peking's forces to the September 8 position. The information received from Peking is that China is prepared for an immediate ceasefire but holds to its own interpretation of the Indian forces' position on October 20. Once again, the three proposals by Chou En-lai—including withdrawal by 20 kilometres from the "line of actual control"—are reiterated. It is clear that no rapprochement is possible.

## November 3, 1962

The storm against Krishna Menon has not subsided. He is blamed for India's reverses at the front, and it seems that punishment meted out to him would give vicarious satisfaction to many people, as if to hit him would be to hit China. Some of them sincerely feel that Menon "purposely kept India unprepared so as to benefit Communist China".

Sensing the anti-Menon mood, some senior Congress MPs think of requesting Menon to quit the cabinet on his own. A few persons advance a curious argument to get rid of Menon. They say that since India is getting arms from the West, the person in charge of Defence should be one who has "faith in the West and of the West". Some members of the Congress Parliamentary Party's Executive have decided to address a letter to Nehru asking for Menon's dismissal.

Menon is his own enemy. He is telling all and sundry that the transfer of the Defence portfolio to the Prime Minister has not made any difference. He is functioning in the same old way; Nehru passes no order without consulting him. Whatever be the truth, this talk upsets the MPs even more.

And on top of it, he has the Defence Ministry's spokesman announce: "No separate Ministry of Defence Production is being set up or contemplated. The Defence Ministry, of which Defence Production is a part, continues. Krishna Menon is in charge of Defence Production." This statement is most untimely because the people are now convinced that Menon is still in charge of Defence and Nehru has only made some change in form without altering the substance.

Probably Nehru has smelted this. The personnel of the National Defence Council, meant to advise on military matters, have been changed, and they include retired generals like Thimayya and Thorat. The Prime Minister's endeavour is to convince the people that no important decision can be taken without consulting this body, even though Menon is the Minister for Defence Production. But this does not seem in any way to lessen criticism against him.

Morarji Desai has reportedly met Nehru to ask him to drop Menon immediately. Shastri has also been approached by certain ministers to prevail upon Nehru to let Menon go.

## November 5, 1962

Chou En-lai's much-awaited reply to Nehru's letter of October 27 is conciliatory in tone but does not give an honourable way out to the Indian government. For the first time, Chou En-lai has used words like "imperialism and colonization" to argue that they are the "chief enemies of us newly independent Asian and African countries". New Delhi's interpretation is that the letter is meant on the one hand to stall any move by India to seek assistance from the Western countries—Peking has obviously heard that this may happen if the hostilities continue because Nehru is under constant pressure to seek the West's help—and on the other, to convey to the non-aligned world that Peking is keen to keep out the West from Asia.

Chou En-lai has defined the line of actual control as that "existing on November 7, 1959". New Delhi believes that there was no line at that time, only a series of positions of Chinese forces on Indian territory. The Chinese Prime Minister's letter says that the "line of actual control" "coincides in the main" with the so-called McMahon Line in the Eastern sector. In the western and middle sectors, the line is a "customary" one. What it means is that New Delhi should recognize in the western sector a series of positions of Chinese forces in Ladakh, at Spanggur, Khuranak Fort and Kongka La, not to speak of the main Aksai Chin road. Even if the Chinese forces were to withdraw by 20 kilometres, they would still be positioned at least one hundred kilometres deep in Indian territory. On the other hand, India's withdrawal of 20 kilometres would mean withdrawal from its own territory, vacating posts of Daulat Beg Oldi, Chushul and Hanle, on which Peking had always cast a covetous eye.

In the eastern sector, the Chinese Prime Minister's observation was that Chinese positions have always remained to the north of the highest Himalayan ridge of the border and the alignment of the McMahon Line has never been questioned by China. The Chinese were nowhere in the vicinity of this watershed boundary either in November 1959 or later till September 8, 1962, when they started their aggression into Indian territory in this region.

Peking has never had any authority south of the main Himalayan watershed ridge, which is the traditional boundary in this sector. Some Tibetans, along with some Chinese troops, did intrude into Barahoti on various occasions since 1954; and, in 1958, the two governments agreed to withdraw their armed personnel from the locality. But Indian civilian personnel have throughout been functioning in the area. A conference held in 1958 to discuss the question made clear that the Chinese government didn't even have precise knowledge of the area they were claiming.

There is no doubt that New Delhi would like to make up with Peking, in view of the military reverses. But the line of September 8, 1962, is the minimum which the government has promised the nation. There could be no going back, even though it is obvious that there would be many more reverses at the front.

For Nehru, it is also a crisis of confidence. How could he reconcile himself to accepting the suggestion of Chou En-lai, the man he trusted but who had now betrayed him? Nehru still nourishes the hope that Peking will agree to his September 8 line proposal. Even while discussing Chou En-lai's letter with his colleagues, he had avoided invective. A neighbouring country, however misled, is after all a neighbour and deserves neighbourly consideration.

## November 8, 1962

Krishna Menon has handed in a letter of resignation, reportedly written at the instance of Mrs Aruna Asaf Ali and some other friends to "strengthen" Nehru's hands. The letter has been with Nehru for about a week. Shastri feels the resignation will be accepted but he is keeping his fingers crossed lest Panditji should change his mind at the last minute. The mood of the party is such that it is impossible to retain Menon but Nehru tries his best.

At the meeting of the Executive of the Congress Parliamentary Party* held subsequently in the day, Nehru reportedly vacates the chair to argue that he is as much to blame as Menon and that he too must go. But neither the Executive of the Congress Parliamentary Party nor its general body—both meeting on the same day—withdraw the demand for Menon's resignation. Nehru was conscious of public opinion. He said so at the meeting: "I have my finger on the pulse of the people." He realized that by retaining Menon he would only feed controversy and divert the nation's attention from the real problem of standing united against the enemy.

---

* K.C. Pant, the then Secretary of the Congress Parliamentary Party, literally forced three Executive members to put signatures on the petition asking for the dismissal of Menon. The members were afraid they might annoy Nehru.

For once, the Congress Party has its way. While announcing the acceptance of Menon's resignation, Nehru praised him to the skies and paid tribute to his "great ability and energy". Menon's letter has been released; one of the sentences disliked by senior ministers is: "No one other than you (Nehru) can garner help to maintain that (people's) resoluteness to the fullness of its purpose and without deterioration."

Shastri returned from the meeting quite satisfied. He does not know who would be the Defence Minister. When I asked him for probable names, he said: "Morarji *bhai* will like to become Defence Minister, but Panditji will never make him. Probably, he will call Chavan* sahib from Bombay. Once he mentioned his name in some other connection."

Moscow's response to Nehru's letter is disappointing. Khrushchev's reply contains clichés like "friendship" between two great Asian countries and neighbourly relations, but says nothing in support of India. He asks New Delhi to "negotiate" with Peking without any "pre-conditions". In other words, it means that India should not ask for the vacation of aggression before agreeing to a ceasefire. New Delhi's bigger disappointment is that Moscow is not sending much-needed, much-promised and much-publicized MiGs.

---

* Nehru called Chavan to Delhi on November 10, 1962, and offered him Defence Ministership. Chavan himself announced this before he returned to Bombay.

Word has arrived from Paris that France will supply arms to India on a "priority basis". But the price asked for is stiff, and it has to be paid cash down. An effort is made to have the condition of cash payment waived, but it appears that these "are the instructions of General de Gaulle".

## November 12, 1962

Nehru feels relieved after receiving Ayub's reply to the letter he had written to heads of states. It is pleasant and friendly in tone and specifically mentions that Pakistan considers the conflict between India and China a danger to the whole region. The Press build-up in Pakistan has been rather hostile and had created serious concern about Rawalpindi's intentions. Ayub's letter rules out the possibility of an attack from Pakistan. Deployment of Indian troops can be far easier now, and some will probably be pulled away from the Pakistan front. Kennedy has, in a special message, communicated to New Delhi the assurance he has received from President Ayub that India need not fear an attack from Pakistan. The same assurance has reached New Delhi from London.

Of course, India has to make a formal declaration that the arms received from America will not be sent to the Pakistan front, nor used against that country in future. New Delhi has also agreed to regular inspection by American military officials to ensure that US armaments are supplied only to the forces facing the Chinese.

Shastri suspects that America will sooner or later insist on India discussing Kashmir with Pakistan. He says that hints have already been dropped both by Washington and London. "I think we should have talks with Pakistan," Shastri says. "It is far easier to settle with our kith and kin than with the Chinese."

However, the message received from our mission in Pakistan says that the government there is telling the people through the press that "Pakistan can do without American aid". All think that this is propaganda. But the continuance of the strike of the Pakistani crew of the joint steamer companies, paralysing the river services to Assam, is considered "politically motivated". The government has decided to strengthen roads and bridges in the area to expand road transport between Siliguri and Dhubri.

The Soviet Union has not yet supplied the prized MiG-21 fighters and the factory to manufacture them, even though India has sent many reminders. But what has pleased New Delhi is the rift between Peking and Moscow. The news from diplomatic sources is that China is withdrawing its envoys from many East European countries and that behind the purge in Bulgaria, there was the hand of Moscow because it feared Sofia was increasingly going under the influence of Peking.

It is assumed that before long the Soviet Union will publicly back India against China. And one straw seen in the wind is the unflinching support of the Communist Party of India. China does not like it and has described Indian Communists as "self-styled Marxist-Leninists" who have "departed from the basic principles of Marxism-Leninism and proletarian internationalism".

In the Communist Party there are two factions: one predominantly pro-Moscow, supporting India, and the other, the extremists, questioning the veracity of New Delhi's claims about the border. The Indian Communist Party's National Council has come out unequivocally against the Chinese aggression and has supported Nehru's "stirring appeal for national unity in the defence of the country". But this has widened the gulf in the party. Three prominent members, Jyoti Basu, P. Sundaraya and Harkishen Singh Surjit, have resigned from the party's secretariat. E.M.S. Namboodiripad, general secretary, who belongs to the "centre" group, is understood to have expressed a desire to be relieved of his post.

The Home Ministry has reported that even when China's unprovoked aggression continued, the attitude of a large majority of the party was one of anti-national equivocation and a blind belief that a socialist country could never be guilty of aggression. The Leftists led by E.M.S. Namboodiripad were pro-Peking, while the Rightists under S.A. Dange accused China of creating tension, and came out with sharp condemnation of the Chinese aggression. The Chinese aggression issue was deliberated at a meeting of the National Council of the CPI in Delhi (October 31–November 2, 1962). The consensus, influenced by the Rightists, was to pledge the support of the party to the war measures of the Government of India and to ask the Chinese forces to withdraw to their positions held before September 8, 1962. This resolution was carried. In protest, some Leftist members submitted their resignation from the

Central Secretariat of the party. The Leftists continued to indulge in a scathing criticism of the Indian government as also of CPI leadership.

Shastri is not too happy with the activities of the pro-China lobby in the Communist Party. According to intelligence reports, they are saying that it is not China that is the aggressor but that India is to blame. They also argue that the exact boundaries are not known. Several anonymous documents have come to the possession of the government and they give three points for the guidance of party members. The points are: (a) Expression of the correctness of the Chinese line of action as opposed to the Soviet line at the level of international Communism, and (b) Virulent attacks on the moderate leadership of the CPI with incitement to replace it with a Left-oriented militant section. Anti-Indian propaganda is being smuggled into the country by the Chinese through various agencies. One trick used is to mail literature directly to individuals, schools, colleges, libraries and Communist-run book houses which have figured in the past on the distribution list of various Chinese agencies in and outside India. To beat the censorship on mail coming from China and Hong Kong, propaganda material is sent from West Germany, the UK, Holland, Czechoslovakia, Switzerland, Russia, Japan, Burma, Nepal, Ceylon, Pakistan, Australia and New Zealand.

## November 14, 1962

There have been several discussions in the ECC on the reply to Chou En-lai's letter of November 4. Nehru wanted to say in unequivocal terms that China had been perfidiously dishonest in its assurances of friendship with India. However, he has somewhat toned down the reply which speaks of "the complete loss of confidence in the bonafides of the professions for a peaceful settlement repeatedly made by the Government of China".

The letter says: "This is the basic fact that till September 8, 1962, no Chinese forces had crossed the frontier between India and China in the Eastern sector as defined by India, that is, along the highest watershed in the region, in accordance with the Agreement of 1914." Spelling out what he means by the "line of actual control", Nehru says: "In the Eastern sector, the Chinese forces will go back to the positions they held on November 7, 1959, that is, they will be on the other side of the boundary along the Himalayan watershed which they first crossed on September 8, 1962. In the central sector, the position will be the same, that is, they will be to the north of the highest watershed ridge. In the western sector, the Chinese forces will go back to the positions they held on November 7, 1959, as given in the attached note, that is, along the line connecting their Spanggur post, Khurnak Fort and Kongka La, and then northwards to join the main Aksai Chin road. The Indian forces will go back to the various defence posts they occupied in all the three sectors prior to September 8, 1962."

The consensus at the ECC was to refer appreciatively to the UAR proposals and suggest to Peking that they could form the basis for a settlement. However, in the final draft, Nehru only tells Chou En-lai: "You must have seen in this connection the four-point suggestion made by the President of the UAR."

The China Division of the External Affairs Ministry had been asked to prepare a rebuttal to Chou En-lai's claim in his letter that while "according to the original map, the western end of the so-called McMahon Line clearly starts from 27° 44.6'N, the Indian government arbitrarily said that it started from 27° 48'N and, on this pretext, it not only refused to withdraw the Indian troops from the Kechilang River area north of the Line, but also made active dispositions for a massive military attack, attempting to clear the area of Chinese frontier guards defending it".

The External Affairs Ministry's note, which Nehru has sent now as an annexure to his letter, refutes this contention. It says: "The Agreement of 1914 only formalized what was the traditional and customary boundary in the area which lies along the highest Himalayan watershed ridges. The maps attached to the Agreement were of small scale of 1 inch to 8 miles. They were sketch maps and intended to be only illustrative. All that they made clear was that the boundary ran along the main watershed ridges of the area. The parallels and meridians were "shown only approximately in accordance with the progress achieved at the time in the sphere of scientific surveys. This is a common cartographic feature and the Chinese government have themselves recognized this in Article 48 of their 1960 treaty with Burma. If the maps and the coordinates given therein were taken literally it is impossible to explain the discrepancy between the existing distances and those given in the map between various villages in the area." "Also Migyitun, according to the maps, is at latitude 28° 38′ north while its actual position as ascertained by the latest surveys is much further north. Tulung La has been shown on the 1914 maps at 27° 47′ while its position on the ground is further north of this point. Strict adherence to the coordinates shown on the McMahon Line maps would result in advancing the Indian boundary in both the areas of Migyitun and Tulung La further north, thereby including both these places inside Indian territory. In the area east of Tsai Sarpa, strict adherence to the coordinates of Lola in the McMahon Line maps would result in advancing the boundary of India into this area by at least 7 miles to the north. This would mean including at least 70 square miles of Tibetan territory within India."

> The Government of India recognizing the principle underlying the McMahon Line agreement, that the boundaries lie along the highest watershed ridges, actually confined their jurisdiction to the area south of this boundary and did not try to take over Tibetan territory beyond the highest watershed ridge on the basis of the inaccurate coordinates given in the 1914 maps. This must be known to the Chinese authorities and yet they ignore this and seek to use the inaccurate coordinates given in the maps where they are favourable to their fanciful claims made to support their latest aggression. The Chinese authorities cannot have it both ways. They cannot accept the highest watershed as the boundary in parts of the eastern sector where it suits them though this is not consistent with the coordinates given in the 1914 maps, and quote the coordinates

in these very maps in their favour in other parts of the sector to make demands for territorial concessions from India.

## November 19, 1962

Nehru has sent an SOS to America for massive air help. In an urgent appeal* to President Kennedy he has asked for the US Air Force to come to India's rescue. It is obvious that the US planes when they come are to operate from our airfields even though Nehru has not specifically mentioned anything about the place from where they are to operate. A man who was reluctant to ask anything except small arms at the beginning of hostilities is now desperately looking for all that he can get from any quarter to stem China's rapid advance.

For whatever reasons, Nehru has asked the Prime Minister's Secretariat to retain the copy of his letter to Washington—he never sent one to the Ministry of External Affairs.

(A few years later, in the context of a question raised in Parliament, the Ministry of External Affairs made a request to the US Embassy in New Delhi for the copy of Nehru's letter. Chester Bowles, with whom I checked

---

* Sudhir Ghosh once asked in Parliament about Nehru's request to the USA for assistance. Shastri denied it because the type of question asked by Ghosh provided Shastri with a loophole. Ghosh's question was if Nehru had asked America for a US aircraft carrier. That was not technically correct, and Shastri could easily say there was no request for the aircraft carrier. And that is how Shastri replied.

on March 27, 1969, before he left New Delhi, said: "We (the American Embassy) obtained it from Washington for the EA. Ministry." He told me that Nehru's plan was to use the US planes to protect Indian cities, and to use the Indian Air Force to strike against Chinese territory, particularly Tibet.

When Shastri was the Prime Minister, Dinesh Singh, the then Deputy Minister for External Affairs, wanted to see Nehru's letter. On the advice of his Secretary, L.K. Jha, Shastri said "No" and ordered that the letter should never leave the PM's Secretariat.)

## November 20, 1962

Things look gloomy. A good deal of NEFA has fallen. Indian forces have retreated to Tezpur, near the foot of the hills. The pall of helplessness is spreading and seems to have affected even those who have been putting up a brave front. The Prime Minister remains determined but has no clue about how things might shape up. One MP, Khadilkar (now Deputy Speaker), met him in the lobby and suggested the revival of the "diplomatic front". What about Nasser? Nehru said Nasser had proved to be disappointing. Moscow? "I am not very optimistic." There is a sense of emptiness. He must be the unhappiest man in India today, seeing all that he has built on the basis of peace with China crumbling. His household reports that he is quieter than usual, keeping his thoughts to himself, often in a reverie and sometimes trembling.

Non-aligned countries have been a disappointment. Ceylon's Prime Minister, Mrs Bandaranaike, is sympathetic but her advisers are keeping her away from openly taking sides. She is prepared to go to Peking to find out possibilities of an accord and wants to sponsor a conference of the non-aligned, but nothing beyond it. She is afraid of annoying Peking.

A letter from our High Commissioner in Karachi reports that Pakistan is not worried about Peking's threat; it does not think itself endangered or exposed. But its Foreign Minister, Mohammed Ali, did say that Pakistan would be ready to plan for the defence of the sub-continent if India were to have a settlement with Pakistan over Kashmir. He said these were the views of Ayub, who felt disappointed by Nehru's latest letter, which did not even mention Kashmir.

The Emergency Committee of the cabinet has met to consider the situation. The discussion there brings out the discrepancy in the thinking of Nehru and Shastri. The Home Minister suggests that India should accept the Chinese proposals contained in Chou En-lai's letter dated October 24. The PM says "No". No other cabinet minister says much. In fact, the other ministers support the PM. The President, Dr Radhakrishnan, congratulates the Home Minister on his courage in proposing the best solution.

There is great resentment over the functioning of the top men in the Army. The reverses at the NEFA front are so many and so devastating that the resignation of General Thapar, the Chief of the Army Staff, has been expected for some time. Reports are that he has offered to resign more than once, but is not being allowed to do so. Obviously, things must have reached a breaking point because General Thapar has been allowed to go on leave and Lt General Chaudhuri appointed to officiate and there to succeed.

There have been insistent demands from Gauhati that a senior leader from Delhi should visit Assam. Both the State Chief Minister and the Governor were rather unhappy over the growing anger in Assam that New Delhi did not care for the state. Nehru's broadcast that "my heart goes out to the people of Assam at this hour" had been interpreted as saying "goodbye" to the State. Many Assamese are saying openly that they should join hands with the Chinese and wreak vengeance "on Dilliwallas" for having abandoned the state. Shastri was asked to go to Assam.

## November 21, 1962

I was the first to reach Palam. The newspaper stall at the airport was unusually crowded. With great difficulty I could make my way to buy the morning paper. It carried the dramatic offer of a ceasefire by the Chinese. The news story said:

> "Beginning from December 1, 1962, Chinese frontier guards will withdraw to positions 20 km (12.5 miles) behind the lines of actual control which existed between China and India on November 7, 1959."

The statement said this meant that Chinese forces would withdraw north of the "illegal McMahon Line" on the eastern sector of the border and from their present position on the remaining sectors of the 2,000-mile Himalayan boundary.

The statement also said that "in order to ensure the normal movement of the inhabitants in the Sino-Indian border and to forestall the activities of saboteurs and maintain order there, China will set up checkposts".

The statement said the checkposts would be at a number of places on its side of the line of actual control with a certain number of civil police assigned to each checkpost.

The statement said the Chinese Government was making these actions to reverse the present situation along the border and to bring about realization of its three-point proposals of October 24.

These proposals have already been rejected by the Indian Government but the statement pointed out that after withdrawal "the Chinese frontier guards will be far behind their positions prior to September 8, 1962".

The news relieved the gloom in the atmosphere. Soon L.P. Singh, Additional Secretary in the Home Ministry, and Hooja, Joint Director of Intelligence, reached the airport. I showed them the paper. Surprisingly the bosses of the Home Ministry and the Intelligence were not aware of the ceasefire offer. The Home Minister, who reached exactly on time at 6 a.m. also did not know anything about it. After reading the news, he said: "This does make a difference. Probably I shall have to cancel the visit. But let me find out from the Prime Minister."

A car cavalcade then moved to the Prime Minister's house. Nehru had only just got up but like them did not know of the Chinese offer. This was typical of our intelligence service or of the government. Though reports of the offer had reached newspaper offices probably five to six hours earlier, the government continued to remain unaware of it. Even the official spokesman, whom the pressmen awoke after seeing the story of the Chinese offer, had apparently not communicated with anyone higher up. What a way to fight a war!

Nehru's first remark in Hindi after hearing the news was: "Has it happened? I was expecting it." He, however, wanted to see the newspaper. Shastri asked him if he should cancel his trip to Assam. Nehru's reply was: "No, we cannot give up our plans. But you should come back soon."

We returned to the airport, and there we heard that A. Harriman, President Kennedy's personal envoy, was coming from America. Shastri's immediate reaction was that the Chinese, after humiliating us, must have decided to withdraw to give the USA no reason to send us massive aid by way of armaments, and also to put us in the wrong before the world, especially before the non-aligned countries.

Shastri was inclined to accept the Chinese proposal. When we reached Gauhati, the Chief Minister of Assam, Chaliha, was at the airport. According to Sahay, the state Governor, Chaliha smiled for the first time in days after the Chinese statement. Indira Gandhi, who was also in Gauhati, found the last paragraph of the Chinese statement objectionable because, according to her, control by the Chinese of the area held by them would facilitate indoctrination.

We never realized until we met people in Gauhati how angry they were about the PM's remark in the AIR broadcast that "our heart goes out to the people of Assam at this time of crisis". The Home Minister assuaged their feelings by assuring the people that Nehru never meant to forsake Assam.

## November 22, 1962

We flew to Tezpur. The airport had been saved in the nick of time—a day's delay in the Chinese ceasefire offer and it would have been blown up by a demolition squad. We were received by a posse of Army officers. For the first time, I met Lt General Kaul. How meek he looked for such a controversial figure! I had expected him to be stouter and younger than he turned out to be. His face was pudgy, somewhat loose in the skin. He looked a reserved type, at least behaved like one, but later he opened up. My encounter with him was brief and formal, but he squeezed my arm to show friendship. Shastri, who has never liked his appointment as Commander of the 4th Corps, paid him scant attention.

Lt General Kaul told our pilot that he was going in a helicopter with food, clothes and medicines to contact the men who had been cut off when Bomdi La fell unexpectedly. I knew this information was meant for me, to be passed on to the Home Minister, who was a little away.

The passenger lounge—still displaying a board "Beer Sold Here"—had been converted into a map room. We were told how the debacle took place, which routes the men who had been cut off could possibly take to get back, and where the Chinese soldiers were. The position is worse than we had imagined.

I met a younger crowd in another corner of the lounge. They were bitter and openly talked of how the requirements of senior officers were being carried to the last picket post even when firing was taking place. A captain said: "We are no longer fighters. We think of clubs or restaurants, even in the trenches. We have gone too soft—we're no good."

Accompanying Shastri on this trip is Orissa's Patnaik, likeable but flamboyant, apt to play to the gallery and therefore sounding amateurish even when what he speaks is sound sense. At Tezpur, I met an Army major who belonged to my home town, Sialkot. He said that peace must be bought at any cost because the Army's morale was broken and nobody had the will to fight or the confidence to win. The Chinese had stopped themselves; we did not stop them. He said the troops were thinking of their women and children all the time. The Army should be one of bachelors, he said bitterly. He, like others, wanted to know when the promised arms were coming from abroad.· The much publicized automatic weapons, said the major, did reach Sela pass, 20 lorry-loads of them, but even the grease on them had not been removed when the enemy attacked. His comment was that Kaul should not have been sent back to the front. Harbaksh Singh, who served during Kaul's illness, was far better and showed a good understanding of the soldier's problem.

This is also the impression of some journalists who had gone to the frontline. They say that once Kaul ordered shelling and firing of 25 mortars to give the journalists a sort of exhibition, when the Chinese could have hit back and finished the journalists probably. Kaul is too much of an exhibitionist to be a good General, according to them.

Hearing the news of Shastri's arrival, some civilians reached Tezpur airport. They complained against officials who had allegedly bungled the evacuation. They said that no prior warning was given. Suddenly, one evening, at about 8 p.m., an announcement was made over loudspeakers that the government was no longer responsible for the citizens' life or property. The Deputy Commissioner had fled burning files. Currency notes in the Treasury were burnt. Most cars were requisitioned; others were denied petrol. All persons had to walk, and there was little food, even for children. Government officials, Army personnel, old dusty files and unwieldy furniture had been evacuated, but not the people. Some persons complained to Shastri that vehicles had been found to evacuate even the chickens of the *burra sahib,* but not ordinary people. Prisoners were let off; also mental patients. Hospitals were deserted.

Nobody owned the responsibility of having issued orders regarding the evacuation of the population. A press note said that civilians could leave Assam by air or by special and other trains if they wanted to and that arrangements had been made for their stay at "the other end". This had created panic; the general impression was that the entire state would be emptied.

At the instance of Shastri, the state cabinet had withdrawn the orders. The Home Minister promised a deputation of women that their children would be moved to some safe place in central India. The flamboyant Biju Patnaik meanwhile talked to some military officials; he spoke about "guerrillas". Later, I learnt that he has been allotted a separate room in the Ministry of External Affairs, and was working on some kind of hush-hush project.

Shastri, Patnaik, Chaliha and Kaul have held a marathon conference at the airport itself. This is more of a post-mortem, because everybody has taken it for granted that the Chinese will withdraw and that we will accept the ceasefire without specifically saying so. Shastri has said that India will not pursue or chase the Chinese but await their withdrawal. However, Kaul's estimate is that the Army has been badly bruised, if not broken, and we must have peace at all costs. Other Army officers whom I met also feel that by having a ceasefire we could gain time to prepare. The Home Minister has come to the same conclusion for he thinks there is nothing else one could do. Time must be gained, possibly a year. He has quoted Thimayya, the former Chief of the Army Staff, to say a year is needed, though some others say two years will be needed. Shastri also says that Thimayya is of the opinion that NEFA should have been defended by evacuating half of it and withdrawing to a position below the Sela Pass.

Shastri tells me that he is ready to talk to the various political leaders and persuade them to accept the ceasefire proposals. At least talks should be started, officers sent to Peking, while in the meantime 15 or 20 days can be gained till help from foreign countries arrives. He says he would mention this to the PM. About the positions on the McMahon Line under the Chinese proposals he is unhappy, but does not know what to do about Chushul, which will have to be evacuated when the withdrawal up to 20 kilometres (12.5 miles) is implemented. Malik, Director of Intelligence Bureau, explains that Daulet Beg Oldi will also be lost at some other police posts. And he has fears about Nepal, Bhutan and Sikkim. The State Governor, Vishnu Sahay, does not impress. He is still behaving like a State's Chief Secretary on the verge of retirement, happy to be left alone.

Two telegrams from abroad have been received. One is from Peking in which Bannerjee reports on the talks he has had with Chou En-lai. Chou is happy over Dr Radhakrishnan's speech in Poona that peace is better than war and the Prime Minister's remark that India wants to solve the problem peacefully. Chou says he is ready to fly to Delhi even though he knows he will not be welcomed as a friend. He has complained that his picture has been burnt in several Indian towns. He once again repeats the three-point proposal as well as the warning that China will not accept anything less even if the conflict were to become wider. His view is that there should be a withdrawal of 12.5 miles in the western and middle sectors, on the borders of UP and Himachal also, and, of course, the Chushul side. Chou has expressed the hope that the diplomatic ties will continue. It seems that they are probably fearing that India might break off diplomatic relations.

The other telegram from Indonesia says that Peking is anxious for President Sukarno to visit China and arrange some kind of Bandung Conference of non-aligned countries to intervene in the Sino-Indian dispute. China is anxious to have the non-aligned countries on her side because Nehru's letter to the heads of states has influenced them. China has mentioned that the British High Commissioner in South-East Asia, Malcolm McDonald, understands its point of view and has sent a long letter to 25 countries explaining its case.

## November 23, 1962

The Chinese ceasefire offer has raised many questions. A.P. Venkateshwaran, Deputy Secretary in the Indian Ministry of External Affairs, has approached Yin Shang-chih, First Secretary of the Chinese Embassy in Delhi, for clarification on three points:

1. Which is the line of actual control? The answer given is that the line is described in detail in the letter by Premier Chou En-lai to Prime Minister Nehru on November 4.
2. According to Peking's statement, Chinese frontier guards, after withdrawing 20 kilometres from the line of actual control would be far behind their positions prior to September 8. But even according to the so-called line of actual control claimed by Peking, Chinese troops, after withdrawing 20 kilometres, would still have crossed the line of September 8 at certain places.

   The answer is that in the eastern sector, China would withdraw its frontier guards in Tsayul and Le village; in the western district, many Chinese posts in Chip Chap Valley, Galwan River Valley, Kongka Pass, Pangong Lake and Spanggur Lake areas would be withdrawn.

3. What is the meaning of "possible eventualities" used by Peking in the statement? The Chinese official says—all the replies are given orally—that should the Indian side, taking advantage of the withdrawal by the Chinese side, again advance to the line of actual control or remain on it, this could not but mean that the Indian side's policy is one of deliberately maintaining border tensions, preparing for new intrusions at any moment and provoking clashes.

Meanwhile India has also received from Bannerjee, the Indian Chargé d'Affaires in Peking, the explanation given by Chou En-lai. In substance it is more or less what the Chinese Embassy in New Delhi has said.

There were still many points not clear to the Union Cabinet. Foreign Secretary M.J. Desai has been asked to get in touch with the Chinese Embassy in Delhi. The Chargé d'Affaires of the Embassy has insisted on Desai fixing an appointment with him and meeting him in the Chinese Embassy. Desai has done so but has asked for clarifications only orally.

Once again Desai has asked if the withdrawal of Chinese troops to positions 20 kilometres behind the line of actual control refers to the western sector only. The reply is that the withdrawal would be all along the Sino-Indian border, in the western, eastern and middle sectors. Then Desai has inquired if Chinese troops would pull back behind the positions of September 8, 1962. The Chinese Chargé d'Affaires says that after withdrawing, the Chinese frontier guards would be far behind their positions prior to September 8, 1962. China would, of course, continue to exercise administrative jurisdiction in the area.

One question which the Union Cabinet is carefully studying is where should Indian troops be in order not to provoke the Chinese? The Chinese Chargé d'Affaires says that if Indian troops should continue to attack Chinese frontier guards after their ceasefire and withdrawal, or again if Indian troops advance to the line of actual control or refuse to withdraw, "China reserves the right to strike back in self-defence".

The foreign envoys in Delhi, especially those from America, Britain and the UAR, are anxious to find out India's reaction. It is obvious to them that New Delhi is in no position to reject the ceasefire proposals put forth by Peking. What the western powers are interested to know is whether any negotiations would start between India and China, as is envisaged in the ceasefire proposals. They have been categorically told that India would never agree to talk to China unless it is willing to restore the September 8 positions.

Nehru has expressed his gratitude to countries like America, Britain and Canada for their support and has requested an early supply of defence equipment. The US and British military-cum-diplomatic missions are already in Delhi—Harriman from Washington and General Sir Richard Hull, Chief of the Imperial General Staff, from London. Some other senior British and US military officials are also in Delhi.

In fact, one senior US military official has been sitting in the Ministry of External Affairs. Since his arrival a few days ago, before the ceasefire, he had been wanting full information on the latest situation at the front. I hear that last week when he asked for some information about the fighting, he was told that it would take two to three days to get the details. His reported remark was: "Are you fighting a war or having a picnic?"

Both the US and British military missions have expressed their desire to see things for themselves in Assam and NEFA. Now they have the run of things to such an extent that no objection is raised about the representatives of foreign missions knowing the strength of the Indian Army at the different fronts and the type of weapons they are using.

One official of the Defence Ministry tells me that the USA wants to reorganize the entire intelligence service of India. Indeed the US intelligence service knows much more than ours about Chinese deployment on our borders. I have come to know that an attack by China was anticipated by the US intelligence service and Washington had informed New Delhi before October 20 about the approximate number of troops deployed by the Chinese on the Indian border.

## November 26, 1962

Nehru has received a letter from the most unexpected quarter. This is from President Ho Chi Minh of North Vietnam. He has described the Chinese ceasefire proposals as being "very reasonable and conducive to a peaceful settlement of the border question". There was an appeal made to Nehru not to interfere in any way with the implementation of the Chinese unilateral ceasefire proposals.

What has pained Nehru is that there is not a word about the Chinese occupation of extensive areas of Indian territory.

## November 28, 1962

The government does not show any sense of urgency except in top-level convening conferences and meetings. Shastri complains: "Really, nothing comes out of them."

One result of the half-baked proposals emerging from these meetings has been the arrest of Communists. Their detention is considered necessary because of the pro-China lobby working among them. But nobody in the Home Ministry, right from the Minister to Under-Secretary, saw the list of persons to be arrested. It turns out that the Director of Intelligence had supplied the list, and it was sent as it was to the States, which, although aware of the fact that some of the people listed were not pro-China, had to arrest them because it was the Centre's order.

The Prime Minister has written to the Home Minister that certain persons have been arrested mistakenly. Shastri himself feels that the mass arrests were a mistake. In his letter, the Prime Minister says that indiscriminate arrests would give India a bad name in Communist countries. This is true, and I find journalists from Communist countries talking critically about them.

I learn that when M.S. Namboodiripad was arrested, he was writing for *New Age,* the Communist weekly, an editorial criticising China on the ceasefire proposals. Dange was then leaving for Moscow to put across New

Delhi's point of view and to talk to the Communist representatives gathered there for a conference. He cancelled the trip as soon as he heard of the Communists' arrests and conveyed his decision to the Prime Minister. A few Communists met the Home Minister to press for the release of some of their colleagues. Shastri did not hide his embarrassment and gave them to understand that it would be done. Subsequently, at an informal conference of the Chief Ministers, Shastri admitted that the government had committed a big mistake in making indiscriminate arrests. This had alienated even those who had sympathized with India's point of view. A mass release, it was realized, would be equally embarrassing. Therefore, it was decided to release some Communists, one by one, so that it did not look like rectifying a mistake.

At the instance of Aruna Asaf Ali, Namboodiripad was given facilities like newspapers, more interviews, and so on. The Home Minister had a nagging conscience about E.M.S.'s arrest and felt that his imprisonment was the biggest mistake of all. K.D. Malviya, Union Minister, has written a letter to the Home Minister saying that the few Chief Ministers he had met had said that certain arrests were a mistake. The pressure has told on the government. Some Communists have been released. It has been decided to set E.M.S. free. Surprisingly, Renu Chakravarti, a Communist woman leader from West Bengal, gave Shastri the impression that she was not opposed to the detention of E.M.S.

Diplomatic activity has been in full swing. Indonesia's Foreign Minister, our Ambassador from Jakarta writes, has been approached by Chou En-lai to come to Peking, but he is reluctant to go until he knows that Delhi will back his visit. Soviet Deputy Foreign Minister Malik, in Moscow, has told our Ambassador that India should accept the ceasefire proposals. This time Russia does not say that the border is a legacy of imperialism and should be adjusted mutually.

This time we have been told that China seems anxious to make up with India. Malik says never before in history has a victor withdrawn of his own accord, and announced a unilateral ceasefire. When our Ambassador in Moscow, Kaul, insisted that China should at least accept the September 8, 1962 line, so that its aggression was proved, Malik said that what had been conceded was quite adequate. How could one expect an aggressor not only to vacate territory but also to admit aggression?

Kaul has also informed New Delhi that Russia has refused to send MiGs on the ground that it needs them for its own internal security and external needs. However, it has promised to set up a MiG factory and to give four helicopters and a few transport planes.

At one stage, there was a suggestion to refer the issue of the Chinese aggression to the UN, but New Delhi is not confident about the attitude of the non-aligned nations. The surmise of our permanent representative at the UN is that the Soviet Union, which has not taken sides in public, would tend to oppose the issue being raised in the world body. Were this to happen, the whole thing would become part of the Cold War. New Delhi also realizes that some of the Afro-Asian countries are not really non-aligned. They may embarrass New Delhi by passing some kind of resolution which would go against China but not help India. Thus the conflict might become wider.

I have seen the publicity guidance note sent by the Foreign Secretary to missions. The missions are to insist on the world accepting the September line, because on that day China had left the "way of peaceful negotiations" and switched over to a massive attack. Once again it is to be emphasized that India would not swerve from the path of non-alignment, even after the Chinese aggression. Whatever the merits of the note, the External Publicity Division is as usual locking the stable after the horse has been stolen.

The Home Minister, to whom I talked, says the situation is serious. He fears that hostilities might break out again. There would be further reverses, and in that eventuality, the present government would have to go. He thinks an American-dominated military government would then take over or probably the country would be split like Indo-China, with one half going to China or a government supported by them, and the other going to a government supported by others, possibly Americans.

I asked him about his talks with Duncan Sandys, the British representative, and Harriman, the US envoy-at-large. Shastri says that both Sandys and Harriman, especially the former, had wanted India to make up with Pakistan. But he had told Sandys that India wanted a solution, and an honourable one. When the

Home Minister asked Sandys to devise a solution, he was pleasantly surprised. According to the Home Minister, Sandys was so happy and "impressed" by his talks that he talked to Harriman, whereupon both sought an interview with Shastri. Both said that they found him more receptive and forthcoming than Nehru. Harriman said that India should make up with Pakistan and added that he was happy to see even the Indian press veering round to the same view after all. Sandys said that there was no question of handing over the valley; it meant only marginal changes.

However, Lady Jackson (Barbara Ward), who was in town, has the brain wave that Kashmir should be made independent, with the UN as its guardian. She has also conveyed her view, reportedly through Sandys, to the Government of India, that Ayub is hard-pressed and that if there were no gesture from the Indian side, extremists would take over in Pakistan.

## November 28, 1962

The UAR efforts—encouraged by India—to arrange a meeting of some non-aligned countries to discuss the Chinese ceasefire proposals, are beginning to pay off. Ceylon has agreed to initiate the proposal for a conference.* December 1 has been fixed as the date, but Cairo thinks it is too soon. Nasser wants first to see if the Chinese would fully implement their unilateral

* Mrs Bandaranaike selected five other countries—the UAR, Ghana, Indonesia, Burma and Cambodia—on the basis of their non-aligned policies and their acceptability by both New Delhi and Peking.

offer to withdraw troops in NEFA. Secondly, he wants Peking to indicate on a map its claim to the "actual line of control" and the positions its troops would withdraw to 20 kilometres back from this line.

The UAR also wants other participants* in the Colombo Conference to make behind-the-scenes efforts before assembling at Colombo.

New Delhi is organising a big team to go to Colombo to be in the wings when the six powers discuss the next step. India expects to retrieve part of the honour it lost in the battlefield. If world pressure could rub off the blot of the Suez debacle from the UAR's face, the Colombo Conference could do something similar for India.

## November 30, 1962

After the announcement of a unilateral ceasefire by the Chinese, Nehru had been expecting to hear from China practically every day. The much-awaited letter was delivered at the Ministry of External Affairs the night before. As usual, it was addressed as "Respected Mr Prime Minister".

Chou En-lai has expressed regret that Nehru had not written him after the ceasefire offer. There is the same old rigmarole about the line of actual control. Chou En-lai says:

> The line of actual control of November 7, 1959, had taken shape on the basis of the extent of administration by each side at the time; it existed objectively and cannot

---

* These six powers came to be known as "The inconsequential six".

> be defined or interpreted according to the free will of either side. In withdrawing 20 kilometres from this line, the armed forces of each side would be evacuating areas under its own administration; hence the question of one side achieving gains and the other suffering losses does not arise.

Chou En-lai has stressed that

> withdrawal by China alone of its frontier guards beyond 20 kilometres of its side of the 1959 line of actual control cannot ensure the disengagement of the armed forces of the two sides, nor can it prevent the recurrence of border clashes. On the contrary, in case the Indian side should refuse to cooperate, even the ceasefire which has been effected is liable to be upset. Therefore, the Chinese Government sincerely hopes that the Indian Government will take corresponding measures.

He has specifically proposed that the officials of the two countries should meet to discuss the withdrawal and the establishment of checkposts by each party. After the results of the meeting of officials had been put into effect, the Prime Ministers of the two countries should hold talks "to seek a friendly settlement of the Sino-Indian boundary question".

## December 1, 1962

Nehru is prompt in replying to the letter. His argument is that the boot is on the other foot. He says:

> What you call "the line of actual control as on November 7, 1959" in the western sector, was only a series of isolated military posts. You are aware that in November 1959 there were no Chinese posts of any kind either at

> Qiziljilga, Shinglung, Dehra, Samzangling or any areas to the west of these locations nor did the Chinese have any posts to the south or west of Spanggur. Despite this, "the line of actual control as on November 7, 1959", as your Government now claim in Ladakh, is along the line of control established by your forces after the massive attacks mounted since 20th October, 1962. This is a definite attempt to retain under cover of preliminary ceasefire arrangements, physical possession over the area which China claims, to secure which, the massive attack since 20th October, 1962, was mounted by your forces.

On the preparation front, there is nothing except the talks between India and the UK and the USA on the supply of arms. An agreement is signed between the British Commonwealth Secretaries, Sandys, and Chavan. India has given three assurances: (1) It will not transfer the arms and other equipment received from the UK to anyone else without British concurrence; (2) The UK High Commission's staff in New Delhi will have facilities to inspect arms and equipment supplied by the UK; (3) India will return to the British government arms and equipment no longer needed for the purpose for which they were supplied.

Harriman, leader of the US military-cum-diplomatic mission, is returning to America and has declared categorically at a press conference that the USA is not attaching any political condition in respect of Kashmir to its aid to India.

Both Sandys and Harriman have been formally

informed* that New Delhi has agreed to start discussions with Rawalpindi on "Kashmir and other related matters" so as to reach "an honourable and equitable settlement". First, Ministers would meet and then Nehru and Ayub.

For some time it has been felt that India's case has not been properly explained to the non-aligned countries. The unilateral ceasefire by China has given another boost to Peking's prestige. The ECC has decided to send Asoke Sen, Law Minister, to the UAR and certain other countries, and Mrs Lakshmi Menon, Minister of State for External Affairs, to South-East Asia.

## December 5, 1962

Mrs Lakshmi Menon has written from Indonesia that she has delivered the Prime Minister's and Patnaik's letters to President Sukarno and the Foreign Minister. While President Sukarno, she reports, is happy to get the letter and appreciates India's stand to some extent.

* On Novermber 29, Ayub and Nehru had issued a joint statement that a renewed effort should be made to resolve the outstanding differences between the two countries on Kashmir and other related matters. A day later, Ayub objected to some observations made by Nehru in the Lok Sabha, and said so to Duncan Sandys who was then in Karachi on his way to London. Sandys immediately returned to Delhi and requested Nehru to issue a clarification. The result was another Nehru statement on December 1: "There has never been any question of preconditions or of any restrictions on the scope of the talks which the two friends are initiating."

The Foreign Minister, Subandrio, is more reticent, and said he would reply to the Prime Minister directly.

The telegram sent by Mrs Lakshmi Menon says her visits to Cambodia and Ceylon were successful and these countries support the Prime Minister's stand as explained in his letter of November 14, 1962. She is not sure of Burma which, she says, is sympathetic but uncommitted. Some other source says that these countries have questioned Mrs Menon on the causes of a sudden collapse of the Indian Army. The Burmese leader, Ne Win, according to this source, feels that the Indian Army is probably too conventional a force to withstand any modern manoeuvres.

## December 6, 1962

Asoke Sen has told me on his return from Cairo that Nasser is 100 per cent behind India and has made a proposal* which had been, in fact, suggested to Cairo by New Delhi itself. Since New Delhi wants to remain in the background, Cairo has been asked to own and sponsor it. Azim Hussain, our ambassador to the UAR, has sent a telegram to emphasize that Cairo does not want the secret to leak out. The UAR is trying to arrange a meeting between the Ambassadors of India and China, without any publicity, so that the two could discuss some proposals face to face to find out which was most acceptable to both.

The UAR proposal is to create a demilitarized zone of 12.5 miles in Ladakh and the entire territory occupied

* This subsequently became the basis of the Colombo proposals.

by China since October 20, 1962. The telegram from Cairo says once again that it would need a lot of convincing to establish India's bonafides with other Afro-Asian countries if New Delhi were to reject the Chinese unilateral ceasefire proposals. Cairo says that as far as the UAR is concerned, it could appreciate India's stand, but other non-aligned countries are anxious to have a ceasefire and are impressed by China's dramatic offer followed by the withdrawal of its forces.

Sen says he found Nigeria also on India's side, but he is frank enough to admit that Ghana is not as enthusiastic about New Delhi's stand. He says Nkrumah did express regret over his first statement, which he said was hasty, and added that he had tried to make amends. Sen says it was at Nasser's request that he again stopped in Cairo while on his way to Delhi from Accra.

A telegram sent to Chakravarti, our representative at the UN, explains why the matter cannot be referred to the UN. The main snag seems to be the uncertain attitude of the Soviet Union, which might veto the resolution. A further argument is that either the situation would get frozen in the Cold War or hostilities would erupt to engulf the rest of the world. Interestingly, Chakravarti has not been sent the maps which he has been wanting badly. *The Survey of India* is still busy delineating the lines. He reports that not all the Afro-Asian countries are non-aligned—some are siding with China.

Vinoba Bhave has sent a letter to the Prime Minister to offer his support, but at the same time, he has emphasized the need to desist from resuming hostilities as far as possible. He suggests that the question of the "line of actual control" and where the two sides stood on November 7, 1959, could be settled through arbitration. He is ready to come by air or rail to Delhi if Nehru wants him.

An MP, Sudhir Ghosh, has informed the Prime Minister that the American Ambassador and the UK High Commissioner to India want India to make up with Pakistan because they would find it hard to approach their legislatures for any long and massive aid commitment to India without some rapprochement in the sub-continent. Also, they are not sure of India's long-term policy towards China and want New Delhi to define its overall strategy.

## December 7, 1962

Khrushchev, I am told, has written to the Prime Minister to protest politely against the joint statement of Ayub and Nehru. He is particularly unhappy about raking the subject of Kashmir every now and then. Khrushchev has reportedly informed Nehru that Pakistan has told Russia that it is willing to come out of SEATO and CENTO provided Moscow helps Rawalpindi on Kashmir.

India's High Commissioner to Pakistan, Parthasarathi, now in Delhi, is reported to have said that now is the best time to solve the Kashmir issue. All the officials he had met in Pakistan were certain that India and Pakistan could be friends if the Kashmir problem was solved. He reportedly said that a portion of the valley would have to be given up.

Shastri's* name is mentioned as the leader of the delegation for the talks with Pakistan, but he tells me that it will be Swaran Singh. Swaran Singh, who was finally chosen to head the team, was asked to talk sweetly to Pakistan and as long as it wanted to, but without conceding ground on fundamental issues. Marginal changes in the ceasefire were acceptable, but nothing beyond it.

A telegram received from Djakarta says that after Mrs Menon had explained to Subandrio what the Chinese meant by the withdrawal to the line of actual control of 1959 and what India's position was, he said New Delhi's stand was "reasonable and practical". He said, eventually, China might, with "certain compromises and modifications, leave India to delineate the actual line of control". According to Mrs Menon, between the actual line of control in 1959, as defined by India, and the actual positions on September 8, there would be enough gap to avoid a clash. If advisable, New Delhi has suggested that the patrolling of that gap by friendly neutral countries can be agreed to. Indonesia has asked for an expert team familiar with the border from India to be present in Colombo.

---

* Shastri later told me that during the Chinese attack the Shah of Iran had suggested to Ayub to offer Pakistani forces to India without tagging any condition. Shastri said that had Ayub done so, there would have been so much goodwill for Pakistan in India that people probably would not have considered even Kashmir a big price to pay in gratitude.

## December 9, 1962

A telegram from Peking says the Chinese are seeking to refute the statements made by Indian spokesmen on November 25, 26 and 27. Embassy assessment: The Chinese are worried that the world is realizing that India is the victim and China the aggressor; hence the urgency to "return" to the conference table. The Chinese will permit India to station civil police in checkposts outside the 20 km zone, but not on the border. Mrs Menon's statement in the Lok Sabha that Indian troops will move to the McMahon Line has upset them. The sudden closure of the Consulates-General at Lhasa and Shanghai and asking the Chinese to do the same in Bombay and Calcutta is considered unilateral on the part of India. The Chinese have protested strongly. They say that such an action of the Government of India can be taken only as "a calculated move to worsen relations between the two countries and impair the interests of the two peoples". It is alleged that the Chinese nationals in India are being subjected to all sorts of restrictions and persecutions in contravention of accepted international practice. The Chinese have said it is the government which is pursuing an anti-China policy, not the people of India.

The UAR has informed our team in Colombo, where the conference begins tomorrow, that the Chinese will agree to set up only the minimum number of civilian posts in the area held by them. Nasser and the Chinese Deputy Foreign Minister had discussed this a few days ago in Cairo.

New Delhi is not too confident about the attitude of Prince Norodom Sihanouk from Cambodia. He is against putting forward any concrete suggestion aimed at solving the problem, which, according to him, "is exclusively a Sino-Indian matter". All that the conference should do is to induce India and China to meet to discuss the frontier dispute. How could India do so when China was occupying such a large track of land illegally?

## December 10, 1962

On the eve of the Colombo conference, the Chinese spokesman has issued a 5,000-word statement which New Delhi has described as "an unveiled threat to the effect that peaceful negotiations can be reopened only on the basis of terms dictated by China".

The Chinese Ministry of Foreign Affairs has sent to New Delhi the text of the same broadcast as a memorandum. The three questions posed are: whether the Indian government agrees to a ceasefire; to the disengagement of the armed forces on the two sides drawing back 20 kilometres each from the November 7, 1959 "the line of actual control"; and to a meeting of the two sides to discuss matters relating to withdrawal by both sides to form a demilitarized zone, the establishment of checkposts and the return of captured personnel.

Peking has also announced that Chinese troops, which began withdrawing soon after the unilateral ceasefire, will "withdraw still further".

At the Colombo conference, which has begun from today, the Indian team is in close touch with Ali Sabri and other members of the UAR delegation; the rest of the powers are secretive. Sabri has had talks with Subandrio. Contrary to the assurance given to Lakshmi Menon, Indonesia wishes to propose Indian withdrawal by 20 km behind the September 8 line and the Chinese withdrawal behind their claimed line of 1960. India has already conveyed that the proposal is not acceptable. Subandrio has said that in case India is not agreeable to the proposal, the UAR should take the initiative. India has, however, pointed out that the Indonesian proposal does not result in disengagement but in entanglement.

The UAR proposal is somewhat different from the one discussed with Nasser. Sabri has said that since the restoration of the *status quo* as on September 8 is not acceptable to China, the alternative can be that if it returns to the line of September 8, the posts between that line and the Chinese claimed line of 1960 should be converted into civil posts. India has pointed out that both Chinese and Indian posts were in that area; the withdrawal of forces should be behind those posts. Otherwise the new proposal would be disadvantageous to India, because only the Indian posts between the two lines would be converted into civil. New Delhi has said that it would accept the proposal if the Chinese posts are also converted into civil. Ali Sabri has said that he would try but he has added in the same breath that others in the conference do not seem willing to go even as far as him. Burma is not prepared to commit itself to the proposal. Cambodia and Ceylon are equally undecided. China seems anxious to spin out the discussion and have another conference at Accra. In any case, Ghana has nothing to fear even after talking irrelevance because no record of the talks is being kept and even shorthand reporters have been excluded.

The Governor of Assam has informed the Foreign Secretary that the Chinese are evacuating Bomdi La. New Delhi's instructions are that only the police should go there. Neither the army nor the Assam Rifles is to move up there or other areas vacated by the Chinese till further instructions.

## December 11, 1962

In Colombo, the UAR is trying to be helpful, while Burma is keeping in line with Chinese demands as far as possible. The two countries put forth their peace proposals.

UAR proposal: In Ladakh, Indians are to stay on the Chinese 1960 claim line and the Chinese on their September 8 line. The intervening area is to be demilitarized. In other words, the old Indian military posts are to become civil posts. In NEFA, Indians should go back to the McMahon Line. Except in Longju and in the disputed area south of the Thag La ridge, the Indian military posts are to become civil posts. All nations agree to this except Burma, on the plea that the UAR proposals are too near India's proposals and they had been rejected by China.

Even though Ne Win has returned to Rangoon, Burma has also put up a proposal: In Ladakh, Indians are to stay on the Chinese 1960 claim line and the Chinese are to withdraw 20 kilometres to the east of this line; the intervening area is to be demilitarized. There is no proposal on NEFA, and this means Burma accepts the UAR proposition on that, but not in Ladakh. All delegations except the UAR have accepted this.

Ali Sabri has contacted India to ascertain its reaction. He is told that disengagement could be considered on the basis of the September 8 positions, which must be fully restored. It has been made clear that India attaches great importance to the restoration of the pre-8th September *status quo,* which is its minimum requirement.

New Delhi has received a protest from China about air violation. That was considered an effort to find a pretext to upset the ceasefire should India officially intimate non-acceptance of China's proposal. The Chinese appear to have taken for granted that the crossing of their so-called 1959 line of control constituted a violation of their terms of ceasefire—a warning to the Colombo conference that if the Chinese proposal did not find support, China would depend on her military strength.

Meanwhile, India was preparing. Nehru to MacMillan: "Dear Friend, apart from the immediate situation facing us, the Chinese menace is a continuing affair, and we have to prepare ourselves adequately. I understand a financial ceiling within which the supplies are to be made has to be agreed between the two countries. Hope this ceiling will be a generous one and cover our requirements fully. Indo-Pakistan differences, particularly over Kashmir, have a long and complicated history and none of us can expect quick results. It will require infinite patience and considerable goodwill on both sides to evolve a line of settlement of our differences without causing serious dislocation in the life of the two countries and without prejudicing our defence efforts against the continuing Chinese aggression. I hope all concerned will exercise restraint and patience as the discussions are bound to be long and arduous."

## December 12,1952

Tripathi, the Assam minister, has written to the Prime Minister and has sent a copy of the letter to the Home Minister. He says that the evacuation of Tezpur was done under the Home Ministry's instructions. Therefore, the Centre must defend the State Administration unequivocally; otherwise there would be a lot of demoralization. He has also blamed the military authorities.

An earlier wireless message from the Assam Chief Minister said that criticism of the faulty evacuation of Tezpur by the Prime Minister and the Home Minister was not fully justified because all that the state did was at the instance of the Home Ministry. The instructions it issued on November 17, 1962, ran to a page and a half. They bore the signature of L.P. Singh, Additional Home Secretary. According to Chaliha, the instructions said that the overall evacuation of the threatened area of Tezpur should not be encouraged but young persons should be removed lest they be indoctrinated by the enemy. Currency, secret papers, petrol pumps, the power-house, etc., should be destroyed before moving out. A skeleton civil staff should work till the end and then withdraw. Wives and children of government servants should be evacuated. Technical persons should be moved for use elsewhere. Not much food stock should be left behind.

The Assam government explained that it had acted accordingly.

Currency was destroyed along with official papers. Prisoners were released, as Tripathi's letter explained, to make room for Chinese prisoners (only one prisoner had been captured!). Foodgrains were distributed among the cooperative stores so that the bulk should not fall into Chinese hands. The Deputy Commissioner had not run away from duty as the new Deputy Commissioner was at his post when the former left. Tripathi also gave a chronological description of what happened from the 19th to the 21st before the ceasefire took place. On the 19th night, he and Fakhruddin Ali Ahmed, accompanied by energetic K.D.N. Singh, the Deputy Commissioner, reached Tezpur at 11 o'clock. By that time, the Corps Commander, Lt General Kaul, had gone to sleep. Brig. Verma met them and painted a gloomy picture. The next morning at 8 they met General Kaul and General Sen, who said that things were very bad. Chacko, a place near the foothills, had fallen into Chinese hands with its trucks, jeeps and ammunition, after Bomdi La. The Chinese were advancing 20 miles a day. They were moving faster and in another two hours from then, they would be at the foothills. Kaul was expecting an air raid on Tezpur or an airdrop of paratroopers to end resistance at Missamari, where Sen said Indian troops had been asked to make a stand. They were also told that Corps headquarters would be moved from Tezpur to Gauhati.

An interesting point made by Tripathi in his letter is that in future, arrangements should be made to evacuate ministers safely so that they do not fall into enemy hands. From the morale point of view, this is important, Tripathi has argued. The slogan that everyone must stick to one's post should not be applicable to the ministers because their capture would give the enemy a good propaganda plank as well as cast a slur on the nation. Tripathi has also said that the war could be fought through non-violence. His idea is to start some kind of satyagraha or boycott to get the occupied territory vacated.

## December 13, 1962

New Delhi is unhappy at the outcome of the Colombo conference. The communique the conference has issued says that "their efforts in seeking to bring about negotiations between India and the People's Republic of China should not end with the present meetings in Colombo, but should continue. There can be no final decision until the final settlement of the problem could be negotiated between the Governments of India and the People's Republic of China". The net result is that *de facto* ceasefire has become *de jure*. Nehru thinks Burma and Indonesia have let India down. What has surprised him is that such an obvious case of aggression had neither evoked solid support for India nor a straight condemnation of China. The aggressor and the victim have been put on par. Nehru has come to believe that after all it is the strength of a country which ultimately decides its status or say. Therefore, his mind is working towards training as many people as possible to handle arms.

The Colombo proposals reportedly embody two general principles: One, nowhere will Indian troops be required to make any further withdrawals; two, the McMahon Line will be more or less the ceasefire line in the east. Thanks for these mercies!

In the Ladakh sector, the Chinese will be asked to withdraw 20 kilometres from their 1959 claim line, that is, the present line of control, which at some points will take them back beyond the September 8 line. The zone of disengagement so created will be demilitarized under joint civilian control.

In the central sector, there will be more or less no change.

In NEFA, the Indian Army may advance to the McMahon Line. But this will not give them the right to occupy Dhola or Longju; these posts are to be subject to negotiations. No recommendation has been made for the area around Walong.

Mrs Bandaranaike will visit Peking and Delhi to press for the acceptance of the proposals. It is strange that the Colombo Conference participants expect India to say "yes" because, as one of the members put it, India as a leading Afro-Asian non-aligned country owes it to Afro-Asian countries to accept their recommendations. Yes, it must offer its head to maintain the honour of its friends.

## December 15, 1962

The Prime Minister is reported to have admonished Kaul when he met him after the General had relinquished charge at Tezpur. Nehru's remark is said to have been that he would rather have seen him dead than return as a defeated General. Another rumour afloat is that an inquiry against Kaul is in progress. That is probably not correct. Two brigadiers have been demoted to the ranks of Lt-Col and Major. These officers had been asked to engage the Chinese that tried to outflank Bomdi La; they had 8,000 *jawans* with them but they just did not fight. The Chinese were not more than 3,000. It is said that had they fought, the history of Se La would have been different.

One complaint that Kaul is said to have made is that General Chaudhuri had gone all the way to Tezpur to ensure that Lt General Kaul handed over charge there. Before General Chaudhuri left, the Prime Minister had reportedly told him that he should use persuasion to get General Kaul to hand over charge. Chaudhuri is said to have replied that "persuasion" was not a word used in the Army. "If he disobeys, I shall court martial him," Chaudhuri is reported to have said.

Kaul has also written a letter asking for permission to retire and the reason given was that in the best traditions of the Army, a general should retire if he loses the confidence of his Chief and of the Army. It is said that General Chaudhuri wanted him to go to Jullundur first—where there was no corps to command—and then ask for retirement. Apparently Nehru has intervened and saved Kaul from this humiliation.

Khrushchev's statement warmly welcoming the Chinese ceasefire proposals has not been liked. He had said that there would be people who characterized the Chinese troop withdrawals as a sign of weakness but the Soviet Union hoped that the Chinese and Indian leaders would not be taken in by such provocations and would resort to common sense in settling their differences. According to him, by accepting Western arms and waging war, India would be putting its neck in the imperialist noose and losing its freedom. Mrs Indira Gandhi has mentioned at a number of places that her father is very unhappy over this statement. New Delhi has written to Moscow requesting ground-to-air missiles and Ilyushins.

The Prime Minister is also not happy over Nepal's attitude.

He had written a two-page letter to the King of Nepal. He said that differences among the countries was a normal thing but India had never liked violence to settle them; it was against India's philosophy. Referring to China's aggression Nehru said that a chauvinistic and expansionist China was a threat to the whole of South-East Asia. He expressed the hope that India and Nepal would continue to march together.

The Nepal King's reply was terse, short and curt. He said he was glad that the raids on Nepal "from shelters in India" had stopped, adding, "which you (Nehru) have brought about". Henceforward, the King added, everything would be all right. There was no mention of the Chinese aggression in the letter.

## December 20, 1962

The Indo-Pak talks have started in Rawalpindi. The briefing given to the Indian delegation was that the talks should be continued, not broken. The strategy was to start from the point where President Ayub and Prime Minister Nehru left off in 1960. While there was no hesitation in discussing Kashmir, India wanted to cover other subjects like illegal immigration of Pakistani Muslims into Assam, and evacuee property. The delegation was specifically told not to accept the demand for a plebiscite in Kashmir.

Bhutto, Pakistan's delegate, began the talks with the UNICEF resolution and demand for a plebiscite. Swaran Singh, from the Indian side, spoke of the difficulties in taking such a course. He said that India was a secular state and had therefore to guard against communal riots which might break out once plebiscite supporters were allowed to have a free hand. He argued that a plebiscite would inevitably lead to an appeal in the name of Islam, and this was not acceptable to secular India. Bhutto at one stage, conceded that probably a plebiscite would not be possible, and that some other solution be sought. The Indian side deduced that what he meant was some kind of partition, although he was reluctant to put that in so many words.

The announcement of Pakistan's accord with China on the Sinkiang border was made on the day the Indian delegation reached Karachi. Swaran Singh, without consulting Delhi, decided not to back out of the negotiations on that account, although he said during the talks that the announcement was surprising as well as regrettable. The Ambassadors of America and Britain, who met Swaran Singh later, congratulated him on his restraint.

Within five minutes of the beginning of the conference, there was an urgent message from President Ayub that the heads of the two delegations should meet him. He was apologetic and told Swaran Singh that the timing for the announcement of the Pakistan–China agreement on the border was not in any way intentional. He explained that he had given some broad instructions to his Ambassador in Peking. He thought it would take some time for China to indicate its reaction, but instead it offered such liberal terms and conceded all Pakistan's points that the Ambassador had no choice but to accept it there and then.

President Ayub said that India and Pakistan were dissipating their energies over the Kashmir dispute; in fact, the sub-continent could put its resources to better use. In the conference, Swaran Singh repeated the observation by President Ayub. Bhutto also expressed the same sentiments, but he insisted on taking up Kashmir first; India did not object. Among other problems for discussion, the Farakka barrage was also added.

After the opening meeting, Bhutto said that Pakistan was at first sceptical but now believed that India was sincere and earnest about finding a solution to Kashmir. The starting points were the McNaughton proposals, the Mohammed Ali–Nehru meeting and so on. The first round of talks ended on a note of optimism. India wanted the second meeting to be held in Delhi towards the end of January. But Pakistan wanted a later date. The reason reportedly was that Pakistan wanted America and Britain to take an interest in the talks and to give their own proposals on Kashmir. Incidentally, the Ambassadors of the USA and the UK stayed in the building where Swaran Singh and Bhutto were until the talks concluded.

Before the Indian delegation returned, I found out from the Home Minister that the strategy was to take the talks to the third round without conceding anything. The breakdown should not be in Delhi, he added.

## December 21,1962

A significant statement has been made by the US Information Service in Delhi. It says: "India's only supply route to Ladakh, where so much is at stake, runs out of the vale of Kashmir. The old fortress city of Srinagar is a major supply base. For India, the fertile vale is the lifeline to Communist-threatened Ladakh."

The statement, however, points out Pakistan also had strong traditional economic, legal and religious ties with the valley and possessed "the rugged western approaches" to it. "Thus any settlement of the Kashmir issue as a whole involves an agreement on access to the valley."*

The word "access" has not been defined. But New Delhi is clear that America wants Ladakh to be defended by India with a guaranteed passage through the valley.

---

* Coincidentally, Sheikh Abdullah and Mirza Afzal Beg, after their release in 1968, argued with me on the same lines and said that the border should be "soft" so that Pakistan had an easy access to the valley. Of course, their argument was that the trade requirements necessitated such an arrangement.

As regards the valley, the USA probably wants to go to Pakistan. Of course, officially the USA has made it clear that the initiative for a settlement lay with India and Pakistan and that the USA would not "seek to impose a viewpoint".

## December 29, 1962

I hear that when Bomdi La fell, the President reportedly suggested to the Prime Minister that since Parliament would be increasingly critical of the government in the days to come, it should be suspended. The cabinet could then become an advisory committee to the President with the Prime Minister as the chief adviser. One source says that the President did not make the suggestion himself; it had come through T.T. Krishnamachari, former Union Minister.

The inquiry* into the military reverses and reasons for India's unpreparedness is progressing, with Lt-General Henderson Brooks as the chief inquiry officer. It is said that he found more and more fault with the politicians and some blame was laid on Krishna Menon for "having interfered" too much. Lt General Kaul has put in his explanation. General Chaudhuri has reportedly referred to a graphic field despatch from Kaul which said that bullets were passing to the left of him and bullets were passing to the right of him, and he was on a high ridge, overlooking the rival positions. He reportedly ended the despatch by saying that the situation was desperate and two divisions were required immediately. He was Chief of the General Staff

---

* See Annexure II.

before he became Corps Commandant and knew that India had no more divisions to spare; the two divisions, he pleaded, must be obtained from somewhere, even from a foreign country.

The rumour about Kaul is that he might be posted abroad. He is reportedly meeting Mrs Gandhi often. In fact, she had stayed with him when she visited Tezpur after the ceasefire, and this was objected to by some MPs.

As regards Krishna Menon, the Prime Minister's reported remark that he might join the cabinet again puts life in him and his men, who are saying that he would be in the cabinet much sooner than anybody expects. Nehru is said to have hinted as much to him, according to persons close to Menon. Menon himself is reported to have told Kamaraj that he would be joining the cabinet soon. Shastri has not liked the remarks of the Prime Minister about Menon. He says that the Prime Minister wants to reply to every question a newspaperman puts to him or a Member of Parliament asks. "This often lands us in trouble." He says that if Nehru were to give even one-fourth of the time he devotes to foreign journalists to Indians, the cooperation of the masses would be much better. The Home Minister thinks that the Prime Minister cannot bring back Menon into the cabinet during the term of the present Parliament without endangering his own reputation.

A letter dated 24th December has been received from MacMillan. It is in reply to Nehru's. MacMillan thanks Nehru for the courtesy shown to Sandys and the frank talk Nehru had with him. MacMillan says he has had discussions with Kennedy on India's long-term military needs and the setting up of armament factories. The plans, he says, are being processed partly by American and partly by British military officials. The short-term programme of equipping the Indian Army and finding the armaments it lost in Se La is under way. For the long term, the formula agreed to, he says, is that America and the Commonwealth will share the cost equally. As regards the threat of air raids on civilians and cities, MacMillan says that if Nehru agrees, a joint air mission of American and British officials could visit Delhi to study problems and hold discussions with Indian Air Force personnel.

MacMillan also touches on Kashmir in his letter. He says he and Kennedy both feel that an agreement with Pakistan on Kashmir and other outstanding issues would be good for the sub-continent. A breakdown of talks, he fears, would dampen the enthusiasm of the people in the two countries, America and Britain, because they would have to bear more burdens. They might say India could very easily pull back its forces from the Pakistani front to fight the Chinese. MacMillan also says the talks should not be prolonged, because then the public would lose patience. The British Prime Minister suggests that if Nehru prefers it, the UK is ready to show more active interest because in any case, it would be following the talks closely. He hopes Nehru will keep him informed about the progress of the talks.

A report coming from Kaul, India's Ambassador in Moscow, says he has met Soviet Defence Minister

Malinovsky. Kaul reports having been told that the plan to set up a MiG factory in India has been cleared "knowing how China had committed aggression after aggression in the past". Russia could not, however, spare the latest helicopters because it needed some 4,000 of them itself to lessen its reliance on road and railway transport. At one time during the conversation, the Ambassador used the word "reactionary". The Soviet Defence Minister asked: "You mean the KMT?" Kaul replied: "No, the Chinese." The Defence Minister laughed and seemed to like the remark. According to Kaul, the unconfirmed report in Moscow is that China stopped its advance into India because Russia threatened to cut off its petrol supply. Kaul says the Defence Minister told him that Khrushchev held Nehru in high regard.

Law Minister Asoke Sen tells me that India will accept the Colombo conference proposals. It may seek clarifications, but it will accept them. I hear that T.T.K. and Desai want to go abroad to explain India's case as well as to purchase military supplies for India.

Shastri has told a conference of Chief Ministers that civil defence should go slow in regard to digging of trenches and the blackout. He says that the digging of trenches in Delhi would stop. In any case the trenches dug are not of the proper dimensions. At the conference, Pratap Singh Kairon, the Chief Minister of Punjab, has described in detail how his State would defend itself if Pakistan invades it. He has said that he is having border roads built and trees planted for any future eventuality.

He says it is possible that India may have to pull back to the Beas, but the real fight would be near Panipat, where the tide would be turned. He does not mind what the Centre does about civil defence in other states, but he does not want it to be stopped in his state. The Home Minister has agreed with him and has jocularly drawn the attention of the Assam Chief Minister to the way the chief ministers of other border states are preparing the defence of their areas.

## January 1, 1953

The government is ready to refer the border issue to the International Court of Justice at The Hague if Peking will agree to accept the verdict. Nehru, who made this offer some time ago, has reiterated it to Chou En-lai in a letter.

Two days earlier, Chou En-lai had written to take "note of the fact that the Indian Government has stated that it will not impede the implementation of the ceasefire by China, that it is in favour of the principles of disentanglement of the armed forces of the two States and that it is not opposed to the holding of meetings of the officials of the two States." However, Nehru is opposed to the meeting of officials until China has agreed to restore the *status quo* prevailing on September 8, 1962. Nehru says in his letter*: "That we should have to come into military conflict with our neighbour China, with whom we have sought to develop friendly relations, has caused us great pain. We would certainly

---

* This was Nehru's last letter to the Chinese Prime Minister.

like to find peaceful solutions of any differences that we might have about our frontiers or about anything else."

Nehru and his colleagues are awaiting the visit of the Ceylonese Prime Minister, Mrs Bandaranaike, to discuss the Colombo proposals. New Delhi, which was constantly kept in the picture when the Colombo proposals were finalized, does not seem to have any choice except to accept them. But it is quite clear that India will not sit with Peking's representatives across the same table until China accepts the Colombo proposals *in toto*, a phrase which Nehru has started using and other ministers repeating.

## January 4, 1963

Ambassador Kaul has had a long talk with the Soviet Defence Minister at the Burmese National Day reception. The Soviet Defence Minister said: "We accept the principle that each side should revert to the positions before hostilities started but we are not convinced that September 8 is the relevant date. We do not wish to go into details and the merits or demerits of either side, but would ask you to accept that it is only a border dispute and China has no intention of invading India. Military hotheads may have gone too far but China's unilateral withdrawal was a political decision and showed China's willingness for a peaceful settlement."

Kaul told him that the Soviet government should persuade China to accept the principle of restoring the *status quo ante* hostilities. Once the principle was accepted by China it would be possible for India to talk. But it could not accept any decision unless that principle is accepted and implemented by China. The Soviet Defence Minister shrugged his shoulders and said:

"We are willing to welcome your Foreign Secretary-General. We hope Mrs Bandaranaike will be able to bring both sides together. We welcome the initiative of the Colombo conference." He repeated, "We are convinced China wants a peaceful settlement otherwise we would not say so."

The UAR Ambassador in New Delhi has suggested that India should now accept the proposals, after making suitable reservations. This acceptance, he said, was necessary in India's own interest to enable it to gain time to strengthen its military positions and regain its political prestige. It could later, if necessary, withdraw from negotiations and take military action.

He said that the proposals of the Chinese withdrawal in the western sector to 20 kilometres from that of the November 7, 1959 line, and demilitarization of the area in between, was better for India than that of September 8 line in the eastern sector. Indians should know that once negotiations begin, the Chinese would be prepared for any concession elsewhere in order to gain Aksai Chin, which China wants as a testing ground for nuclear weapons in the context of a nuclear research programme in Sinkiang which they are launching with the help of Chinese scientists returned from the USA and other countries.

## January 14, 1963

Asoke Sen tells me that India has accepted the Colombo proposals, though officially it is being said that the government's "final response" to them will be available after Parliament has considered it on January 21. Whatever information has been picked up on the Congress Party's reaction indicates that the vocal section is opposed to the acceptance of the proposals in their present form. It seems the government will have to disclose the clarification that Mrs Bandaranaike offered during her recent talks in Delhi.

According to the clarification, India is entitled to revert to her military control in NEFA right up to the McMahon Line. Exception is, however, made in respect to two areas in the eastern sector. They are Thagla Ridge and Longju. The control of these two areas is to be settled through negotiations between India and China.

By the Thagla Ridge area, the Colombo conference means the narrow strip between the Ridge and the Namkachu river. According to Indian maps, the McMahon Line runs along the Ridge.

As regards the western sector, the Indian military posts may be re-established up to the border of the demilitarized zone proposed to be created through the Chinese withdrawal.

The Chinese are called upon to withdraw 20 km in Ladakh from their line of actual control as on November 7, 1959. This is taken as an indirect confirmation of the Indian allegation that what Peking calls the November 7 line is in reality the same as the line of control that the Chinese established as a result of their massive aggression since October 20, 1962.

The setting up of posts in the territory vacated by China has been the main hitch in the acceptance of the

Colombo proposals. In NEFA, the Chinese have laid down that Indian forces should not occupy the area they had vacated. Delhi has totally accepted it, and has issued instructions to the Governor of Assam to ensure that no Indian force goes there. The cabinet was, however, divided on this, and T.T.K. had reportedly opposed this. The Cabinet also discussed that NEFA be merged with Assam and that people, particularly ex-Servicemen, be settled there. The latter proposal was accepted.

Meanwhile, the activity of the hostile Nagas has increased. The Assam governor has informed New Delhi that the withdrawal of forces from Nagaland for operations elsewhere has created a vacuum and has made the hostiles bold. They are killing people and destroying property.

## January 18, 1963

On his arrival in Delhi, Bhutto met Shastri. Shastri told him that he considered the talks with Pakistan more important than those with China. This might be because he is Home Minister and has to look more within than without. Shastri requested Bhutto not to allow the Indo-Pakistan talks to break down. Bhutto agreed with him but added that something tangible should be achieved, something concrete. The Pakistan High Commissioner, present at the meeting, complained that the pace of the talks was very slow. But he added that he would rather see slow progress than a breakdown. Shastri said he was looking forward to the outcome of the third round in Pakistan. He said, "You have to carry the people with you in your country, and we in ours." It was a difficult problem. Bhutto told Shastri a story circulating in Pakistan, that left to Shastri, he would have a settlement with Pakistan in no time. Saying this, Bhutto added that the purpose was not to in any way embarrass the Home Minister.

Shastri told me that when he, Swaran Singh and Foreign Secretary Gundevia talked to Nehru, he was firmly against making any concession to Pakistan. The Prime Minister was not accepting anything beyond a minor adjustment to the ceasefire line. However, Shastri attached great importance to a rapprochement with Pakistan.

At a meeting with the editor of a paper in Delhi, Bhutto said Pakistan must have some portion of the valley; otherwise it would be difficult to win over public opinion in Pakistan. Spelling out his scheme, Bhutto reportedly said that Pakistan would like to have Srinagar but would give Pahalgam to India and the way to Ladakh for defence purposes. The editor's impression was that Pakistan might also agree to give Baramula to India.

During the Indo-Pakistan talks, a map was prepared by the Indus Water Commission showing the line along Rajouri, Poonch and Akhnur. This line was reportedly drawn at the instance of Delhi.

It seems as if India is willing to go to the extent of making the watershed of Srinagar and the hills around as the dividing line. Pakistan, it is said, wants Chhamb as the dividing line.

## January 23, 1963

A telegram has been received this morning from the Ceylonese Prime Minister, Mrs Bandaranaike, that the Chinese have not fully accepted the proposals and the clarification given by the Colombo conference leaders in Delhi recently. However, she says that Chou En-lai has informed her that China has accepted the proposals "in principle".

Nehru's inference is that China has not accepted the Colombo plan. He had told the Colombo conference leaders when they were in Delhi that any acceptance in part would mean rejection as a whole. The reaction of Peking as indicated by Mrs Bandaranaike should naturally mean that China has rejected the proposals.

China is still maintaining that no Indian post should be set up in the demilitarized zone in Ladakh, nor does it agree to joint control.

New Delhi may not be in a position to establish the posts at this time but it can at least declare that it will not accept any change in the proposals, nor will it sit with China across the same table until it accepts the proposals *in toto.* And this is what Nehru has made the plank of his future policy.

## February 11, 1963

Colombo's reaction, received through our High Commission, is not very encouraging. One report says that Felix Bandaranaike, Ceylon's minister without portfolio, might be visiting China soon to give his interpretation of the Colombo conference proposals. He told the High Commissioner that things would be easier if he were allowed to convey Prime Minister Nehru's assurance that India would not take its troops right up to the McMahon Line even though the Colombo proposals allowed this.

Shastri has told me that in principle, India has been allowed to take its forces up to the Dhola post. But the Colombo conference representatives had said in Delhi that though India had the right, China would like to talk about it. If New Delhi were to give an undertaking that it would not exercise that right, Felix Bandaranaike felt that it would facilitate matters. He said that China had accepted the proposals in principle but had started thinking afresh noticing that the Indian press was supporting them unreservedly. He said that the volte face of the Indian press was interesting. He asked why India and its leaders were talking of "preparedness" all the time. This only made China angry.

Czechoslovakia is being approached for the supply of rifles, following France's curt rejection of Nehru's request not to insist on cash payment. B.K. Nehru has reported from Washington that there is no prospect of getting additional military assistance till there is a solution on Kashmir. The State Department now plainly says that it is not possible to get Congress approval. Meanwhile, there is only a trickle of economic aid coming in.

Marshal Tito has sent a letter to Nehru pointing out that the Russians and Chinese are going further apart, and that more would be heard on the subject as the days go by. He appreciates India's point of view and thinks India has done well in accepting the Colombo proposals. He says he would be writing to non-aligned countries asking them to support the proposals.

## February 16, 1963

Bannerjee, our Chargé d'Affaires, has called on Prince Sihanouk in Peking. The Prince has told him that he had had many hours of discussion on the Sino-Indian border with Chou En-lai, who, he said, still insisted mainly on one point, namely, the setting up of posts in the demilitarized zone in the western sector. Chou En-lai had called the eastern sector a point for negotiation. He had said he now understood that the Colombo powers had in mind only a stop-gap arrangement, not a settlement. The Cambodian Prince said that some participants to the Colombo conference had given some clarifications regarding the conference proposals. Chou En-lai was not happy over the clarifications. The Prince has said it was for the two countries, to accept them; the Colombo powers could not set themselves up as judges or arbitrators. They had to leave it to India and China to settle things between themselves through talks. He has said that representatives of the two countries can go to the negotiating table with their own interpretations. This is contrary to the views expressed by the representatives of the Colombo powers in New Delhi.

The Colombo powers were still waiting for the Chinese prime minister to write to them to clarify his stand, after which they should either meet again or have further correspondence among themselves on what further steps to take. Prince Sihanouk said that this was a slow process and would naturally take up an enormous amount of time. He had proposed that the leaders of Asian countries should meet periodically, not with the spotlight of publicity on them as was the case at the

Bandung conference, but privately, to discuss common problems. The Prince praised India for having accepted the Colombo powers' proposals *in toto*, and China for having declared a unilateral ceasefire and withdrawal. He emphasized that it was necessary for Cambodia to be strictly neutral over the Sino-Indian border question if she was to be of any use in finding a settlement.

The Russian Ambassador in Jakarta, Mikhailov, told our Ambassador in Indonesia that Russia was not at all optimistic about proposals for Sino-Indian talks on the border question. Russia did not expect any solution of the problem so long as both India and China considered Aksai Chin as their own territory. The Indonesian Foreign Minister, Subandrio, was, however, optimistic, but he conceded that there would be no solution for a long time to come.

Dr Belber, the Yugoslav Ambassador to Indonesia, has reported that at a secret meeting of east European Ambassadors to analyse the world situation, Mikhailov had said that Russia feared China might again pursue its "adventurist" policy and launch an offensive against India in April or May, and after such an offensive, follow the same tactics of advance and withdrawal to force India to come to the conference table on her own terms. Most probably, Liu Shaochi would visit Indonesia in May. The visit would coincide with such moves. Sikkim and Bhutan might also be attacked by China to put pressure on India.

## February 17, 1963

Our Ambassador in Cairo, Azim Hussain, has written that the Foreign Minister, Ali Sabri, has intimated that after the meeting of some Colombo conference participants in Delhi, a telegram was sent by Mrs Bandaranaike to Chou En-lai asking China to accept the Colombo proposals in the same way as India had done. Up to now, no reply has been received. Instead, he (Sabri) has been invited to Peking. He is willing to go but has asked if China accepts the Colombo proposals in the light of the clarifications given.

Peking's silence appeared deliberate. From this, President Nasser and Sabri have deduced that, contrary to their earlier impression, the Chinese do not care for the Colombo proposals, or indeed, any negotiations. Having achieved their objective in humbling India, the Chinese seem satisfied with the present situation which keeps the position fluid and leaves the initiative in their hands. Azim Hussain has reported that Nasser and Sabri have said the Chinese leaders are making confusing statements about India, accusing it of not having accepted the proposals and of not wishing a peaceful settlement and so on.

The UAR is not happy about this and feels the stage has been reached when the Colombo powers should clarify the correct position, asking the Chinese to accept the proposals in full or to let it be known to the world that they have rejected them. Cairo is considering two alternatives: First, it is thinking of an appeal to the Chinese to accept the proposals, with clarifications, *in toto*. This appeal would be made publicly, so as to put the onus squarely on the Chinese, and to remove the impression of any of the Colombo powers having different views.

Sabri is not sure if all the six powers will agree to this proposal. Alternatively, since the six had entrusted Mrs Bandaranaike with the task of writing to Chou En-lai, she should write on their behalf for a reply requesting China to accept the Colombo proposals in the same way as India had done. Nasser is said to be in favour of the second alternative and wants the other Colombo powers to be consulted informally on the second proposal. New Delhi also accepts the second alternative. What other choice does it have? There is no will to fight; in fact, every leader is bending backwards to ensure that the Chinese ceasefire proposals are not violated in any way.

## February 19, 1963

Jakarta's Ambassador in New Delhi, Laliov, feels that Dr Soekarno and Subandrio are "a bit suspicious" of China's politics and tactics. The assessment of Moscow's Ambassador is that China will not accept the Colombo proposals *in toto*, and also will not launch an attack. China may prepare for all eventualities, but will not repeat the "mistake" of invading India, he says.

## February 20, 1963

New Delhi's request to Mrs Bandaranaike through Kapur, our envoy in Colombo, is that she should not make any proposals which may directly or indirectly deviate from the Colombo powers' proposals. In any case, she has said that she cannot do so, even if she wishes to, without consulting the other five Colombo conference participants.

Sudhir Ghosh has written a letter to Nehru after talks with Ambassador Kaul in Moscow. Kaul has reportedly said that the friendly relationship between Nehru and Khrushchev are of great value not only to India but to the non-Communist world including America. Nothing should be done which might in any way injure that relationship. Kaul feels that the informal assurances of Khrushchev and other Communist leaders like the Yugoslav leader, Edward Kardelj, and Rapacki suggest that there is little likelihood of a repetition of Chinese aggression against India. They say that they are going to do whatever they can to restrain aggressive Chinese leaders. Khrushchev believes that the invasion of India by China was a direct result of the Sino-Soviet rift and what was invaded was non-alignment, not India. The Sino-Soviet quarrel in its present intensity is not the cause but the effect of the invasion of India by the Chinese. This is what Moscow has began saying now.

According to Sudhir Ghosh, Kaul thinks this should be taken with a pinch of salt. Kaul's assessment is that India must assume that the violation of India's territorial integrity by China is bound to be repeated—perhaps in the very near future. The Chinese will shrewdly choose their own time. New Delhi must do everything in its power to increase its military strength and should get aid from both sides. Why not get 100 MiGs instead of 12 is Kaul's suggestion.

## February 22, 1963

Nehru has written a letter to the State Chief Ministers, saying that he is not optimistic about a long-term settlement with China. He does not know whether the Chinese will accept the Colombo proposals. If they do, it will be a diplomatic victory for India because the line mentioned in the proposals is better than the one of September 8; if they do not accept them, even then it will be a diplomatic victory because it will put Peking in the wrong. The Prime Minister says that the question is not one of territory alone; it is deeper. It is an offshoot of the struggle for supremacy by China, a vast and powerful Asian country. He emphasizes that Russia and China are drifting apart. Russia and America may get together to contain China. He says that America and Britain are helping India, while Russia is doing so indirectly by not helping China.

Nehru again and again refers to the estrangement between Russia and China and says the rift will grow. But whatever the situation, India has to strengthen itself economically and militarily. He says he wished military preparations could go faster. He is happy that the Third Plan would cover more or less the main economic and transport aspects, the sinews of defence. He says that friendly countries were helping but essentially the country should be self-sufficient, because dependence on others is bad and creates a defeatist attitude. More burdens must be carried; foreign countries should be convinced that we are ready to bear them.

Nehru regrets that some newspapers have criticized the Colombo proposals without understanding them. His main objection is that the countries have been condemned just because they have not come forward in favour of India or the Colombo proposals. He thinks this is bad propaganda for India. Nehru says that the problem will be with India for years and preparations should be on this basis. The emergency will continue, although some critics want the emergency to go, but the sense of urgency has to continue.

Regarding Pakistan, Nehru says in his letter that India will never accept anything on the basis of the two-nation theory. India wants good relations with Pakistan but not by compromising on secularism. He thinks that the difficulties with China run parallel to those with Pakistan. It has developed Gilgit into a big military base with the help of America; the territory Rawalpindi has given to China which is near Gilgit and Peking will also develop it into a military base. Nehru also refers to Pakistan's propaganda that all the stones of China's aggression are make-believe and in fact India wants to arm itself only against Pakistan to "keep" Kashmir. The Prime Minister says that he has again made the offer of a no-war pact to Pakistan and also declared that India will not ever attack Pakistan unless it attacks first.

The Prime Minister also says in his letter that if the Chinese decide to attack it would be at a time when heavy rain and storms make military movement difficult (Shastri had earlier told the chief ministers at a Southern Zone Council meeting that he feared that the Chinese might attack India in the rainy season to prove that nothing was difficult for them).

Cairo has told our Ambassador that China is probably not agreeable to the Colombo proposals. Nasser is of the view that China would like to reap the benefits of the situation and retain the initiative. He has repeated his earlier suggestion that a joint telegram on behalf of the six Colombo powers be sent to China to ask if it accepts or rejects the proposals. The telegram should be made public to exert the necessary pressure. Alternatively, Mrs Bandaranaike should write on behalf of the six and ask China for a categorical reply.

The UN Secretary-General, visiting Cairo, says that Peking is deliberately misrepresenting India's stand on the border and the Colombo proposals.

Our envoy in Ceylon has been asked to inform Felix Bandaranaike that New Delhi's undertaking given to the Colombo conference participants on not taking troops right to the McMahon Line should not be conveyed to Peking because this is a bargaining point which India does not want to lose before the negotiations start. The Foreign Secretary has also emphasized upon our envoy that the setting up of Indian and Chinese posts in the demilitarized zone in Ladakh is an integral part of the Colombo proposals, not a clarification.

Meanwhile, China has rejected India's note of protest on the Sino-Pak border agreement. China has said that it had not brought up with Pakistan the question of the status of Kashmir. Peking has, however, charged India with exacerbating its relations with Pakistan. China has welcomed the Indo-Pakistan talks; it says that it had always hoped for it in the past. Our embassy has informed New Delhi that Bhutto might be visiting Peking.

## February 23, 1963

Bannerjee, our Chargé d' Affaires, has sent a cable from Peking to convey that the Ceylonese Ambassador to China has met Chou En-lai yesterday and is leaving for Colombo with a personal message for Mrs Bandaranaike. This is on the same lines as was Prince Sihanouk's impression after his talks with Chou En-lai. The point that China is making is that different clarifications of the Colombo proposals have been given at Delhi and Peking. Chou En-lai has favoured combined efforts by the Colombo powers through diplomatic channels to bring India and China to the conference table rather than another conference in Colombo or elsewhere. Ghana is interested in holding a conference of the Colombo powers in its own country as a matter of prestige.

## March 27, 1963

A telegram received from our embassy in Peking is disturbing. It gives details of a protest note dated March 25 alleging that India is repairing pillboxes on the border of Sikkim and China, has set up a communication centre for long entrenchment, has set up one defence post north of Nathu La in Chinese territory, has sent a party to reconnoitre and chart out the terrain north of Nathu La, has committed air violations and, has encouraged "Tibetan bandits" to attack. The note describes India's allegation that the Chinese are building up their military strength on the Sikkim border as "making white black", injuring China's friendly relations with Sikkim. It asks New Delhi to withdraw its own forces from what India considers as its own territory and to stop building pillboxes there.

The note protests the publication of the Tibetan Constitution by the Dalai Lama in India. China says that

India has never been reconciled to the merger of Tibet with China. The Tibetan Constitution has been drawn up at the instance of India which is encouraging the "Tibetan bandits". It recalls the oft-repeated statements of some Congress leaders that Tibet must be liberated. The note alleges that the Dalai Lama is being exploited, and mentions Patnaik's visit to America "to get more American aid". This shows the intention of India, it says.

A telegram received from Indonesia says that Subandrio claims to have taken up with the Chinese President, Liu Shao-chi, the Colombo proposals, and has asked him to accept them "without reservations". Subandrio says: "It was Pakistan which has put pressure on China to reject the Colombo proposals." To quote the Pakistan Ambassador, their acceptance "would mean our death". The Chinese Ambassador in Indonesia has said that India could stick to its own interpretation in the eastern sector but let China stand by its own in the western.

If China's reply to Mrs Bandaranaike's letter is any guide it means that Indian forces can go up to the McMahon Line. But in Ladakh, China has the unfettered right to set up checkposts; it plans to set up posts only at seven places where it had them before, and not the 43 other places where India had posts.

While Nehru has said in Parliament that the Colombo proposals are an advance, China seems inclined not to accept them. Subandrio has said that China might accept the proposals without reservation provided the details of "implementation" are disclosed, probably meaning the assurance India had given that it would not exercise its right to advance its troops beyond the places where they were—that is, not right up to the McMahon Line, even though on paper it could do so.

Another telegram from Peking speaks of the celebrations held on Pakistan's National Day. The Pakistani Ambassador said on the occasion that the Sino-Pak treaty did no harm to India. Chen Yi said that China was willing to settle* border differences with all, not with Pakistan alone. He said that India was not interested in a settlement and was increasing its military power and was using the "Tibetan bandits". Bannerjee did not walk out, nor did he join in the exchange of toasts.

China has also complained that Chinese internees in India are not being treated well. It had sought permission for two officers to visit the camp but the request had been rejected. Chou En-lai is sending a ship to pick up the internees.

With Shastri, I once visited their camp in Madhya Pradesh. The internees were rude to us and their rooms were plastered with the pictures of Mao and Chou.

---

* Peking's contention is that there are no historical or traditional boundaries; only mutual agreements should determine them. To support this theory, China has signed pacts with Pakistan and Burma. Peking's effort has been that New Delhi should also accept its premises. Somehow, the Indian officials' team which discussed the boundary question with the Chinese officials saw through this game and refused to yield.

## March 28, 1963

The reply sent by Chou En-lai to Mrs Bandaranaike is insolent and disrespectful. Chou En-lai has said in the seven-page letter that he was not able to reply earlier because he was busy holding talks with Prince Sihanouk. Chou En-lai has alleged that what he was told in Peking by Mrs Bandaranaike and what was later sent to him in writing on behalf of the Colombo powers are quite different—they are two sets of clarifications, one given to Delhi and the other to Peking. He says his belief is that things were changed in Delhi in deference to Indian pressure. Ceylon had no right to do so. The proposals only outline principles, they are not an award. No country can change them as Colombo is trying to do. Other countries are not so rigid. Chou En-lai says that Colombo's request that the proposals be accepted *in toto* means it is an award. The conference participants are not arbiters. China will never accept arbitration. It will not accept arbitration by the Hague Court either, as India had suggested, Chou En-lai says.

## May 4, 1963

The Prime Minister has sent a letter to President Soekarno, thanking him for the honour he had shown to Appa Pant, India's new envoy in Jakarta. Nehru has said that the Sino-Indian issue is not one of the border alone; it is one of checking an enemy who has a very large land army and believes it can dominate the world through force.

# Epilogue

The only thing I heard of after writing the diary was a fresh approach by Ceylon's Prime Minister to New Delhi in April 1964 asking whether she could take up with Peking the question of China's vacating the seven posts in Ladakh as a preliminary to Sino-India negotiations. The posts mentioned were Shensenwian, Tienweniian, Hot Springs, Kongka Pass, Nyagzu Pass, Khurnak Fort and Spanggur.

Mrs Bandaranaike had addressed the request to Nehru. In her letter she had said that she felt encouraged by the statement that Nehru made in the Lok Sabha on the subject on April 12.

Nehru had then said that India would consider negotiations with China on the basis of the withdrawal of the late Chinese posts from the demilitarized zone in Ladakh provided the Peking Government made "a proper approach" in the matter.

Earlier also, the Ceylonese Prime Minister had written to Nehru about a feeler that the Chinese might vacate the seven posts in Ladakh if India was willing to come to the negotiating table.

The feeler was said to have come from Chou En-lai during his talks with Mrs Bandaranaike when he visited Colombo last. However, when he returned to Peking he reportedly insisted that New Delhi should first come to the negotiating table; only then would China announce the vacation of the seven posts.

This is not acceptable to New Delhi, which has repeatedly said that China must accept the Colombo proposals *in toto* without any preconditions.

I also remember that when Shastri was returning to India in December 1964 from a visit to Britain, he stopped at Cairo. Nasser came to meet him at the airport. As chance would have it, Chou En-lai was leaving Cairo Airport at that time for Peking. Nasser asked Shastri if he would like to meet Chou En-lai. Shastri thought for a minute and said: "No."

Relating this incident to me, Shastri said that knowing the mood of Parliament, he did not think it advisable to meet the Chinese Prime Minister. Shastri said when he once remarked in the Lok Sabha that India should do some re-thinking on its relationship with China, almost the entire House protested against the use of the word "re-thinking" in the absence of Peking's acceptance of the Colombo proposals *in toto*. Naturally, Shastri said, no purpose would have been served in meeting Chou En-lai.

Nearly two years ago, there was an uproar in Parliament when it learnt that Indian officials had signed receipts, to get back from the Chinese, the bodies of Indian soldiers killed near Nathu La and Cho La. The government in Delhi said that no receipts* were signed.

* Facsimile of the receipts—containing the Chinese and the Hindi texts—signed by the Indian Army officers at Nathu La and Cho La at the time of receiving the bodies of Indian soldiers in October, 1967, is given as Annexure III.

# Annexure I

My dear Jawaharlal,

Ever since my return from Ahmedabad and after the Cabinet meeting the same day which I had to attend at practically fifteen minutes' notice and for which I regret I was not able to read all the papers, I have been anxiously thinking over the problem of Tibet and I thought I should share with you what is passing through my mind.

I have carefully gone through the correspondence between the External Affairs Ministry and our Ambassador in Peking, and through him, the Chinese government. I have tried to pursue this correspondence as favourably to our Ambassador and the Chinese government as possible, but I regret to say that neither of them comes out well as a result of this study.

The Chinese government have tried to delude us by professions of peaceful intentions. My own feeling is that at a crucial period they managed to install into our Ambassador a false sense of confidence in their so-called desire to settle the Tibetan problem by peaceful means.

There can be no doubt that during the period covered by this correspondence, the Chinese must have been concentrating for an onslaught on Tibet. The final action of the Chinese, in my judgement, is little short of perfidy.

The tragedy of it is that the Tibetans put faith in us, they chose to be guided by us, and we have been unable to get them out of the meshes of Chinese diplomacy or Chinese malevolence. From the latest position, it appears that we shall not be able to rescue the Dalai Lama.

Our Ambassador has been at great pains to find an explanation or justification for Chinese policy and actions. As the External Affairs Ministry remarked in one of their telegrams, there was a lack of firmness and unnecessary apology in one or two representations that he made to the Chinese government on our behalf. It is impossible to imagine any sensible person believing in the so-called threat to China from Anglo-American machinations in Tibet. Therefore, if the Chinese put faith in this, they must have distrusted us so completely as to have taken us as tools or stooges of Anglo-American diplomacy or strategy. This feeling, if genuinely entertained by the Chinese in spite of your direct approaches to them, indicates that, even though we regard ourselves as the friends of China, the Chinese do not regard us as their friends. With the Communist mentality of "Whoever is not with them being against them", this is a significant pointer, of which we have to take due note.

During the last several months, outside the Russian camp, we have practically been alone in championing the cause of Chinese entry into the UNO and in securing from the Americans assurances on the question of Formosa. We have done everything we could to assuage Chinese feelings, to allay their apprehensions and to defend their legitimate claims, in our discussions and correspondence with America and Britain and in the UNO. In spite of this, China is not convinced about our disinterestedness; it continues to regard us with suspicion and the whole psychology is one, at least outwardly, of scepticism perhaps mixed with a little hostility.

I doubt if we can go any further than we have done already to convince China of our good intentions, friendliness and goodwill. In Peking, we have an Ambassador who is eminently suitable for putting across a friendly point of view. Even he seems to have failed to convert the Chinese. Their last telegram to us is an act of gross discourtesy not only in the summary way it disposes of our protest against the entry of Chinese forces into Tibet but also in the wild insinuation that our attitude is determined by foreign influences.

It looks as though it is not a friend speaking in that language but a potential enemy.

In the background of this, we have to consider what new situation now faces us as a result of the disappearance of Tibet, as we know it, and the expansion of China almost up to our gates. Throughout history, we have seldom been worried about our northeast frontier. The Himalayas have been regarded as an impenetrable barrier against any threat from the north. We had a friendly Tibet which gave us no trouble. The Chinese were divided. They had their own domestic problems and never bothered us about our frontiers.

In 1914, we entered into a convention with Tibet which was not endorsed by the Chinese. We seem to have regarded Tibetan autonomy as extending to an independent treaty relationship. Presumably, all that we required was a Chinese counter-signature. The Chinese interpretation of suzerainty seems to be different. We can, therefore, safely assume that very soon they will disown all the stipulations which Tibet has entered into with us in the past. That throws into the melting pot all frontier and commercial settlements with Tibet on which we have been functioning and acting during the last half a century.

China is no longer divided. It is united and strong. All along the Himalayas in the north and north-east, we have, on our side of the frontier, a population ethnologically and culturally not different from Tibetans or Mongoloids.

The undefined state of the frontier, and the existence on our side, of a population with its affinities to Tibetans or Chinese, have all the elements of potential trouble between China and ourselves. Recent and bitter history also tells us that Communism is no shield against imperialism and that Communists are as good or as bad imperialists as any other. Chinese ambitions in this respect, not only cover the Himalayan slopes on our side but also include important parts of Assam.

They have their ambitions in Burma also. Burma has the added difficulty that it has no McMahon Line round which to build up even the semblance of an agreement.

Chinese irredentism and Communist imperialism are different from the expansionism or imperialism of the Western powers. The former has a cloak of ideology which makes it ten times more dangerous. In the guise of ideological expansion lie concealed racial, national and historical claims.

The danger from the north and north-east, therefore, becomes both Communist and imperialist. While our western and north-western threats to security are still as prominent as before, a new threat has developed from the north and north-east. Thus, for the first time after centuries, India's defence has to concentrate itself on two fronts simultaneously. Our defence measures have so far been based on the calculations of a superiority over Pakistan.

In our calculations we shall now have to reckon with Communist China in the north and north-east—a Communist China which has definite ambitions and aims and which does not, in any way, seem to have a friendly disposition towards us.

Let me also consider the political considerations of this potentially troublesome frontier. Our northern or north-eastern approaches consist of Nepal, Bhutan, Sikkim, Darjeeling and the tribal areas in Assam. From the point of view of communications, they are weak spots. Continuous defensive lines do not exist. There is an almost unlimited scope for infiltration. Police protection is limited to a very small number of passes. There, too, our outposts do not seem to be fully manned.

The contact of these areas with us is, by no means, close and intimate. The people inhabiting these portions have no established loyalty or devotion to India. Even Darjeeling and Kalimpong areas are not free from pro-Mongoloid prejudices. During the last three years, we have not been able to make any appreciable approaches to the Nagas and other hill tribes in Assam. European missionaries and other visitors had been in touch with them, but their influence was, in no way, friendly to India or Indians. In Sikkim, there was political ferment some time ago. It is quite possible that discontent is smouldering there. Bhutan is comparatively quiet, but its affinity with Tibetans would be a handicap. Nepal has a weak oligarchic regime based almost entirely on force: it is in conflict with a turbulent element of the population as well as with enlightened ideas of the modern age.

In these circumstances, to make people alive to the new danger or to make them defensively strong is a very difficult task indeed and that difficulty can be got over only by enlightened firmness, strength and a clear line of policy. I am sure the Chinese and their source of inspiration, Soviet Russia, would not miss any opportunity to exploit these weak spots, partly in support of their ideology and partly in support of their ambitions.

In my judgement, therefore, the situation is one in which we cannot afford either to be complacent or to be vacillating. We must have a clear idea of what we wish to achieve and also of the methods by which we should achieve it. Any faltering or lack of decisiveness in formulating our objectives or in pursuing our policy to attain those objectives is bound to weaken us and increase the threats which are so evident.

Side by side with these external dangers we shall now have to face serious internal problems as well. I have already asked Iyengar to send to the External Affairs Ministry a copy of the Intelligence Bureau's appreciation of these matters. Hitherto, the Communist Party of India has found some difficulty in contacting Communists abroad, or in getting supplies of arms, literature, etc, from them. They had to contend with difficult Burmese and Pakistan frontiers on the east or with the long seaboard.

They will now have a comparatively easy means of access to Chinese Communists, and through them, to other foreign Communists. Infiltration of spies, fifth columnists and Communists would be easier. Instead of having to deal with isolated Communist pockets in Telengana and Warangal, we may have to deal with Communist threats to our security along our northern and north-eastern frontiers where, for supplies of arms and ammunition, they can safely depend on Communist arsenal in China.

The whole situation thus raises a number of problems on which we must come to an early decision so that we can, as said earlier, formulate the objectives of our policy and decide the methods by which those actions will have to be fairly comprehensive, involving not only our defence strategy and state of preparation, but also problems of internal security to deal with which we have not a moment to lose. We shall also have to deal with administrative and political problems in the weak spots along the frontier to which I have already referred.

It is, of course, impossible for me to be exhaustive in setting out all these problems. I am, however, giving below some of the problems, which, in my opinion, require early solution and around which we have to build our administrative or military policies and measures to implement them.

(a) A military and intelligence appreciation of the Chinese threat to India, both on the frontier, and to internal security.

(b) An examination of our military position and such redisposition of our forces as might be necessary, particularly with the idea of guarding important routes or areas which are likely to be the subject of dispute.

(c) An appraisement of the strength of our forces and, if necessary, reconsideration of our retrenchment plans for the Army in the light of these new threats.

(d) A long-term consideration of our defence needs. My own feeling is that unless we assure our supplies of arms, ammunition and armour, we would be making our defence perpetually weak and we would not be able to stand up to the double threat of difficulties both from the west and north-west and north and north-east.

(e) The question of Chinese entry into the UNO. In view of China's rebuff and the method which it has followed in dealing with Tibet, I am doubtful whether we can advocate its claims any longer. There would probably be a threat in the UNO virtually to outlaw China, in view of its active participation in the Korean war. We must determine our attitude on this question also.

(f) The political and administrative steps which we should take to strengthen our northern and north-eastern frontiers. This would include the whole of the border, that is, Nepal, Bhutan, Sikkim, Darjeeling and the tribal territory in Assam.

(g) Measures of internal security in the border areas as well as the states flanking those areas such as Uttar Pradesh, Bihar, Bengal and Assam.

(h) Improvement of our communications, road, rail, air and wireless, in these areas, and with the frontier outposts.

(i) Policing and intelligence of frontier posts.

(j) The future of our mission at Lhasa and the trade posts at Gyangtse and Yatung and the forces which we have in operation in Tibet to guard the trade routes.

(k) The policy in regard to the McMahon Line.

These are some of the questions which occur to my mind. It is possible that a consideration of these matters may lead us into wider questions of our relationship with China, Russia, America, Britain and Burma. This, however, would be of a general nature, though some might be basically very important, for example, we might have to consider whether we should not enter into closer association with Burma in order to strengthen the latter in the dealings with China. I do not rule out the possibility that, before applying pressure on us, China might apply pressure on Burma. With Burma, the frontier is entirely undefined and the Chinese territorial claims are more substantial. In its present position, Burma might offer an easier problem for China and, therefore, might claim its first attention.

I suggest that we meet early to have a general discussion on these problems and decide on such steps as we might think to be immediately necessary, and direct quick examination of other problems with a view to taking early measures to deal with them.

Vallabhbhai Patel
7th November,1950.

# Annexure II

## Extracts from the Report of Lt General Henderson-Brooks

Our basic training was sound and the soldiers adapted themselves to the mountains adequately. The training of our troops did not have an orientation towards operations vis-à-vis the particular terrain in which the troops had to operate. Our training of the troops did not have a slant for a war being launched by China. Thus our troops had no requisite knowledge of Chinese tactics, and ways of war, their weapons, equipment and capabilities. Knowledge of the enemy helps to build up confidence and morale, so essential for the *jawan* on the front.

There is certainly need for toughening and battle inoculation. It is, therefore, essential that battle schools are opened at training centres and formations so that gradual toughening and battle inoculation can be carried out.

The main aspect of training as well as the higher commanders' concept of mountain warfare requires to be put right.

Training alone, however, without correct leadership will pay little dividends. Thus the need of the moment, above all else, is training in leadership.

The second question was about our equipment. There was indeed an overall shortage of equipment both for training and during operations. But it was not always the case that particular equipment was not available at all with the Armed Forces anywhere in the country. The crucial difficulty in many cases was that, while the equipment could be reached to the last point in the plains, or even beyond it, it was another matter to reach it in time, mostly by air or by animal or human transport to the forward formations, who took the brunt of fighting. This position of logistics was aggravated by two factors:

i. The fast rate at which troops had to be inducted, mostly from plains to high mountain areas; and
ii. Lack of properly built roads and other means of communications.

This, situation was aggravated and made worse because of overall shortage as far as vehicles were concerned and as our fleet was too old and its efficiency not adequate for operating on steep gradients and mountain terrain.

Thus in brief, an overall shortage of equipment; it has also revealed that our weapons were adequate to fight the Chinese and compared favourably with theirs. The automatic rifle would have helped in the cold climate and is being introduced. There is the need to make up deficiencies in equipment, particularly suited for mountain warfare, but more so to provide means and modes of communication to make it available to the troops at the right place at the right time. Work on these lines has already been taken in hand and is progressing vigorously.

## System of Command

There is basically nothing wrong with the system and chain of command, provided it is exercised in an accepted manner at various levels. There is, however, need for a realization of responsibilities at various levels which must work with trust and confidence in each other. During the operations, difficulties arose only when there was a departure from the accepted chain of command. There again, such departures occurred mainly due to haste and lack of adequate prior planning.

The practice has crept in at the higher army formations, of interfering in tactical details even to the extent of detailing troops for specified tasks. It is the duty of the commanders in the field to make on-the-spot decisions, when so required, and details of operations ought to have been left to them.

It is axiomatic that an unacclimatized army cannot be as fit as one which is. Despite this, our troops, both officers and men, stood up to the rigours of the climate, although most of them were rushed at short notice from the plains. Thus, in brief, our troops were physically fit in every way for their normal tasks, but they were not acclimatized to fight at the heights at which some of them were asked to make a stand. Where acclimatization had taken place, such as in Ladakh, the height factor presented no difficulty. Among some middle-age-group officers, there had been a deterioration in standards of physical fitness. This is a matter which is being rectified. The physical fitness among junior officers was good and is now even better.

By and large, it has been found that the general standard amongst the junior officers was fair. At unit level there were good and mediocre commanding officers. The proportion of good commanding officers and not-so-good was perhaps the same as obtained in any army in the last World War. At the brigade level, but for the odd exception, commanders were able to adequately exercise their command. It was at higher levels that shortcomings became more apparent. It was also revealed that some of the highest commanders did not depend enough on the initiative of the lower commanders, who alone could have the requisite knowledge of the terrain and local conditions of troops under them.

## Other Aspects Examined

As regards our system and organization of intelligence, it is known that in the Army Headquarters, there is a Directorate of Intelligence under an officer designated as Director of Military Intelligence, briefly known as DMI.

The collection of intelligence in general was not satisfactory. The acquisition of intelligence was slow and the reporting of it vague.

The second important aspect of intelligence is its collection and evaluation. Admittedly, because of the vague nature of intelligence evaluation may not have been accurate. Thus, a clear picture of the Chinese build-up was not made available. No attempt was made to link up the new enemy build-up with the old deployment. Thus, field formation had little guidance whether there were fresh troops or old ones moving to a new location.

The third aspect is dissemination of intelligence. It has come out that much faster means must be employed to send out processed and important information to field formations, if it is to be of any use.

There is no doubt that a major overhauling of the intelligence system is required. A great deal has been done during the last six months. The overhauling of the intelligence system is a complex and lengthy task and, in view of its vital importance, I am paying personal attention to this.

Now about our staff work and procedures. Much more attention will have to be given, than was done in the past, to the work and procedures of the general staff at the Services Headquarters, as well as in the command headquarters and below, to long-term operational planning, including logistics as well as to the problems of co-ordination between various Services Headquarters. So one major lesson learnt is that the quality of general staff work, and the depth of its prior planning in time, is going to be one of the most crucial factors in our future preparedness.

That brings me to the next point which is called the higher direction of operations. Even the largest and the best equipped of armies need to be given proper policy guidance and major directives by the government, whose instrument it is. These must bear a reasonable relation to the size of the army and state of its equipment from time to time. An increase in the size or improving the equipment of army, costs not only money but also needs time.

## Last Year's Reverses

The reverses that our armed forces admittedly suffered were due to a variety of causes and weaknesses as stated above. While this inquiry has gone deeply into those causes, it has also confirmed that the attack was so sudden and in such remote and isolated sectors that the Indian Army as a whole was really not tested. In that period of less than two months last year, only about 24,000 of our troops were actually involved in fighting. Of these, those in Ladakh did an excellent job even when overwhelmed and outnumbered. In the easternmost sector, though the troops had to withdraw in the face of vastly superior enemy strength from Walong, they withdrew in an orderly manner and took their toll. It was only in the Kameng sector that the Army suffered a series of reverses. These battles were fought on our remotest borders and were at heights not known to the army and at places which geographically had all the disadvantages for our troops and many advantages for the enemy. But such initial reverses are a part of the tides of war and what matters most is who wins the last battle.

(Original receipts in Chinese and Hindi)

由边防部队交給印度方面代表在
一九六七年十月一日，印度军队在卓拉山口
越入中国境内进行军事挑衅时遗
弃在中国境内的尸体及军用物资計
印军尸体 5具　　望远镜 1具
輕机枪 1挺　　冲鋒枪1支，子弹30发
半自动步枪7支，子弹169发，弹夹12个

चीन की सीमा रक्षक टुकड़ी ने भारतीय पक्ष के प्रतिनिधि
को लाशें और सैनिक सामग्रियाँ लौट दे दी हैं जो एक
अक्तूबर उन्नीस सौ सड़सठ को जोला दर्रे में तैनात भारतीय
सेना ने चीन भूमि में अनधिकार प्रवेश करके सैनिक चुनौती
करते समय छोड़ दी हैं।

संख्या :
भारतीय सैनिक लाशें 5　　दूरबीन 1
हल्का मशीनगन 1　　सब मशीनगन 1
अर्ध स्वचालित रायफल 7　　गोलियाँ 30
गोलियाँ 169　　गोली - कारतीव 12

Dead Bodies - 5
LMG - 1
Rifle Semi automatic - 7
Binocular - 1
Sten Mechanic Carbine - 1.
Rifle Magazines - 12
Rounds 9MM - 30
Rounds 7.62 169
Received
Signed, Major.

中国人民
解放军駐卓拉山口边防部队代表 Signed
印度方面代表 Signed
Major, Indian Army.
一九六七年十月四日
4 अक्तूबर 1967

चीनी जन मुक्ति सेना की जोला दर्रे
में तैनात सीमा रक्षक टुकड़ी
के प्रतिनिधि　　Signed

भारतीय पक्ष के प्रतिनिधि　　Signed Major, Indian Army 4 October 1967

# Annexure III

(Facsimiles of the receipts containing the Chinese and Hindi texts signed by the Indian Army officers at Nathu La and Cho La at the time of receiving the bodies of Indian soldiers in October last.)

Chinese border guards have returned to the representative of the Indian side the dead bodies and military equipment which were left behind in the Cho La Valley on October 1, 1967, by Indian troops during the time they intruded into Chinese territory to offer a military challenge.

| | |
|---|---|
| Dead bodies | 5 |
| Light machine gun | 1 |
| Sub-machine gun | 1 |
| Semi-automatic rifle | 7 |
| Telescope | 1 |
| 9 mm rounds | 30 |
| 7.62 mm rounds | 169 |

Representative of border guard detachment of Chinese People's Liberation Army posted in Cho La Valley.

Signed

Received

Representative of Indian side

Signed
(Major)
Indian Army
October 4, 1967

The Chinese border guards detachment handed over to the representative of the Indian side corpses and military equipment which were left on Chinese territory on September 11, 1967, when Indian troops engaged in military provocation across the border.

| | |
|---|---|
| Bodies of Indian troops | 14 |
| Rifles | 2 |
| Sub-machine guns | 9 |
| Rounds | 85 |
| Semi-automatic rifles | 13 |
| Rounds | 333 |
| Mortars | 9 |
| Steel helmets | 12 |

Signed by representative of border guard detachment of Chinese People's Liberation Army stationed in Nathu La Valley.

Ma Sho-ched

Received

Representative of Indian Side

Signed Major 16.9.1967

中国边防部队交给印军方面代表。在一九六七年九月十二日，印度军队越过中国境内进行军事挑衅时遗弃在中国境内的屍体及军用物资即：屍体14具，半自动枪13支，步枪2支，子弹333发，冲锋枪9支，子弹85发，手榴弹9枚，鋼盔12顶

चीनी सीमावर्ती रक्षक टकड़ी ने भारतीय पक्ष के प्रतिनिधि को लाशें और फौजी सामान दीं, जो ग्यारह सितंबर उन्नीस सौ सड़सठ को भारतीय सेना द्वारा सीमा लाइन के . . . चीन के इधर फौजी उकसाते करते समय चीन की भूमि में छोड़ दिये गये हैं: निम्न लिखित

भारतीय सेना की लाशें १४

राइफिल २

सब मशीन गन ९

गोलियाँ ८५

अर्द्ध स्वचालित राइफ़िल १३

गोलियाँ ३३३

हथ गोला ९

इस्पाती टोप १२

中国人民解放军 驻乃堆拉山口边防部队代表: Signed

印度方面代表: Signed Major.

一九六七年九月十六日

नाथूला दर्रे तैनात चीनी जन-मुक्ति सेना की सीमावर्ती रक्षक टुकड़ी के प्रतिनिधि: मा शो-चेङ Signed.

भारतीय पक्ष के प्रतिनिधि: Signed Major

1967.9.16

# Acknowledgement

I am grateful to my talented colleague, Mr Dilip Mukerjee for his assistance in making this book possible. I also thank Mr Trevor Drieberg and Mr V. Achuta Menon who have read parts of my manuscript, Mrs G. Barrett and Miss Veena Malhotra, my two secretaries, who have done all the typing uncomplainingly, Mr Kotru and Mr Ismail, who have gone through proofs, and Mr M. Chalapathi Rao, who has suggested the title for this book.